1971

ECONOMIC CRITICISM
IN
AMERICAN FICTION

1792 TO 1900

ECONOMIC CRITICISM
IN
AMERICAN FICTION

1792 TO 1900

Claude Reherd Flory

NEW YORK / RUSSELL & RUSSELL

FIRST PUBLISHED IN 1937
REISSUED, 1969, BY RUSSELL & RUSSELL
A DIVISION OF ATHENEUM PUBLISHERS, INC.
BY ARRANGEMENT WITH
THE UNIVERSITY OF PENNSYLVANIA PRESS
L. C. CATALOG CARD NO: 68-25075
PRINTED IN THE UNITED STATES OF AMERICA

ACKNOWLEDGMENT

This study was begun under the direction of Dr. Arthur Hobson Quinn. His wide knowledge of American fiction was particularly helpful in the developing of my bibliography. The work in its final form, however, owes most to the sound criticism and generous guidance of Dr. Paul H. Musser. Dr. S. Howard Patterson gave me much helpful information and advice, and very kindly read my completed manuscript. To these in particular, and to all others who facilitated my work, I express my sincere appreciation.

CLAUDE R. FLORY

CONTENTS

ECONOMIC CRITICISM
IN
AMERICAN FICTION

1792 TO 1900

ERRATA

Page 186, line 23, *for* 1889 *read* 1899
Page 231, line 7, *for* 1882 *read* 1845
Page 245, *for* Adams, Henry: *Democracy*. New York, 1908
    read Adams, Henry: *Democracy*. New York, 1880
Page 250, *for* Walch, Caroline C.: *Doctor Sphinx*. New York, 1898
    read Walch, Caroline F.: *Doctor Sphinx*. New York, 1898

INTRODUCTION

CHAPTER ONE

The Problem as the Novelists View It: Man's Inhumanity to Man

I. Class consciousness as depicted in the novel: Who is my neighbor?
   A. General class distinctions as pictured in American fiction.
      1. Social divisions based upon differences in wealth
      2. Pauperizing attitude of charity and the Church
   B. Special race problems treated in American fiction
      1. The Indian
      2. The Negro
      3. The immigrant

II. Industry in government as represented in the novel: The Invisible Empire
   A. Legislators economically incapable — both unable to grasp the country's needs, and subject unknowingly to fraud, American fictionists declare
   B. Public officials subject to direct willful influence for the profit of private interests, the novelists charge

III. General economic injustice and unhappiness as treated in the novel: The whole truth
   A. The effect of the industrial age in building up a disagreeable and oppressive relationship of capital to labor, as reflected in American fiction
   B. Financial chicanery as revealed in the novel
   C. Depressing conditions of living in city and country, as represented in the American novel.
   D. Fictional defenses of the present capitalistic order of society.

CHAPTER TWO

<small>THE ANSWER AS THE NOVELISTS GIVE IT: SIGNPOSTS TO UTOPIA</small>

I. Reforms suggested by the general novelist
   A. Chronological survey of the novels proposing remedies for the conditions described
   B. Summary of the reforms advocated in this fiction
      1. A spirit of rehabilitation to be substituted for the usual pauperizing attitude of charity
      2. Christian Socialism
      3. Cooperative industry
      4. Tax reforms
      5. Government ownership and operation of public utilities
      6. National socialism

II. The program of the utopian novelists
   A. Chronological survey of utopian fiction in America
   B. Summary of the reforms recommended in American utopian fiction
      1. The practical application of the Christian principles of brotherhood
      2. A program of modified socialism—many variations
      3. Complete national communism

CHAPTER THREE

<small>LITERARY CHARACTERISTICS OF AMERICAN FICTION TREATING ECONOMIC THEMES: THE EXPRESSION OF THE PROBLEM AND THE ANSWER</small>

I. Seeds of realism to be found in the elements of economic criticism in fiction, 1792 to 1860
   A. Chronological survey of the general novel treating economic themes in this period
   B. Fiction treating the problem of the Negro race predominantly romantic

II. The developed realism in the economic novel, 1860 to 1900

III. The utopian novel a peculiar continuation of romanticism

CONCLUSION

INTRODUCTION

.... Of grief and anger, grown to fierce revolt,
And hatred of the invisible force which holds
The issue of men's lives, and binds us fast
Within the net of fate.

It must be clear, first of all, that the submitting of this study as an English thesis presupposes an acceptance of the dictum that literature is a criticism of life. It is the matter rather than the method that interests us in this summary of how the novelists during the first hundred years of the history of our fiction looked at the American social scene, what faults they found in it, and what remedies they suggested for its puzzling problems. The selective principle here has not been an esthetic one. But if literature be made for man as well as man for literature then this fiction — much of which the sophisticated litterateur would dismiss with the derogation 'sub-literary' — is still worthy of our consideration. For these novelists of economic protest have been very serious. They have looked at life with as critical eyes as writers of fiction may, hesitating not to preach with the fist however greatly the finer elements of art have suffered in their vigorous polemics. And one begins to feel justified in recalling to the memory of literary history many of these forgotten novels when tracing in the identifiable backgrounds of their critical pronouncements he discovers in the broader fields of our political, social, and economic development the forces which stand anterior to the literary schools and movements with which the narrower belletrist usually contents himself, and from which literary culture eventually springs; charming child whose now so remote grandparent is forgotten.

An examination of the economic criticism in American fiction is a timely task. For five years the nation has been passing through a period of economic stress, and it has always been true that under similar conditions men have paused to inquire into the short-comings of the social system under which they lived. Some particularly unsettled time is the explanation of the majority of utopian ventures, imaginary or real, of which we have record: Plato's *Republic* has as its background the social disintegration following the Peloponnesian war; the theocracy which Savanarola established in Florence from 1495 to 1497 was essentially a middle-class reaction against the aristocratic domination of the Medici; Sir Thomas More sought to span the gap between the old order of the Middle Ages and the new interests and institutions of the Renaissance; the outburst of utopian fiction in America is the last quarter of the nineteenth century arose from the growing complexity of industrialization and the discovery that for the first time in its history the country no longer had a frontier to serve as the solvent for its economic ills.

A reading of the two hundred fifty novels on which this study has been based will disclose that much — though by no means all — of the most trenchant and memorable economic criticism in our fiction is to be found in the novels customarily described as utopian — picturizations of an ideal Nowhere. These are in the large, however, most accurately interpreted as attempts to satirize existing conditions rather than to recommend the literal application of the schemes they set forth. The heart of their message is that Utopia is the principle of all progress. "Without the Utopians of other times," in the phrasing of Anatole France, "men would still live in caves, miserable and naked. . . . Out of generous dreams come beneficial realities." "Nowhere may be an imaginary country, but News from Nowhere is real news," insist these critics of our social structure. However, not all of the economic judgments set forth in our fiction are in condemnation of the current version of capitalistic civilization. As Whittier pointed out at a time when utopian fiction was beginning to reach its widest popularity in America, there is a class of people who "themselves generally enjoying whatever of good belongs to the political or social system in which their lot is cast . . . are disposed to look with philosophic indifference upon the evil which only afflicts their neighbors."[1] The capitalistic order has its positive defenders, too. They

1. "Utopian Schemes and Political Theorists." *Works* 7:199.

maintain that the faults of the system are exaggerated in the propaganda of self-deceived prophets crying in a wilderness that does not exist. Modern wealth is democratic they say, repeating after Henry C. Carey that "capital gets less and labor more as the world grows older" — that is, capital gets relatively less but absolutely more, while labor gets both relatively more and absolutely more out of a constantly increasing product; they discover willful falsehood in the utopian cry of anguish that the rich are growing richer and the poor poorer: both are growing richer; they hold that "all possible perfection of the race will be attained under the present forms of development."[2] There are capitalistic refutations also for many of the economic criticisms of the general novelist who has not clothed his reform ideas in utopian garb. Both positive and negative views on the several economic problems of our democracy are recorded in this study, for it purports to be a summary of all viewpoints rather than the tracing out of a particular theme. But since the burden of proof lies with those who would produce a change the larger amount of criticism is condemnatory rather than approving.

It must be borne in mind that this study had no opportunity of achieving relative balance from an economic point of view. Rarely does one find a novelist who is more than an amateur in economics. And it is their opinions and prejudices, the materials employed by these writers of the novel of economic criticism that have determined the content of this thesis. I have organized this definitely limited material on a two-fold basis: what evils do the novelists see in the American social scheme, and what remedies do they propose for them. Class distinctions based on superior economic power used for selfish ends seem to the novelists to be the fundamental background of nearly all of our social ills. The subtle and insidious control of our nominally democratic government by large industrial interests receives wide condemnation in the pages of our critical economic fiction. Many other ills of varying size and significance are pointed out in our body social, and solutions suggested, a very welter of ideas on how to make the most out of the

---

2. Sanders, George A., *Reality: A Reply to Edward Bellamy's Looking Backward and Equality*, p. 10.

welter of industry. These reform ideas, whether of the general critical novelist or of the avowed utopian, I have thought of as signposts to the ideal Nowhere. They vary from a mild, indefinite Christian program, teaching submission to one's lot and improvement through self-education, to the espousal of unqualified communism which has repudiated the last vestige of individual right and willfully forgotten every tenet of religion. Thus do the economic critics in American fiction treat the thousand natural ills the flesh is heir to.

But however strongly one emphasizes the economic thought content of these novels rather than the technique of their composition as art efforts, however resolutely he holds to his attitude that literature is made for man much more than man for literature, some appraisal of these novels from the literary standpoint is necessary to to the identification of this study as an English thesis. The appraisal, however, is here only very broadly done. It consists largely of description of type and tracing of general method, rather than of minute analysis; for those novels, containing elements of economic criticism, which at the same time have distinct literary merit have been elsewhere examined more adequately than the scope of this study permits — emphasizing as it does the problems that have been fundamental in the life, and consequently the thought, of the people as a whole rather than the philosophy and composition skill of a few artists — while those lesser novels of economic theme of which belletristic history preserves no record are for the most part unworthy of analysis as literature. They can be dismissed in a sentence. To give them more attention would be an unprofitable squandering of everybody's time, for not infrequently the author's introduction specifically denies any attempt at literary merit — and judging from the accomplishment many others might well have been similarly prefaced. Often the authors — even Bellamy in regard to *Looking Backward,* the most famous of these economic novels — point out what the reader soon discovers as truth, that "barely enough story was left to decently drape the skeleton of the argument, and not enough, I fear, in spots, for even that purpose."[3] Many of these novels were bound only in paper, and privately printed; the less literary ranged in price from ten cents to a dollar.

The most significant general facts from the standpoint of literary technique that can be cited concerning the novels treated in this study relate to romantic-realistic distinctions. In the novels of the first half-entury of our fiction the seeds which were later to develop into the sturdy stalk of American realism are found more clearly in the elements of economic and social criticism than anywhere else. And it is in the marked development from these seeds that we see, beginning with Rebecca Harding Davis in the early 1860's, that economic protest in the general novel is probably the most pronounced phase of the new realism in American literature. The attitude of the novelists is: "You shall know the truth and the truth shall make you free" — a philosophy of composition conducive to good art. But when we observe economic criticism carried to its ultimate extent — in the definitely utopian novels — we see a thread in our fiction pattern which judged by literary standards is peculiarly though unmistakably romantic, paradoxical as that may at first seem. It is along the line of these three general distinctions that my brief literary analyses have been made. Many of these writers have had visions as one at Patmos but not all have written worthily of them.

---

3. Bellamy, Edward, "How I Came to Write *Looking Backward*", *Nationalist* 1:3, May, 1889.

CHAPTER ONE

THE PROBLEM: MAN'S INHUMANITY TO MAN

I

CLASS CONSCIOUSNESS AS DEPICTED IN THE NOVEL: WHO IS MY NEIGHBOR?

GENERAL CLASS DISTINCTIONS AS PICTURED IN AMERICAN FICTION

The thing which most clearly distinguishes modern life from the life of the ancient world is the decisive importance of industrial resources and efficiency in determining the history of nations. In earlier times military skill and personal courage were the determining factors in the fate of governments, but in the modern age the balance of power rests with that people who have superior skill in applying the accomplishments of modern science and organizing the service of supply. Not those who are willing to die for it, but those who are willing to work for it are a nation's heroes; the race is not to the strong, but to the provident. In this is the essential distinction between the age of feudalism and the age of industrialism —the fundamental human impulses of self-interest and acquisitiveness remaining essentially unchanged.

The history of the United States is in a very singular sense an expression of this new emphatically economic phase of the world's record of life. The Past here was brief and negligible; we were born only a day before the Present began. American industry with its huge resources of wood, oil, coal, metals, and waterways began to mass and differentiate early. Awkward at first, of course, the economic nation boomed steadily after 1790, encouraged by the ratification of a constitution favorable to the property classes. The America that came out of the second war with Britain was an eager, restless nation; the optimism of youth facing romantic opportunity surged in its soul. It frankly acknowledged acquisitiveness as a fundamental force in its make-up, and insisted that such acquisitiveness was a cardinal virtue. It saw acres of diamonds in the unexploited resources of a continent and with the magnificent prodigality of speculative short-cuts proposed to gather only the largest gems; the conservative philosophy of a drab agrarianism was to have little place in the future.

During 1819 infant capitalism persevered over rudimentary banking methods with its definite emergence from a domestic to a factory stage. Manufacturing assumed strength as iron and textiles began to direct tariff policies: a century of invention was beginning to revolutionize the steel and loom industries. The water power of New England was being harnessed to cotton and woolen mills, and tanneries. Immigration from wartorn Europe was increasing. "New York had begun that marvelous growth which made the city in the course of a few decades the financial capital of a hemisphere. So rapidly were people flocking to New York that houses had tenants long before they had windows and doors, and streets were lined with buildings before they had sewers, sidewalks, or pavements."[1] New commonwealths were rising in the wilderness: Pittsburgh and Cincinnati were emerging from 'settlements' into manufacturing towns of importance. "In 1820 it was estimated that 200,000 persons and a capital of $75,000,000 were employed in manufacturing. In 1825 the capital used had been expanded to $160,000,000 and the number of workers to 2,000,000".[2]

Recovery from the panic of 1837 was swift; commercial forces assumed more adult strength with the development of western markets, the railroad, the telegraph, the postal system, and express companies. The Civil War saw further acceleration in the growth of the machine system caused by a shortage of labor due to the military demand for men. Indeed "the eight years in America from 1860 to 1868 uprooted institutions that were centuries old, changed the politics of a people, transformed the social life of half the country, and wrought so profoundly upon the national character that the influence cannot be measured short of two or three generations".[3] The Old South, last frontier of feudalism, was metamorphosed into the New South, increasingly strong competitor in the race for industrial suprem-

---

1. Samuel P. Orth, *The Armies of Labor*, p. 25.
2. McMaster, *History of the People of the United States*, 5:230.
3. M. Twain and C. D. Warner, *The Gilded Age*, v. 1, pp. 200-201.

acy.[4] In the North the manipulation of war finances enabled
a clique of New York bankers to gain a position of conspicuous
domination within the capitalistic ranks. It was the beginning
of the age of trusts, headed by such industrial dinosaurs as
Carnegie, Rockefeller, Hill, Harriman, and Morgan; and despite
two panics industry continued to grow with logarithmic speed.
The country's need of facilities for communication and transportation was so great that grants of the public domain to railroad companies were almost universally approved at the beginning — however severely they were condemned later by our economic critics in fiction, and others. These marvelous communication and transportation developments created a new demand
for capital for themselves and also reacted on already established industry. Where a manufacturer had formerly made
products practically to order for a limited number of known
customers, now he manufactured on a speculative basis counting upon finding a large number of unknown buyers in distant
markets. The banker who formerly loaned money on local
security now gave credit to great projects in far quarters. New
industrial processes and new inventions brought on new speculations.

In the fifty years preceding 1910 the United States built half
as much railroad mileage as all the rest of the world together.
"Population trebled. This fact stands alone in the data of
vital statistics. Yet even more remarkable were the alterations
of human activity. The number of city dwellers increased three
and one half times faster than the population; the number of
wage-earners two times faster; miners three times faster; clerks,
salesmen, and typists six and a half times faster; transportation
workers twenty times faster; and the number of independent
farmers decreased. Wealth in this time increased from about
$500 to more than $1500 per capita".[5]

But average wealth statistics are misleading: in comparison
with labor conditions abroad wages were high in the United
States; but as compared with the rise in rent and profits in this
country wages' rate of increase was slow. These inequalities

---

4. Cf. Holland Thompson, *The New South,* pp. 86-128.
5. Harold E. Stearns, *Civilization in the United States,* pp. 403-404.

are well illustrated by the estimate made several years ago that seven-eighths of the families in the United States owned but one-eighth of the national wealth. A later study made in 1915 estimated that sixty-five per cent of our population—the poor class, but not paupers—possessed no property; that fifteen per cent composed the lower middle class whose wealth was below $1000; that eighteen per cent made up the upper middle class whose wealth ranged from $2000 to $40,000; that only two per cent of our total population were wealthy in the modern sense of the term. This two per cent owned three-fifths of the entire property of the United States.[6] Significantly contributory to this concentration of wealth—pronounced and perilous, if our novelists are to be believed—have been the subsidation of railroads, exhaustion of free lands in the West, the strangling of the farmer, the adaptation of electricity, the rise of corporations with their piratical gulping of small firms, political manipulation of the dollar, laxity of government control of business, and the *laissez faire* attitude of court decisions. It is in the economic inequalities builded upon these foundations that our critic-novelists see class distinctions which they variously condemn, according to their individual tempers, as mildly shameful to being absolutely intolerable. "Class consciousness in its early stages means that the members of a social or economic group are so impressed with their own moral superiority to the rest of the community that they care relatively little what the rest of the community thinks or what becomes of it. In its later stages it means that they become so absorbed in the wishes and aspirations of their own group that they mistake these for facts and acquire a mental blindness which prevents them from taking any other kind of facts into account".[7] It is this class consciousness of our plutocracy which the critical novelists see as basic

---

6. For a further elaboration of this see S. Howard Patterson *Social Aspects of Industry* (1929), chapter V: "The Diffusion of Our National Prosperity", pp. 99-122.

7. A. T. Hadley, *Economic Problems of Democracy*, p. 133.

in all our economic ills.[8]   And that they have written seriously
upon the problem is proof that they believe these class distinctions must be made less pronounced if not entirely obliterated.
Their program varies from a pleading "for higher and nobler
thoughts in the souls of men,"[9] to a bold threat of redistribut-
ing the social surplus through the complete confiscation of capital by labor—Marxian war until the bourgeoisie are wiped out
by death or unconditional surrender and the proletariat remain
supreme and alone.[10]   Surely we need not come to this; surely
the church can do something through its teaching of brotherhood to erase the feeling of class consciousness; something to
call back the rich young ruler who hearing truly who is his
neighbor has turned away.   But the church itself has "no god
but gold",[11] and the attitude of its charity increases rather than
lessens the consciousness of economic class distinctions.[12]   There
are to be sure many confident priests among our novelists who
see the alleviation and final cure of all our ills in the teaching
of the greater Founder of the church; but a heavy chorus reading the notes of things as they are gives priest and church the
lie.   How can the principles of Christ prevail upon Wall Street
when there are money changers in the Temple.   Class consciousness in its acute stage of utter inconsideration and injustice
of the strong toward the weak, say our novelists of economic
criticism, is the fundamental ill in our social body and no

8.   This general summary of American economic history has been based on
Bogart, *Economic History of the United States;* A. M. Simons, *Social Forces
in American History;* Burton J. Hendrick, *The Age of Big Business;* Harry
Hartwick, *The Foreground of American Fiction;* V. L. Parrington, *Main
Currents in American Thought,* and the other authorities listed in previous
footnotes.

9.   Ignatius Donnelly, *Caesar's Column,* p. 5.

10.   The date set by our utopian novelists for a revolution in the social
order varies from 1900 to 2021.   The most anarchical pictures of the predicted revolution are to be found in Anna Bowman Dodd's *The Republic of
the Future* (1887), p. 48 ff; Ignatius Donnelly's *Caesar's Column* (1890), p.
52 ff, and Albert Adams Merrill's *The Great Awakening* (1899), p. 49 ff.
On the whole, however, our novelists of economic criticism concur in the
hope and belief of Bellamy and Howells that the socialistic order can be
achieved by a peaceful vote of the people.

11.   S. B. H. Judah, *The Buccaneers* (1827) p. 6.

12.   Cf. J. G. Holland, *Nicholas Minturn* (1876), Helen Campbell, *Mrs.
Herndon's Income* (1886), H. H. Boyesen, *Social Strugglers* (1893). and others; Chapter Two, section I of this study.

force in modern society, not even the church, is working toward its cure.

Is the evil greater today in the view of our fictionists than it was yesterday? The view of Wolfert in *John Marvel, Assistant* is typical of the opinion of most of the characters in these economic novels:

"There was never so selfish and hypocritical a society on earth as this which now exists. In times past under the feudal system, there was apparently some reason for the existence of the so-called upper classes — the first castle built made necessary all the others—the chief, at least, protected the subjects from the rapine of others, and he was always ready to imperil his life; but now—this! When they all claim to know, and do know much, they sit quiet in their own smug content like fatted swine, and let rapine, debauchery, and murder go on as it never has gone on in the last three hundred years." . . .[13]

The "rich and successful", it has been charged, have "formed a kind of secret society, pledged to advance any member, to keep the others out by indifference. When the others manage to get in, for any reason, they lend them aid to the exclusion of those left outside".[14] This is class consciousness and class practice of economic injustice as the novelists see it. But only a few recognize that it is also the explanation of why that consciousness and injustice continue. Granting that the capitalistic system is in the large undesirable it still offers the compelling romance of individual opportunity for personal profit. The weakness of the Marxian conception of life on a two-class basis has been that it disregarded that very significant third class which in the past has been constantly just in the act of stepping across the imaginary line between the proletariat and the bourgeoisie.

But let us see in approximate historical sequence how the novelists have chronicled the evils of economic class distinctions in our democracy. Here as elsewhere in this study it will be pointed out that the criticism varies in scope from being the primary purpose of the novel to being merely incidental. Since the sharply defined lines of economic class distinctions arose only with the beginning of the age of big business the problem

---

13. Thomas Nelson Page, *John Marvel, Assistant*, p. 33.
14. Robert Herrick, *The Web of Life*, p. 133.

it presents is reflected in our fiction only after the nineteenth century had turned into its last quarter. Where earlier writers like Brockden Brown, Judah, Judd, and Cummins observe that all men are not neighbors, they dismiss the matter with only passing comment for it was a condition that had not yet become acute. It was the first of these, Brown, who in our early fiction most clearly comprehended the problems of class distinctions, and most forcefully protested against them; notably in *Arthur Mervyn* (1799). The title hero is a Godwinian figure. His soul is filled with brotherhood; every instinct leads him to the espousal of justice; his whole life is an implied criticism of all that is mean and sordid. "Wealth has ever been capriciously distributed", he observes. "The mere physical relation of birth is all that entitles us to manors and thrones".[15] Economic class distinctions have no rational basis and cannot promote the greatest good of the greatest number. The increasing poverty of the weak is not compensated for by increasing charity of the strong; indeed, "the frequency of the spectacle of distress seems to lessen the compassion with which it is reviewed".[16]

That some of our early fictionists were aware of what many have observed in later days, that the church has not done its theoretical duty in keeping down economic class distinctions but on the contrary has actually fostered them, is rather clearly to be read in certain comments of Samuel B. H. Judah. He charges that even the priest-hood has "no God but gold", that ".... in numerous instances, religion hath been made an article of traffic, and bought and sold as if it were a carnal thing".[17]

Something of the growing scope of the trades unions in 1850 is reflected in the analysis of class division which Captain Creamer owner of Green Mill gives Richard Edney, in Sylvester Judd's novel of that name: " 'Tis Labor against capital. Labor is ravenous; it scratches Capital, as the poets say, like a fowl on a dunghill".[18] A figure closer both to the truth and the ideal is Thomas

---

15. Brown, *Arthur Mervyn* (1799), v. 1, p. 56.
16. *Ibid.*, v. 2, p. 4.
17. S. B. H. Judah, *The Buccaneers* (1827), p. 6.
18. *Richard Edney and the Governor's Family* (1850), p. 45.

Bailey Aldrich's conception of Capital and Labor as Siamese twins—if you pinch one it hurts the other as well.[19]

Insipid and uneconomic Maria Cummins is disposed to think that social classes are mutually unenvious: "As long as one class is distinguished by education and refined manners, and another is marked by ignorance and vulgarity, there must be a dividing line between the two, which neither perhaps would desire to overstep".[20]   But she surprisedly discovers that economic power and unimpeachable virtue are not synonymous.   And so Willie Sullivan is made to observe: "I have seen more ignorance, more ill-breeding, meanness, and immorality in the so-called aristocracy of our country than I should have believed it possible would be tolerated there .... high position is no security against such contamination of the soul as unfits it for an exalted place hereafter".[21]   Miss Cummins believes that those are happiest "who have learned submission; those who in the severest afflictions, see the hand of a loving Father, and obedient to his will, kiss the chastening rod".[22]   A far cry this from the Marxian doctrine of uncompromising class war espoused by some of our later novelists.

Edward Eggleston in *The Mystery of Metropolisville* (1873), principally intended as a satirization of speculative land manipulations along the Middle Border, comments briefly on a very fundamental factor in the preservation of class distinctions. Albert Charlton is pictured as a young man full of ideas; the "most fundamental was of course his belief in the equality and universal brotherhood of man".   But his author observing Charlton's conduct remarks: "But the most democratic of democrats in theory is just a little bit of an aristocrat in feeling— he doesn't like to be patted on the back by the hostler".[23]   A comment that seems to call up a picture of William Dean Howells.   And in contrast to the inherent aristocrats with democratic pretences, and the aristocrats who are frankly so, is always "that curious poor-whitey race which is called 'tar-heel' in the

---

19. *The Stillwater Tragedy*, p. 191.
20. *The Lamplighter* (1854), p. 314.
21. *Ibid.*, p. 315.
22. *Ibid.*, p. 95.
23. *The Mystery of Metropolisville*, p. 21.

northern Carolina, 'sand-hiller' in the southern, 'corn-cracker' in Kentucky, 'yahoo' in Mississippi, and in California 'pike'."[24] The poor you have with you always.

Nor does Eggleston overlook the fact that the church often falls short in its duty of preventing class barriers by being more interested in business than in brotherhood: "The minister of the church in which the Hilbroughs had taken pews sent his wife to call on Mrs. Hilbrough, and two of the church officers, knowing the value of such an acquisition to the church, showed their Christian feeling in the same way".[25]

J. G. Holland in *Nicholas Minturn* (1877) continues the attack on an active class consciousness and the spirit of pauperism fostered by the church.

"Rich people, surrounded with their comforts try to make themselves more comfortable in their minds by sharing a portion of their wealth with the poor. Their dinners taste better after having fed a beggar. . . . Society cannot afford to have the vice of pauperism nourished for the small compensation of gratifying the benevolent impulses of the rich. . . . Pauperism grows by what it feeds on, and it feeds on the benevolence of the rich, and on benevolence which, like some of our Christianity, is fashionable."[26]

Holland charges that the mission church of New York is making no real effort to rehabilitate or develop, but simply to keep its poor dependent upon itself. Minturn is made to declare:

"There is one field, it seems to me, which Christian benevolence has never properly occupied. It has fed the mouth and clothed the back, and thus nursed the very greed it might to have destroyed; when it has done this, it has undertaken to give to the pauperism it has helped to develop, the Christian religion. I don't believe it can be made to grow on such a stock. . . . I feel sure that if three-quarters of the money that has been expended upon food and clothing and Sunday-schools and preaching, had been devoted to the enterprise of placing the pauper population in better conditions,—to giving them better tenements, better furniture, instructions in the facts and possibilities of common life, entertaining books, suggestive pictures, and training in household arts,—the good results of religion itself would be ten-fold greater than they are."[27]

The satirization of the charity practices of a class conscious society is not often better done than in H. H. Boyesen's

---

24. Edward Eggleston, *Roxy*, p. 183.
25. *The Faith Doctor* (1891), p. 61.
26. *Nicholas Minturn*, pp. 173-174.
27. *Ibid.*, p. 270.

Falconberg (1879).   He pictures a thriving Minnesota town in which charity faces adverse circumstances.

"In fact paupers were very scarce in Hardanger, as labor was abundant and wages very high, and of really worthy objects of charity the village hardly contained a single one.   These were hard facts to cope with for a charitable association, but Helga and her co-laborers were not easily daunted and they persevered in the face of all difficulties".[28]

Thus far the novelists of economic criticism here surveyed have protested against class distinctions and their fostering forces more or less incidentally.   Rarely has this specific criticism been the important theme of a book.   But hereafter it does become the primary purpose of many novels.

George Thomas Dowling's *The Wreckers* (1886), "a social study", sees the situation in a comprehensive but hopelessly visionary way:

"If men could only emphasize the things we human beings have in common, instead of dwelling always upon the points in which we differ, all classes could understand one another so much better."[29]

Joaquin Miller continues the attack against the forces which support unjust and unchristian class distinctions in *Destruction of Gotham* (1886) and *The Building of the City Beautiful* (1893). The former depicts a conflict of the upper and lower stratas of society in New York City, ending in final disaster when the poor revolt from their economic confinement to the Bowery and swarm up Fifth Avenue destroying with fire the palaces of their oppressors.   Can such an outcome of growing class differences be prevented?   *The Building of the City Beautiful,* a semi-utopian, religious fantasy offers a partial answer: only if man can somehow be recalled from his inhumanity to man, and the church recalled to the spirit of its Founder.   There must be a change; for under the present order

"We claim to build those temples for the people; yet the people are broken in body and in spirit.   Some of them will sleep in the streets and alleys tonight, while every church and temple stands empty and bolted against God's poor.   The rich must have a place where they can come and find God now and then.   And so God's houses are bolted and barred, while God's poor sleep in the rain and frost before the bolted doors."[30]

---

28.   *Falconberg,* p. 109.
29.   *The Wreckers,* p. 133.
30.   *The Building of the City Beautiful,* pp. 33-34.

Annie Kilburn (1888) is of the seven economic novels of
William Dean Howells included in this study perhaps the best
example of his protest against willfully maintained class distinctions. All of his novels could of course be treated under
this head, as indeed could all the economic novels in American
fiction, since the matter of class inequalities in its final ramifications is basic in all our economic ills. The utopian novels, *A
Traveller from Altruria* (1894) and *Through the Eye of the
Needle* (1907), of course propose the re-making of society into
one class, but they are comprehensive in their program; *Annie
Kilburn* is a protest against class consciousness in a more limited
sense. The problem here is, essentially, what can be done within
the present order. The Reverend Peck, who largely represents
Howells' personal view, occasionally sees the future in terms of
revolution rather than reform:

"We live in an age of seeming preparation for indefinite war. The lines
are drawn harder and faster between the rich and the poor and on either side
the forces are embattled. The working-men are combined in vast organizations to withstand the strength of the capitalists, and these are taking the lesson and uniting in trusts. The smaller industries are gone and the smaller
commerce is being devoured by the larger."[31]

There is effective satirization too of those who are particular
in choosing their neighbors, in Annie's memory of Judge
Kilburn's saying that "the great superiority of the American practice of democracy over the French ideal was that it didn't in-
volve any assumption of social equality. He said that equality
before the law and in politics was sacred, but that the principle
could never govern society".[32] Howells rarely accomplished a
more blighting caricature than his drawing of Gerrish in this
protest against the injustices of class. Gerrish had arisen from
a proletarian clerkship to a bourgeois store-ownership standing
in the New England town of Hatboro. When it is proposed
that a public gathering should be held at his home in the interests of a worthy social project, he declares: ". . . I do not
believe in pampering those who have not risen, or made no
effort to rise. . . . I will meet them at the polls, or at the

---

31. *Annie Kilburn,* p. 241.
32. *Ibid.,* pp. 63-64.

communion table, or on any proper occasion; but a man's home is sacred".[33]   Charity that is given only to glorify the giver is no charity at all, declares Howells in this novel, and any effective social union founded on social disunion an impossibility.   The hope of a future better than the past is resident in "not the justice of our Christless codes, with their penalties, but the instinct of righteous shame which, however dumbly, however obscurely, stirs in every honest man's heart when his superfluity is confronted with another's destitution, and which is destined to increase in power till it becomes the social as well as the individual conscience".[34]

Mark Twain has nothing but scorn for the "sarcasm of law and phrase" that calls wage-slaves 'freemen', if we may draw a contemporary inference from *A Connecticut Yankee in King Arthur's Court* (1889).   Seven-tenths of the population were "free and independent paupers dominated by the other three-tenths".   "The priests had told their fathers and themselves that this ironical state of things was ordained of God, and so, not reflecting how unlike God it would be to amuse himself with sarcasms, and especially such poor transparent ones as this, they had dropped the matter there and become respectfully quiet".[35]   The Clemmens conception of class distinctions and injustices is further set forth in a reference to the French Revolution: "There were two 'Reigns of Terror', if we would but remember it and consider it; the one wrought murder in hot passion; the other in heartless cold blood; the one lasted mere months, the other had lasted a thousand years, . . ."[36]   In *The American Claimant* (1892) Twain brings Howard Tracy, an Englishman, into an American atmosphere in order to contrast our theory with our practice.   Tracy observes: "I came away from England to get away from artificial forms . . . and here you've got them too".[37]   It is a significant and striking fact that no matter at what level you take society there is always a

---

33. *Ibid.*, p. 86.
34. *Ibid.*, p. 240.
35. *A Connecticut Yankee in King Arthur's Court*, p. 101.
36. *Ibid.*, p. 103.
37. *The American Claimant*, p. 90.

classification of upper and lower within the segment selected.
In *The American Claimant* Tracy finds social inequalities even
among the residents of his four dollar a week Washington boarding house.

Kate Douglass Wiggin tells the same story of the
slums of San Francisco. Mis' Mooney in the front of No. 32
Anna street looks down with superior despising on Mis' Kennett
who lives in the rear of No. 32 Anna street, and the latter
explains it thus: "You see her husband was in the rug, sack,
and bottle business, 'm, 'n a wealthy gintleman friend set him
up in a fish-cart, an' it's kind of onsettled her, 'm! Some folks
can't stand prosperity. If 't hed bin gradjooal like she might
have took it more natcheral; but it come all of a sudden, an'
she's that purse-proud now. . . ."[38] It is a testimony cor-
roborated by Campbell and Riis, and by almost any social
worker one can meet. Its tendency is to reconcile one to the
social inequalities against which most of our economic novelists
so strenuously protest. If there is no brotherhood among those
who are equally weak how can there be between the strong and
the weak?

Charles Dudley Warner's *A Little Journey in the World*
(1889) is "an attempt to trace the demoralization in a woman's
soul of certain well-known influences in our existing social life",
specifically the disintegrating effect of " 'prosperous' marriages,
and association with unscrupulous methods of acquiring money".
Here, as in *The Golden House* (1894) and *That Fortune* (1889),
is depicted class consciousness from the perspective of the strong.
And Warner is apparently more interested in drawing an attractive and rather authentic picture of the society he treats than
in mitigating the economic injustices done by that society. His
satire is never stinging, annihilating, in its force. He is content
"with observing life and criticizing it, humorously sometimes, and
without any serious intention of disturbing it".[39] There is however, fine irony in his analysis of the manner in which the church
acknowledges and fosters class distinctions based upon wealth.
He recalls that the meeting-house at Pilgrim, Massachusetts,

---

38. *The Story of Patsy,* p. 44.
39. *A Little Journey in the World,* p. 16.

"had a committee for seating people according to their quality. They were very shrewd, but it had not occurred to them to give the best pews to the sitters able to pay the most money for them".[40]

A darker view of the present and the future can scarcely be found even among the most pessimistic of our economic novelists than that of Ignatius Donnelly in *Caesar's Column* (1890). And it is in the class injustices of the age of big business that the problem consists.

"I seek to preach into the ears of the able and rich and powerful the great truth that neglect of the sufferings of their fellows, indifference to the great bond of brotherhood which lies at the base of Christianity, and blind, brutal, and degrading worship of mere wealth must—given time and pressure enough —eventuate in the overthrow of society and the destruction of civilization . . . . life is a dark and wretched failure for the great mass of mankind. The many are plundered to enrich the few. Vast combinations depress the price of labor and increase the cost of the necessaries of existence. The rich, as a rule, despise the poor, and the poor are coming to hate the rich. . . . These conditions have come about in less than a century; most of them in a quarter of a century."[41]

The novel develops into an extravagant utopian tale of the years from 1988 to 1995, but the conception of class injustice is definitely its background and its message.

Albion W. Tourgée in emphasizing his plea for the erasing of economic class lines (*Murvale Eastman, Christian Socialist,* 1890) declares that "the Christ whom being risen we worship, we would not take to our table being incarnate".[42] The man Jesus who walked the streets of Nazareth would not be recognized as a neighbor by the rich young rulers of America's Wall Streets, nor even by the professing Christians of the Church of the Golden Lilies. Only the things of Caesar receive consideration here. But despite the deplorable manner in which the present church fostered class distinctions arising from economic bases, Murvale Eastman still felt that the world's greatest hope lay in the teaching of the Nazarene. "He fell to comparing the Christian idea as he understood it with these pro-

---

40. *Ibid.,* p. 17.
41. *Caesar's Column,* pp. 3-4.
42. *Murvale Eastman,* p. 61.

posed systems of government and society, (from Plato's day until the present) and in so doing was more and more struck with its wisdom and simplicity in dealing not with methods, but with men, not with theories, but with individuals; not with conditions, but with motives. . . . 'Whatsoever ye would that men should do to you, do ye even so to them' is a universally beneficent principle, subject to no variation because of age, condition, race, or clime. Whatever government, form of society, or economic condition promotes the practical application of this idea is good; whatever hinders it is bad. This was Murvale Eastman's philosophy".[43]

In a book dedicated to the Farmer's Alliance whose "aims and achievements" have the author's "respect and sympathy" Mary H. Ford resumes the denouncement of class consciousness on a more economic basis. *Which Wins?* (1891) is a protest against a system of civilization that will allow thousands to starve while plenty exists in the land. John Thurston, inheritor of a comfortable New York legacy, finds a growing socialistic philosophy in his soul; he feels that he can "never be happy" until he has stripped himself of everything and stands "on an equality with the poorest son of Mother Earth".[44] He establishes himself on a Nebraska farm, believing that from the fresher soil of the West can most effectively be raised the beautiful flower of a new order. But he reckoned without the railroads and wheat barons who for a few more points of personal profit force western farmers to leave their grain unharvested while hundreds starve in New York's slums.

It is in the economic oppression of the weak by the strong that Dan Beard, also, sees the failure of American democracy. Using the figure of a picture which turned for a long time toward the wall fades. but turned again to the light renews its colors, Beard declares: "There is a wall called Vested Rights, which prevents nature's sun from shining on our fellow-men, but, thank God! good workmen are busy at its foundation: it is already undermined and *must* fall. Then and then only will the poor tramp, the beggar, and the white slave begin to show the true

43. *Ibid.*, pp. 86-87.
44. *Which Wins?* p. 14.

color of their manhood".[45] Referring to Thomas G. Shearman
and statistics compiled by him Beard further points out that
the "whole wealth of country is practically owned by two hundred and fifty thousand persons, or one in sixty of the adult
male population, and he predicts, from the rapid recent concentration of wealth, that under present conditions, fifty thousand persons will practically own all the wealth of the country
in thirty years—or less than one in five hundred of the adult
male population".[46] Such inequalities of economic classes cannot but be detrimental and disintegrating to the unity of the
state.

Margaret Sherwood (pseudonym: Elizabeth Hastings) is another novelist who places social purpose above art, although
she writes better than the majority of our economic fictionists.
The injustice perpetrated by economic power is her theme—
specifically, as applied to the department store. She sees their
'bargains' made possible only by forcing the women who have
made, and the girls who sell their articles, to live on a killing
wage. Economic organization is such that "the only people
who can make money are those who don't need it".[47] Miss
Sherwood protests, too, against the pauperizing attitude of charity. When society goes into slum work, she points out, they
are always, perhaps unavoidingly, patronizing; they even seem
to patronize the Creator by reminding Him that He is being
recognized by one of the first families.[48]

The Descendant (1897) is an extremely provocative novel but
Miss Glasgow's social purpose is always subservient to her novelist's art. She is wont to see the injustices of life not in the
oppression of the weak by the strong but in the organization of
society, a great seeming force beyond the control of either
class. Michael Ackershem represents the author's attitude: "It
was the system that he hated—the system . . . that protected
oppression in the name of liberty, and injustice in the name of
law".[49] Miss Glasgow, of course, does not subscribe to the com-

---

45. *Moonblight and Six Feet of Romance*, p. xiii.
46. *Ibid.*, pp. 88-89.
47. *Henry Worthington, Idealist*, p. 59.
48. Cf. *An Experiment in Altruism* (1895), p. 3.
49. *The Descendant*, p. 31.

munistic programs of such characters as Semple and McTibbs in this book. She feels that these agitators she has created exaggerate class evils, but nevertheless that "our condition is sufficiently serious".[50]

Hamlin Garland's economic criticism may be most definitely described as a protest against the oppression of the Middle Border farmer by the railroads and eastern mortgage companies. Basic to this but less tangible is a sense of class consciousness and injustice. This more comprehensive and general view of the ills of society is given best in Walter Reeves' article for the "Events", in *Jason Edwards* (1897). Seeing and feeling from a point of vantage on the new Brooklyn Bridge, whose opening he has gone to report, Reeves wrote:

"I saw men rushing to and fro there in those gloomy scenes, like ants in the scoria of a volcano. I saw pale women sewing in dens reeking with pestilence and throbbing with heat. I saw myriads of *homes* where the children could play only on the roof or in the street . . . and I said, man has invented a thousand new ways of producing wealth, but not one for properly distributing it. I don't understand the problem, but it must be solved."[51]

This is the Garland conclusion.

There is perhaps no more stinging condemnation of the uncharitable charity that so effectively supports economic class distinctions than in *The Milltillionaire* (1898) of Albert Waldo Howard. Writing from the perspective of a remotely future Utopia he exclaims with deep feeling:

"The charity of the Church Societies and Municipal organization of the Past, a mockery of true love, which employed itself with vain, empty words and abominable dispensations of watery soup, coffee, and stale bread, or of some dirty, ragged clothes, to the poor with these mottoes staring you in the face from their portals; 'Half-a-loaf is better than no bread', or rather, as they verified it 'A smell of soup is better than no soup' . . . 'Slow poison is better than food' . . . an emphatic manner of preparing them to meet death—fortunately, this exists no more."[52]

There is something of the economic determinist in Robert Herrick, as there is in Ellen Glasgow—as indeed there must be in any thinker who penetrates beyond the obvious superficialities

---

50. *Ibid.*, p. 128.
51. *Jason Edwards*, p. 43.
52. *The Milltillionaire*, p. 13.

of life. Herrick like Glasgow, just cited, conceives of society
as a machine, a system, greater than any class.[53] Of course there
are those who govern the machine, who run it, and oil it, and
turn it to their own pleasures. It is the soullessness of these
that Herrick denounces.

"Wealth has ever been capriciously distributed. The mere
physical relation of birth is all that entitles us to manors and
thrones"[54] was quoted from the character Arthur Mervyn at
the beginning of this survey of fictionist protest against economic
class distinctions and injustices. And in 1900 Christopher Kenyon
is repeating: "I am living on an income of twenty-five thousand a year at the lowest, and Jimmie Casey is living on an income of seven hundred and fifty a year; and the chief
reason is because my father owned the mill and handed it over
to me, and Jimmie's father didn't. And I can't seem to make out
a good and sufficient reason".[55] The problem, then, is an old one,
much older far than American fiction, but it has undoubtedly
grown more acute with the yearly progress of the age of big
business. "The people of the Republic are divided into two
classes; the employers and the employed"[56] and machinery is
increasing the latter. The capitalists are banded together for
the "oppression and degradation of the honest poor".[57] Thousands
of our brothers' children in the great cities must live in leaky,
unheated, vermin-haunted houses and feed from garbage cans
because there is no work, while "not a mile away the rich are
lazy in luxury".[58] This is the charge of our economic critics
in fiction. Is the church not doing something, the novelists ask,
to mitigate this inhumanity of man toward man? No, they
answer, the money-changers are even in the temple; and the
reason they cannot be driven out is that they own the temple.
Must we then accept class injustice to class; must we "bow
in the House of Rimmon, or go and live in the woods like

---

53. Cf. *The Web of Life*, p. 201.
54. Charles Brockden Brown, *Arthur Mervyn* (1799), v. 1, p. 56.
55. Florence Converse, *The Burden of Christopher* (1900), p. 57.
56. Milan C. Edson, *Solaris Farm*, p. 301.
57. Alexander Craig, *Ionia*, p. 43.
58. Hervey White, *Differences*, p. 54.

Thoreau and eat dried peas"?[59]   The novelists of economic criticism in American fiction have written seriously, not because they believed only that something should be done, but that something could be done to alleviate the ills they have described. Their intention is to provoke the thought of the people that from much thinking may eventually come a more equitable distribution of wealth, a more equalitarian class philosophy.

SPECIAL RACE PROBLEMS TREATED IN AMERICAN FICTION: THE INDIAN

In addition to social class distinctions arising from superior economic talent or uncurbed selfishness our fiction also reflects certain class problems based upon race.   The principle of the survival of the social fittest has been augmented by the factor of skin pigment or country of origin.   The Indian, the Negro, and the immigrant represent the different phases of this problem.

There has been only one significant novel within scope of this thesis which had as its fundamental purpose a protest against our ill usage of the Indian through a 'century of dishonor'.   That book, of course, is Helen Hunt Jackson's *Romona* (1884).   But injustice to the Indian had been criticized incidentally and occasionally by our writers of fiction almost from the beginning of the novel in America.   Indeed in *Modern Chivalry* (1792) we find a satirical comment on the way our promises to the Indian were being nullified by our practices toward the Indian. Brackenridge reveals the custom of certain promoters of rounding up fake Indian chiefs, whom they introduce to the government and with whom they make treaties, getting for themselves such considerations as the government records showed were given to the Indians in exchange for the concessions of the treaties. Weavers and pedlars with peculiar hair-cuts were most easily disguised.   Teague O'Regan here as in the other chapters of this picaresque romance moves toward the center of the stage: a plan to make him a 'Kickapoo' chief falls just short of consummation.   Brackenridge comments on the general conduct of Indian affairs:

---

59. Margaret Deland, *The Wisdom of Fools*, p. 128.

"The policy of treating with the Indians is very good; because it takes off a good deal of loose merchandise, that might otherwise lie on our hands, and cuts away superfluities from finances of the government at the same time; as every fresh treaty lays the foundation of a new war, it will serve to check the too rapid growth of the settlements. The extremities of a government, like the arm or ankle of an individual, are the parts at which blood is to be let."[60]

Washington Irving, too, in his *Knickerbocker History* (1809) takes cognizance of the white man's propensity for disestablishing the Indians from "the vast regions they pretended to hold".[61] We note also the high moral integrity with which the white man's commerce with the red was always carried on:

"A brisk trade for furs was soon opened: the Dutch traders were scrupulously honest in their dealings and purchased by weight, establishing it as an invariable table of avoirdupois, that the hand of a Dutchman weighed one pound, and his foot two pounds. It is true the simple Indians were often puzzled by the great disproportion between bulk and weight, for let them place a bundle of furs, ever so large, in one scale, and a Dutchman put his hand or foot in the other, the bundle was sure to kick the beam—never was a package of furs known to weigh more than two pounds in the market of Communipaw!"[62]

John Neal—*Logan* (1822) and *Brother Jonathan* (1825)— is another commentator in our earlier fiction who criticizes— somewhat casually, to be sure, in the midst of his Byronic romances—the injustice which has been done to the Indian, "the native and legitimate proprietor of the western world, unto whose fathers it was given by the Great Spirit, ages and ages ago." Neal's indefinite hope for the future of the Indian race is given in the dying words of Logan, the white chief, to his son: "Harold, remember England . . . . Go there. Learn all that white men know. Return and emancipate the Indians. Do this! and thy father's blessing shall be upon thee . . . . "[63]

It is obvious, of course, that in these early novels injustice to the Indian is only touched upon and is not the central theme of the books. But after Brackenridge, Irving, and Neal the Indian cause had even less support by our social critics in fiction.

---

60. *Modern Chivalry*, v. 1, p. 80.
61. *Knickerbocker History*, p. 133.
62. *Ibid.*, p. 94.
63. *Logan*, v. I, p. 110.

The idealization of the Indian to be found in Cooper's romances might lead one to expect from him some criticism of our Indian policy and practice. However, when he spoke specifically and clearly on the matter his opinion was that the Indian had not been handled with undeserved harshness and that the United States government had always remained well within its international rights. He found the Indians "all alike, a stunted, dirty, and degraded race". . . . and held "that neither the United States, nor any individual State, has ever taken possession of any land that, by usage or construction, might be decreed the property of the Indians, without a treaty and a purchase"; that "a good deal is endeavoured to be done in mitigating the sufferings and in meliorating the condition of the Indians" by the 'office of the Indian affairs'. . . . "at the rate of a little more than a million of dollars a year". "The Indians", Cooper said, "have never been slain except in battle, unless by lawless individuals, ... or in any manner aggrieved, except in the general, and, perhaps, in some degree, justifiable invasion of a territory that they did not want, nor could not use".[64]

It is therefore not until Helen Hunt Jackson's *Romona* (1884) that we have an uncompromising, fully developed espousal of the Indian's case against the white man.[65] The full implications of the grave charges this romance carries so easily are only realized when one interprets it in the light of Mrs. Jackson's *A Century of Dishonor* (1885). This latter volume may be compared in idea with Mrs. Stowe's "A Key to Uncle Tom's Cabin", except that it is an independent book and has considerable merit as a propagandistic essay.

"It is a government of thieves and robbers" is Father Gaspara's indictment of the United States.[66] And Mrs. Jackson proceeds to demonstrate the truth of the charge as particularly seen in southern California in "the downfall of the Missions, the loss

---

64. *Notions of the Americans*, v. II, pp. 281-285.
65. In "Quella" (1875) Rebecca Harding Davis had made a forceful plea for the education of the Cherokees in North Carolina. Her indictment of the social injustice that was being done these Indians was serious in its purpose but comparatively brief and undeveloped. Cf. *Lippincott's Magazine*, November, 1875, p. 576 ff.
66. *Romona*, p. 293.

of their vast estates, and the growing power of the ungodly in the land".[67] The lands which Allesandro and his bronze-skinned fathers before him have held with unselfishness, philanthropy, and justice toward all their people have been taken, "all taken, sold, resold, and settled by greedy speculators; the Indian converts disappearing, driven back to their original wildernesses".[68] The seriousness and comprehensiveness of Mrs. Jackson's criticism here is revealed when we find her noting in *A Century of Dishonor* that there have been some three hundred tribes of Indians in the United States and that "there is not among these three hundred bands of Indians one which has not suffered cruelly at the hands either of the Government or of white settlers. The poorer, the more insignificant, the more helpless the band, the more certain the cruelty and outrage to which they have been subjected. This is especially true of the bands on the Pacific slope . . . . The story of one tribe is the story of all, varied only by differences of time and place . . . . Colorado is as greedy and unjust in 1880 as was Georgia in 1830 and Ohio in 1795; and the United States Government breaks promises now as deftly as then, and with an added ingenuity from long practice."[69]

The Indian lands have been taken through 'regular conveyances', 'extinguishing claims' and 'extending purchase'.[70] The Government's attitude toward these defenseless children of the Great Spirit is well expressed in the instructions given the Commissioners who were to further disestablish the Sioux in Minnesota in 1849:

"Though the proposed purchase is estimated to contain some twenty million acres, and some of it no doubt of excellent quality, there are 'sound reasons why it is comparatively valueless to the Indians, and a large price should not be paid for it. . . . The extent of the proposed cession should be no criterion of the amount that should be paid for it. On a full consideration of the whole matter, it is the opinion of this office that from two to two and a half cents an acre would be an ample equivalent for it'. If the Indians object too strenuously the commissioner may advance the price but any such

---

67. *Ibid.*, p. 44.
68. *Ibid.*, pp. 44-45.
69. *A Century of Dishonor*, pp. 337-38.
70. *Ibid.*, p. 37.

increase in price must be 'based on such evidence and information as shall fully satisfy the President and Senate'."[71]

To the assertion that the red man is lazy, shiftless, and unresponsive to the manners and methods of civilization Mrs. Jackson replies:

"Why should the Indian be expected to plant corn, fence lands, build houses, or do anything but get food from day to day, when experience has taught him that the product of his labor will be seized by the white man to-morrow?"[72]

The solution to this problem of our economic and moral injustice to the Indian, Mrs. Jackson saw in giving to them the property rights of citizens: "All judicious plans and measures for their safety and salvation must embody provisions for their becoming citizens as fast as they are fit . . . ."[73]

This then is the significant criticism of our economic injustice to the Indian. He receives only passing notice in our other social protest fiction. Chauncey Thomas, a utopian novelist— *The Crystal Button* (1891)—in a chapter on the history of the world as looked back upon from the forty-ninth century records a revolt of the Indians "against the Government of Washington and consequently all its white people, on the ground that solemn pledges had been broken and treaties trampled upon whenever the wishes of the whites came in conflict with those of their humble wards".[74]

Mark Twain with characteristic satire exposes at once the useless expense of the army and the ill-treatment of the Indians; Colonel Sellers has persuaded himself into a belief that he can 'materialize' almost anything he desires—"take the army, for instance; now twenty-five thousand men; expense, twenty-two millions a year. I will dig up the Romans, I will resurrect the Greeks, I will furnish the Government for ten millions a year, ten thousand men drawn from the victorious legions of all the ages—soldiers that will chase Indians year in and year out on materialized horses, and cost never a cent for rations or repairs".[75]

---

71. *Ibid.*, p. 147.
72. *Ibid.*, p. 339.
73. *Ibid.*, p. 341.
74. Chancey Thomas, *The Crystal Button*, p. 148.
75. Mark Twain, *The American Claimant*, p. 33.

But there is perhaps no more surprising—and pathetic—picture of the Indian than that of a colony of bronze-skinned people in a New York tenement district drawn by Jacob Riis:

"They are Indians, a handful of Mohawks and Iroquois, whom some ill wind has blown down from their Canadian reservation, and left in these West Side tenements to eke out a living as they can, weaving mats and baskets, and threading glass pearls on slippers and pin-cushions, until one after another, they have died off and gone to happier hunting-grounds than Thompson street."[76]

It is the end of a race. But that is the order of life.

THE NEGRO

Thou spot of hell, deep smirched on human kind
The uncur'd gangrene of the reasoning mind . . .

Thus did Timothy Dwight[77] brand the institution of Negro slavery in the United States. Nor was his the first pen in American literature to write so positively upon the issue that later led to the Civil War. But the first declaration on the subject in our critical fiction expressed an opposite and approving view. Since in general Captain John Farrago in *Modern Chivalry* is Brackenridge's drawing of himself the Captain's view as he discusses the slavery question with a Quaker may well be taken as Brackenridge's own opinion:

"I should think myself justifiable in making any man a slave to answer my purposes, provided I treated him well while he was such. . . . There is no man would be more disposed to treat a slave with tenderness than myself, but to deny me of my right altogether, of making one, or of trafficking for one when made, is carrying the matter too far."[78]

In general, however, the novelists who definitely mentioned the issue were interested in modifying or abolishing the institution, for only such as approve the status quo many remain passive. We find the translator of *Memoirs of the Year 2500* (1795) expressing an almost militantly abolitionist view:

"How can the princes of the North refrain from covering themselves with immortal glory by banishing slavery from their dominions, by restoring to the laborer of the land at least his personal liberty? How can they be deaf

---

76. Jacob A. Riis, *Out of Mulberry Street*, p. 26.
77. *Greenfield Hill* (1794), p. 38. Cf. also Freneau, *Emigration to America*, etc.
78. *Modern Chivalry*, v. I, p. 157.

to the cry of humanity which constantly excites them to that act of glorious beneficence? By what motive can they be induced to hold in an odious servitude, and one that is contrary to their real interest, the most industrious part of their subjects, when they have before their eyes the example of those Quakers who have given liberty to all their Negro slaves? How is it possible for them not to be sensible, that their subjects will be more faithful by being more free: and that they must cease to be slaves ere they can become men."[79]

Dr. Updike Underhill in *The Algerine Captive* (1797) when told of his privilege to take aboard ship a number of slaves for his own profit, declares: "I would sooner suffer servitude than purchase a slave";[80] he later refers to the captured Africans as "these my brothers of the human race".[81] That Tyler was serious in these sentiments of Underhill I think we may assume, especially in view of his rather graphic pictures of family associations being sundered, and the Negroes trying to strangle themselves in the ship's hold by twisting their necks in the iron collars that held them together.[82]

Conscious critic though he was of many phases of our national life James Fenimore Cooper apparently never inserted into his fiction any developed analysis of the slavery problem. His views on the question are, however, explicitly set forth in *Notions of the Americans* (1828). He held that since recognition of slavery was a condition of southern entrance into the union it was while inconsistent with ideal democracy quite consistent with the Constitution of the United States. "Equal rights do not . . . . imply a broad, general, and unequivocal equality".[83] To Cooper's eyes the slaves were in general quite satisfactorily dealt by; indeed he observed that " a very numerous class ("the domestic servants, and those who labor as mechanics and artisans") . . . . are far better instructed, better clothed, and better fed, and . . . . are altogether a superior race to the lowest class of European peasants".[84] However, he felt that "general emancipation . . . must sooner or later arrive". But that this should be immediate, complete, and general was unthinkable, both because of the

79. *Memoirs of the Year 2500*, p. 335.
80. Royall Tyler, *The Algerine Captive*, p. 98.
81. *Ibid.*, p. 101.
82. *Ibid.*, p. 98.
83. *Notions of the Americans*, v. II, p. 265.
84. *Ibid.*, v. II, p. 260.

character limitations of the slaves—"their ignorance and animal qualities"—and because of the economic effect upon the slave-holders. Cooper takes pride in the fact that it is the "glory of the institutions of this country that they have never run into practical excesses", and he believes that the problem should and will work itself out in gradual emancipation.[85]

Slavery as an economic institution was obviously dependent upon a few semitropical plantation crops. At the time the Constitution was framed, rice and indigo, produced principally in Georgia and South Carolina, were the two most important. Indigo declined in importance and sugar greatly increased, especially after the annexation of the Louisiana Purchase. But the crop which most significantly affected slavery was, of course, cotton. The labor of half the slaves of the entire country came finally to be employed by this single product. It is reasonable to surmise, therefore, "that had it not been for the unforeseen development of the cotton industry, the expectation of the founders of the Republic that slavery would soon disappear would actually have been realized".[86] The relation between this notable development of cotton-raising in the South and the contemporary industrial expansion of England and the North is found in the invention of the cotton-gin and the ever wider use of improved power-looms. Send us cotton, cried the mills. The problem therefore became more acute; the price of slaves increased from a few hundred to a thousand or twelve hundred dollars, and the statute which Congress had passed in 1807 prohibiting the African slave-trade remained continually violated.[87] The controversy took a decided turn toward more serious proportions in the year 1831: in January William Lloyd Garrison began the publication of the *Liberator;* in August there occurred at Southampton, Virginia, a slave insurrection led by Nat Turner, a negro, in which sixty-one white persons were massacred.[88]

The growing acuteness of the problem was not, however, immediately reflected in our fiction. The picture of slavery which

---

85. Cf. *Ibid.*, v. II, pp. 265-267.
86. Jesse Macy, *The Anti-Slavery Crusade*, Chronicles of America, v. 28, p. 22.
87. *Ibid.*, p. 23.
88. *Ibid.*, p. 54.

John Pendleton Kennedy drew in *Swallow Barn* (1832), is if not idyllic still far from squalid. His study is quiet, compromising, tactful. Here is his reaction to the slave quarter, the master, and the slave:

"Some few were built after the fashion of the better sort of cottages. . . . But the more lowly of these structures, and the most numerous, were nothing more than plain log cabins. . . . The insides of these dwellings were furnished according to a very primitive notion of comfort. . . . Swarms of little negroes basked on the sunny sides of these cabins . . . prolific mothers of this redundant brood . . . a few reverend, wrinkled, decrepit old men . . ."

"Meriwether . . . is a kind and considerate master. It is his custom frequently to visit his slaves in order to inspect their condition, and, where it may be necessary, to add to their comforts or relieve their wants."[89]

Kennedy observes in the scene about him an "air of contentment and good humor and kind family attachment." He will not say, however, that "in a high state of cultivation and of such self-dependence as they might possibly attain in a separate national existence, they might not become a more respectable people;" but he is "quite sure they never could become a happier people" than he finds them here. He feels that the Negro "is in his moral constitution a dependent upon the white race; dependent for guidance and direction even to the procurement of his most indispensable necessaries". The "direct broad emancipation of these people" would, therefore, be the "most cruel of all projects."[90]

The views of Meriwether are recorded as typical of the Virginia planter; his ideas for slave reform apparently meet with Kennedy's approval. "Extreme poverty," Meriwether avers, "is, perhaps, always a wrong done to the individual upon whom it is cast. Society can have no honest excuses for starving a human being . . . . Slavery, as an original question, is wholly without justification or defense. It is theoretically and morally wrong," but a violent removal of the slaves or a general emancipation would be alike calamitous. "Considerate kindness" should in the meantime be practiced. Harshness of the master is an accusation with "much more malice or invention than truth." There should be legislation to prohibit cruelty. "We owe it to humanity and to the sacred obligation of Christian ordi-

---

89. *Swallow Barn,* pp. 449 ff.
90. *Ibid.,* p. 454.

nances," Meriwether declares, "to respect and secure the bonds of husband and wife, and parent and child. . . . We have no right to put man and wife asunder. . . ." He proposes

"to establish by law an upper or privileged class of slaves—selecting them from the most deserving above the age of forty-five years. These I would endue with something of a feudal character. They should be entitled to hold small tracts of land under their masters, rendering for it a certain rent, payable either in personal service or money. They should be elevated into this class through some order of court, founded on certificates of good conduct, and showing the assent of the master."[91]

Expression on the slavery question becomes more militant in the fiction of Nathaniel Beverly Tucker on the one side, and Lydia Maria Child on the other. We begin to see here the taking of stands which no compromise could reconcile. A more assertive defense of states rights or a more scathing denouncement of Yankee personalities and principles than *The Partisan Leader* (1836) cannot well be imagined. Tucker's agrarian philosophy had a deep-seated hatred for industrialism; a protective tariff that lays a tax on the planter to aid the manufacturer is blightingly condemned. The rights of Virginia can only be adequately protected by insisting upon the sovereignty of her power:

"As long as we let the Yankees hold James river, we must make up our minds to eat our hogs when they are fat, and to do without salt to our bread. But it is not worth grumbling about; and bread without salt is more than men deserve that will give up their country without fighting for it."[92]

Jeffersonian in the background of his thought Tucker corrects Jefferson's error in believing that the gradual extinction of slavery would be a good thing. The slaves, better treated than the peasantry of most countries are characterized by a "proud humility" rather than a "servile sulkiness".[93] The loyalty of the slave and the generosity of the master are the fundamental forces in a more benevolent civilization than the mercenary Yankee can understand.

---

91. *Ibid.*, pp. 455-460.
92. *The Partisan Leader*, p. 13.
93. *Ibid.*, p. 99.

Less militantly abolitionist in her fiction than in her essays[94] Lydia Maria Child must be noted as a reputable novelist who expressed at this time the belief that immediate, complete emancipation was the only solution to the slavery problem. *Philothea* (1836) is Greek in setting, but that its treatment of the slavery question was meant to have reference to the American situation is made clear by appendix notes.[95] Mrs. Child holds that "the Athenian slave laws were much more mild than modern codes", for "if a servant complained of being abused his master had no power to retain him".[96] Mrs. Child further espoused the abolitionist cause in two short stories, "The Quadroons" and "The Black Saxons", in *Fact and Fiction* (1846).

It must be apparent that as between the economic and the moral arguments for the abolition of slavery the moral was likely to receive the preponderant emphasis in fiction dealing with the problem. It could be easily presented through dramatic contrasts. By heightening the virtue of the southern black and exaggerating the vice of the southern white the abolitionist could work a powerful effect through his fiction. And that is in essence the method of *Uncle Tom's Cabin* (1852) and most of the other anti-slavery novels that trailed in the wake of Mrs. Stowe's famous work. The economic argument was much more difficult to dramatize, harder to adapt to the purposes of fiction. Indeed we can often comprehend its elements in these novels only by inference from other abolition writings: the fiction is fully understood only by analysis of the whole body of thought on which it is based.

The economic argument for emancipation stems rather largely from Adam Smith's *The Wealth of Nations*. Smith had said:

"The experience of all ages and nations, I believe, demonstrates that the work done by slaves, though it appears to cost only their maintenance, is in the end the dearest of any. A person who can acquire no property can have no other interest but to eat as much and to labour as little as possible. Whatever work he does beyond what is sufficient to purchase his own maintenance,

---

94. Cf. "An appeal in Favor of that class of Americans called Africans", Boston, 1833; "Anecdotes of American Slavery", Newburyport, 1835; "Anti-slavery Catechism", Newburyport, 1836; "The Evils of Slavery and the Cure of Slavery", Newburyport, 1836.
95. Second edition, 1839, used in this study.
96. *Philothea*, p. 283.

can be squeezed out of him by violence only, and not by any interest of his . . . .
The pride of man makes him love to domineer, and nothing mortifies him so
much as to be obliged to condescend to persuade his inferiors. Wherever
the law allows it, and the nature of the work can afford it, therefore, he will
generally prefer the service of slaves to that of free men. The planting of
sugar and tobacco can afford the expense of slave cultivation. The raising of
corn, it seems, in the present times, cannot. In the English colonies, of which
the principal produce is corn, the far greater part of the work is done by
freemen. The late resolution of the Quakers in Pennsylvania to set at liberty
all their negro slaves, may satisfy us that their number cannot be very great.
Had they made any considerable part of their property, such a resolution could
never have béen agreed to. In our sugar colonies the whole work is done by
slaves, and in our tobacco colonies a very great part of, it . . . . Both can afford
the expense of slave cultivation, but sugar can afford it still better than
tobacco. The number of negroes, accordingly, is much greater, in proportion
to that of whites, in our sugar than in our tobacco colonies."[97]

The abolitionists pointed out that the capital tied up in slaves
was large, and that the cost of maintaining the sick and the
superannuated greatly impaired the return upon that capital.
While the slaves could not work systematically all the year,
still they must be kept all the year. The presence of slaves
discouraged the growth of manufactures, and resulted in the
deterioration in social position of the 'poor whites'. To support these contentions the agitators for emancipation made com-
parisons, North and South, regarding the value of property,
rate of population increase, and size of cities. Among the benefits from abolition would be these: increased production, rise
in land values, agricultural improvements, smaller holdings, re-
lease of capital for manufacture and commerce, revival of a
spirit of industry, the accumulation of property by negroes and
their consequent greater personal interest in the security of
property. This, in outline, is the economic brief of the anti-
slavery advocates.[98]

The social philosophy of the South in this period was an

97. *Wealth of Nations,* p. 298. See Benjamin Franklin's "Observations
Concerning the Increase of Mankind and the Peopling of Countries" (1751)
for a strikingly similar and much earlier statement of the economic significance
of slave labor. Quoted in S. Howard Patterson, *Readings in the History of
Economic Thought,* pp. 93-94.

98. Cf. Carrie M. Lewis, "A History of the Literature of Abolition", un-
published history thesis, Cornell University, 1917. In Cornell University
Library.

integration of Jeffersonian democracy and slave economy: an approximation of the Greek ideal of democracy. It conceived of the patriarchal system existing in the South as the best possible adaptation of government for securing the greatest good for the greatest number. This was accomplished by having a humane and cultivated society—set free from the narrower exactions of economics, for the cultivation of the higher virtues and arts of civilization—which at the same time benevolently assumed responsibility for all who were economically, intellectually, and morally inferior. Southern social thinkers frankly pointed out what northern opinion failed to concede: that civilization both South and North was based upon labor exploitation; that there can be no such thing as free labor in any complex, industrialized society. The wage-slavery of the North they insisted was attended by more poverty and injustice than could be found under the Southern system. "In the South . . . there was no waste in the labor turnover, no ugly labor scrap-heap, no ruthless efficiency in using up the human material".[99] The young and the old were cared for alike; the sick were kindly and carefully treated; living conditions were usually pleasant; here stalked no spectre of economic insecurity. In the North the laborer was not only enslaved by his limited wages but by his effort to maintain or raise those wages: he "bartered off liberty" to the trade unions, and "slavery to an association is not always better than slavery to a single master".[100] But even so insecurity was a constant menace; "the situation of the laborer at the North [is] as precarious as in Europe, and produces a desire for some change that shall secure him employment and support at all times. Slavery alone can effect that change; and towards slavery the North and all Western Europe are unconsciously marching":[101] The plantation system approached close to the Utopian conception of life: "a well-conducted farm in the South [was] a model of associated labor that Fourier might envy".[102] And furthermore conditions were growing even

---

99. V. L. Parington, *Main Currents,* II: 101.
100. George Fitzhugh, *Sociology for the South,* p. 44.
101. *Ibid.,* p. 45.
102. *Ibid.,* p. 45.

better. "Our slaves are treated far better than they were forty years ago, because they have improved in mind and morals, approached nearer to the master's state of civilization, and thus elicited more of his interest and attachment".[103]   If the abolitionist rails at the condition of sex morals in the South the pro-slavery defender points out as even worse the prostitution which results from the callous exploitation of female labor in the textile shops of the North.[104]   When advocates of emancipation cited the fact that wealth in the North was increasing much more rapidly than in the South, the pro-slavery defender had the conclusion of the argument in the observation that while the economic returns of wage-slave industrialism might be greater, the returns in civilization were far less.

These were the economic arguments on slavery, pro and con, which formed the background of a considerable group of novels —about twenty pro-slavery novels can still be rather readily obtained, and a slightly smaller number of anti-slavery novels[105] —dealing with this problem in the last decade before the Civil War. In many of the novels the respective arguments are lifted almost bodily into the framework of the story by having two or more characters engage in debate on the issues involved; but in others the economic ramifications of the problem are only perceived through inference. The obvious emphasis in these novels, as has already been pointed out, especially in the anti-slavery ones, is upon moral rather than economic issues, because the moral were more readily adapted to fictional treatment.

The Fugitive Slave Act of 1850 introduced a greater bitterness into the controversy because it gave definite national authority to the hunting and retrieving of some twenty thousand escaped slaves then living in the northern states.[106]   The im-

---

103. *Ibid.,* p. 211.
104. Cf. " 'Hon.' Charles Sumner, and 'The Barbarism of Slavery' " in *The Plantation,* v. II, No. 2, December, 1860, pp. 373-403.
105. Cf. Jeanette Reidy Tandy, "Pro-Slavery Propaganda in American Fiction in the Fifties", *South Atlantic Quarterly,* January and March, 1922, and Francis Pendleton Gaines, *The Southern Plantation,* chapter III.
106. Jesse Macy, *The Anti-Slavery Crusade,* Chronicles of America, v. 28, p. 129.

plications of the issue were brought to the northern consciousness more directly than they had ever been. And this as much
as the dramatic qualities of the book itself accounts for the
phenomenal interest in Harriet Beecher Stowe's *Uncle Tom's
Cabin* (1852), and the anti-slavery novels which immediately
followed it.

The economic argument of *Uncle Tom's Cabin* must
largely be perceived by inference. In general it follows
the pattern already outlined. Mrs. Stowe felt that the
free labor economy of Ohio was superior in every way to the
slave economy of Kentucky;[107] and that the "oft-fabled poetic
legend" about "slavery as a patriarchal institution" under which
the strong benevolently assumed the economic responsibilities
of the weak, was invalidated by the "portentous shadow" of
slave law.[108] Mrs. Stowe has unbounded confidence in the economic and artistic potentialities of the colored race. She looks
for them in that bright future day when oppression shall be no
more to "awake new forms of art, new styles of splendor, and
of human life".[109] *Dred* (1856) was designed to complement
Uncle Tom's Cabin throwing the weight of argument on the
deterioration of society resting on a slave basis. There is an
attempt to substitute some economic argument for the more
general humanitarian appeal of the earlier novel. Mrs. Stowe
holds that slavery is a wasteful system and that the southerners
must abolish it for their own future economic good. Her realization of the complexity of the problem and the futility of the
argument are shown in the observation of Judge Clayton that
"the system though ruinous in the long run to communities is
immediately profitable to individuals".[110] The problem's solution offered here is very similar to that suggested by Kennedy
in *Swallow Barn* more than thirty years before: a gradual
paternalistic program of emancipation granted in accordance
with the educational attainments and character qualities of the

---

107. Cf. *Uncle Tom's Cabin*, v. I, p. 119.
108. Cf. *ibid.*, p. 11.
109. *Ibid.*, p. 236.
110. *Dred*, v. II, p. 151.

individual. Mrs. Stowe's short story, *"The Two Altars"* (1852) is a humanitarian appeal rather than an economic argument.

The economic implication of slavery receives treatment in some of its more detailed phases in F. C. Adams' *Manuel Pereira* (1853). It is an indictment of the manner in which the laws of South Carolina foster the slave business, assuming that any person white or black is saleable if he does not have iron-clad proof of his whiteness.[111] There is a protest, too, against the severe taxes levied upon free Negroes;[112] and the graft which they are forced to pay to county and state officers is condemned.[113]

Walter Sketch's *The Down-Trodden* (1853) emphasizes the general economic argument that free labor is superior to slavery in building a progressive civilization. Mr. Duverne insists that

"Slavery is a curse to our state; because free labor cannot come into competition with slave labor, and therefore very few migrate to Kentucky in search of employ . . . . We have a great evil among us—this is shown in the case of Ohio and Indiana—Kentucky is much the oldest state, and was thickly settled when they had no settlements within their territory. But mark the result— they have out-stripped us in every improvement, and to use an expression, "Old Kentuck is no-whar".[114]

Emancipation will produce a new era, economically and socially, of benefit to white and black alike.[115]

Almost nothing is added to the general economic argument already outlined, by Mary Langdon's *Ida May* (1855), James T. Trowbridge's *Neighbor Jackwood* (1857) and *Cudjo's Cave* (1863), M. R. Delany's *Blake; or the Huts of America* (1859) Mrs. M. V. Victor's *Maum Guinea's Children* (1861), James R. Gilmore's *Among the Pines* (1862) and Epes Sargent's *Peculiar* (1864).[116] It should perhaps be noted that of all the anti-slavery novelists Sargent is the most rabid condemner of the southern slave-holders. They are bloodier villains than even Sargent's tongue can give them out. If there was any kind-

---

111. *Manuel Pereira*, p. 53.
112. *Ibid.*, p. 84.
113. *Ibid.*, p. 283
114. *The Down-Trodden*, p. 10.
115. *Ibid.*, p. 76.
116. Cf. Francis Pendleton Gaines, *The Southern Plantation*, chapter III, for titles and description of other anti-slavery fiction.

ness among them it was based on the "intense selfishness" of a belief "that good treatment would pay. Humanity was gauged by considerations of cotton."[117] When Sargent is told that the Scriptures justify slavery, he answers: "If Scripture authorized murder, then it would not be murder that would be right, but Scripture that would be wrong".[118]

It must be borne in mind that these slavery novels are significant in this study of economic criticism in American fiction even when their economic arguments are indirect and largely by inference. Even when they emphasize almost exclusively the moral reasons for emancipation they are depicting class distinctions based on unequal economic power: the oppression of the weak by the strong. In seeking to change those economic class distinctions they are in relation to this study classifiable as economic criticism, whatever the direct grounds of their appeal for emancipation.

The pro-slavery reply to abolitionist propaganda, based on a conception of the southern social system in terms of the Greek ideal of democracy and holding that the slaves were economically better off than the industrially exploited laboring classes of the North, began to find definite expression in fiction in 1852. The wide popularity of *Uncle Tom's Cabin* aroused the advocates of slavery to a militant defense through the same medium. A number of the novels specifically acknowledged themselves replies to Mrs. Stowe's book. *Antifanaticism* (1853) by Martha Haines Butt is perhaps the most forceful example of this:

"Mrs. Stowe and other fanatics, blinded by ignorance and swayed by prejudice, may conjure up their 'thousand and one' Uncle Tom stories, with which the imagination of novel writers abounds, to deceive those who are as ignorant as themselves, and, perhaps as reckless of truth; but no reasonable person who has ever been at the South long enough to become acquainted with its usuages will give credit to the descriptions which Mrs. Stowe, and those of her stripe, give of the treatment of slaves at the South . . . . Our slaves are infinitely better off than the white servants of the North . . . . [119]

The general content of the pro-slavery argument has already been outlined. It was characteristically introduced into these

---

117. *Peculiar*, v. I, p. 55.
118. *Ibid.*, v. I, p. 59.
119. *Antifanaticism*, p. v.

novels of defense through a more or less formal colloquy between Southerner and Northerner, with, of course, the former invariably demonstrating the superiority of his view. The method of contrast, showing the advantages of the southern system, was employed in many of these novels—as even a perusal of their titles will disclose. Among the more important volumes of pro-slavery fiction were: Caroline E. Rush's *The North and South or Slavery and Its Contrasts* (1852), J. Thornton Randolph's *Cabin and Parlor* (1852), Mrs. M. H. Eastman's *Aunt Phillis' Cabin; or Southern Life As It Is* (1852), Robert Criswell's *Uncle Tom's Cabin Contrasted with Buckingham Hall* (1852), W. L. A. Smith's *Life at the South: or, Uncle Tom's Cabin As It Is* (1852), Sarah Josepha Hale's *Liberia* (1853), John W. Page's *Uncle Robin in His Cabin in Virginia, and Tom Without One in Boston* (1853), Martha Haines Butt's *Antifanaticism* (1853), J. H. Ingraham's *The Sunny South* (1853-54), Lucien B. Chase's *English Serfdom and American Slavery* (1854), Thomas Bangs Thorpe's *The Master's House* (1854), M. Southwood's *Tit for Tat, A Reply to Dred* (1856) *The Olive-Branch; or, White Oak Farm* (1857)—anonymous, S. H. Elliot's *New England Chattels* (1858), W. T. Thompson's *The Slave-Holder Abroad* (1860), Mrs. G. M. Flanders' *The Ebony Idol* (1860) and Nehemiah Adams' *The Sable Cloud* (1861).[120] The discovery made by Hattie in the last named book is what all of these movelists have attempted to reveal in their stories. She has gone South to visit her aunt and uncle and observes: ". . . What I have seen here in fifteen minutes shows me that at least one half of that which I have learned at the North about the slaves is false".[121]

While in general the pro-slavery novelists followed the economic argument already outlined, that the slaves were on the whole better off than the exploited industrial laborers of Northern and European society, that "if the Northern people have any sympathy to spare, let them give it to their poor white servants,

---

120. For other pro-slavery novels see Jeanette Reid Tandy, "Pro-slavery Propaganda in American Fiction in the Fifties", *South Atlantic Quarterly*, January-March, 1922, and Francis Pendleton Gaines, *The Southern Plantation*, chapter III.

121. *The Sable Cloud*, p. 61.

for our slaves do not stand in any need of it at all",[122] they did not unanimously disapprove of modifying slavery. Indeed two of the novelists already referred to, W. L. G. Smith and Sarah Josepha Hale, definitely subscribe to Henry Clay's plan of colonization in Liberia. But a general freedom for the Negro as a part of American society was unthinkable. Yet that by the Emancipation Proclamation was the outcome of the controversy.

There were those who believed that a stroke of the presidential pen would solve the problem of the Negro race in America. But they were woefully wrong. Indeed Thomas Nelson Page could still write in 1904 that the Negro question was "one of the most vital and pressing problems which has ever confronted a people", that "after more than thirty-five years of peace and of material prosperity, the Question is apparently as live as it was over a generation ago when national passion was allowed to usurp the province of deliberation".[123]

The leading chroniclers in our fiction of the after-the-war problem of the Negro have been J. W. DeForest, Albion W. Tourgée, Mrs. J. H. Walworth, Annie Jefferson Holland, Thomas Nelson Page and George W. Cable. The last two are strictly speaking historical in their fiction—writing near the end of the century about events which occurred during the first decade after the War—but their essays show that they see the problems treated in their novels as continuing very much to the time of their writing.

DeForest's most significant treatment of the Reconstruction problem is contained in *Miss Ravenel's Conversion from Secession to Loyalty* (1867). Dr. Ravenel believes that the slaves have been better off in America than they would have been in Africa, and now that they are free "we must civilize and Christianize them. And we must begin this by teaching them the great elementary duty of man in life—that of working for his own subsistence".[124] His idea is that the freed slaves should be put immediately to work, and he accordingly takes, under the super-

---

122. Martha Haines Butt, *Antifanaticism*, p. 268.
123. *The Negro: the Southerner's Problem*, pp. vii, ix.
124. *Miss Ravenel's Conversion*, p. 250.

vision of the Federal troops commander at New Orleans, an abandoned plantation and an assignment of negroes. He tells them his plan:

"You must not leave the plantation during the day without permission. You will work ten hours a day during the working season. You will be orderly, honest, virtuous and respectable. In return I am to give you rations, clothing, quarters, fuel, medical attendance, and instruction for children. I am also to pay you as wages eight dollars a month for first class hands, and six for second class. Each of you will have his little plot of land. Finally, I will endeavor to see that you are all, old and young, taught to read".[125]

DeForest then records the success of the experiment.

"The negroes were ignorant of their duty, and often thoughtless of it, but they were at bottom zealous to do right, and honestly disposed toward people who paid them for their labor . . . . Under no urgency but that of their own thankfulness, the Doctor's negroes did more work that summer than the Robertsons had ever got from double their number by the agency of a white overseer, drivers, whips, and paddles."[126]

In *The Bloody Chasm* (1881) DeForest shows much less concern about adjusting the Negro to the conditions of his new life. The story is decidedly historical and pictorial; there is no analysis of the Federal Reconstruction program as there is later in Page and Cable treating the same material.[127]

The Reconstruction Act went into effect March 2, 1867; it provided a comprehensive military government for the Confederate states during the succeeding ten years and declared that "the restoration of the states should be effected only after reorganization on the basis of general Negro enfranchisement and limited rebel disfranchisement".[128] As an officer in the Reconstruction administration went Albion W. Tourgée to Charleston. His plan of reform, essentially in accord with the northern policy of Reconstruction, provided equal civil and political rights, abolition of property qualifications for voters, officers and jurors,

---

125. *Ibid.*, p. 264.
126. *Ibid.*, p. 265.
127. See, however, DeForest's "Drawing Bureau Rations" (*Harper's*, June, 1868) and "A Bureau Major's Business and Pleasures" (*Harper's*, November, 1868) for essay treatments of his reaction to Reconstruction conditions. Though himself an officer of the Federal administration at Greenville, South Carolina, he points out some of the Freedman's Bureau's errors that Page and Cable later condemned emphatically.
128. W. A. Dunning, *Reconstruction Political and Social*, p. 93.

election of all officers by the people, penal reform, a uniform system of taxation, and an effective system of public schools.[129] However, by the time he had written his first significant novel, *The Fool's Errand* (1879), he had realized the fundamental error of the Reconstruction Act. Servose, his author's mouthpiece, observes near the end of the book:

"We tried to superimpose the civilization, the idea of the North, upon the South at a moment's warning. We presumed, that, by the suppression of rebellion, the Southern white man had become identical with the Caucasian of the North in thought and sentiment: and that the slave, by emancipation, had become a saint and a Solomon at once. So we tried to build up communities there which should be identical in thought, sentiment, growth, and development, with those of the North. It was A Fool's Errand".[130]

Hereafter Tourgée is interested almost exclusively in a program of education for eliminating the social and economic inequalities of the South:

"The Nation nourished and protected slavery . . . . Now, let the Nation undo the evil it has permitted and encouraged. Let it educate those whom it made ignorant, and protect those whom it made weak. It is not a matter of favor to the black, but of safety to the Nation. Make the spelling-book the scepter of national power. Let the Nation educate the colored man and the poor-white man because the Nation held them in bondage, and is responsible for their education; educate the voter because the Nation cannot afford that he should be ignorant."[131]

The plea for Negro education is also the chief burden of *Bricks Without Straw* (1880):

"The Nation gave the jewel of liberty into the hands of the former [slaves], armed them with the weapons of self-government and said: 'Ye are many, protect what ye have received'. Then it took away its hand, turned away its eyes, closed its ears to every cry of protest or of agony and said: 'We will not aid you nor protect you. Though you are ignorant, from you we will demand the works of wisdom. Though you are weak, great things shall be required at your hands'. Like the ancient taskmaster, the Nation said: 'There shall no straw be given you, yet shall ye deliver the tale of bricks' " [132]

Pactolus Prime (1890) is a ridiculous romance, but at moments continues advocacy of the Tourgée educational program as the cure for the ills of the Negro race. Here, as in *Bricks Without*

---

129. Roy F. Dibble, *Albion W. Tourgée*, p. 66.
130. *A Fool's Errand*, p. 361.
131. *Ibid.*, p. 366.
132. *Bricks Without Straw*, p. 400.

Straw, Tourgée proposes a national educational appropriation to be "applied to each county in proportion to its illiteracy, and in each school district according to its illiteracy".[133]

Tourgée rebukes the American people for continuing to sanction the old distinctions bred of slavery: for looking down on, and keeping down the colored race. He would promote their economic and social power by a program of education. He appeals to fair-mindedness in abolishing class inequalities based on the color of skin.[134]

Mrs. J. H. Walworth's fascinating romance, *Without Blemish* (1886) is a further consideration of what its author calls 'today's problem'. Her program for raising the economic and social status of the Negro is essentially like Tourgée's though less definitely worked out: education. The author's view is represented by Dr. Robert Maddox, Eustis Stanhope, and Olga, who work to promote the economic and political equality of the colored people. That their desire is not a unanimous one in the South Mrs. Walworth well knows; in Waring Trowbridge she represents the white attitude of exploitation which looks on every move toward colored education as an effort "to ruin every nigger in the country".[135]

In an essentially bitter book Annie Jefferson Holland has words of condemnation still for those who freed the slaves. She calls *The Refugees* (1892) "a sequel to 'Uncle Tom's Cabin' from a southern standpoint", and shows that in destroying the slave economy of the South the forces of abolition destroyed the finest civilization of the new world. Upon the downfall of such as the Carringtons "is to be evolved the coming 'Anglo-African race', a foundation of Parian marble for the erection of a mud hut".[136]

Page and Cable it has been pointed out are in their fiction

---

133. *Pactolus Prime*, p. 121. Cf. also *Bricks Without Straw*, p. 519.
134. Cf. Holland Thompson, "Educational Progress", Chap. VIII in *The New South*, Chronicles of America Series 42: 157-190 for a concise summary of what has been done toward promoting negro education in the South.
135. *Without Blemish*, p. 378.
136. *The Refugees*, p. 179. See a similar but decidedly milder view of this problem in "Chivalrous and Semi-chivalrous Southrons," by J. W. DeForest, *Harper's*, January, 1869, p. 192.

essentially historians rather than critics of their own times. The volume *In Ole Virginia* (short-stories, 1887-92-96) for example, avowedly written to "bring about a better understanding between the North and the South" is still only a picture of "the social life of the old South",[137] rather than an analysis of the economic and social problem whose earlier phase had caused the intranational antagonism. In *Red Rock* (1898) Page denounces the Reconstruction administration in the South. That he intended this work as more than a chronicle of the after-the-war decade is proved by a later volume of essays in which he traces the continuing compass of the negro problem as due in large measure to the fundamental errors of the Reconstruction government. The Negro

"was taught that the white man was his enemy when he should have been taught to cultivate his friendship. He was told he was the equal of the white when he was not the equal; he was given to understand that he was the ward of the nation when he should have been trained in self-reliance; he was led to believe that the Government would sustain him when he could not be sustained. In legislation, he was taught thieving; in politics, he was taught not to think for himself, but to follow slavishly his leaders (and such leaders!); in private life, he was taught insolence. A laborer, dependent on his labor, no greater misfortune could have befallen him than estrangement from the Southern whites. To instil into his mind the belief that the Southern white was his enemy; that his interest was necessarily opposed to that of the white, and that he must thwart the white man to the utmost of his power, was to deprive him of his best friend and to array against him his strongest enemy."[138]

Provost Leech is the arch-villain of *Red Rock* the "supreme carpet-bagger dictator", "the vampire sucking the life-blood of the people, the harpy battening on the writhing body of the prostrate State . . . " He is shown "summoning the negroes and enrolling them by hundreds, exciting them with stories of what the Government proposed to do for them, and telling them the most pernicious lies: that they need not work, and that the Government was going to feed them and give them all 'forty acres and a mule apiece' ".[139] Small wonder then that "contemporaneously with this, an unprecedented amount of lawlessness

137. *In Ole Virginia*, pp. x, xi.
138. *The Negro: The Southerner's Problem*, pp. 47-48.
139. *Red Rock*, pp. 103-104.

suddenly appeared: chicken-houses were robbed; sheep and pigs and even cattle were stolen, without there being any authority to take cognizance of the thefts or any power to punish".[140]

No small part of the explanation of how "the conflict with the North set the South back thirty or forty years while the remainder of the country was increasing in wealth"[141] is to be found in the ruinous governmental financing of the carpet-bagger reign. The northern dictators "had an act passed making the State guarantee the bonds" of the railroad they were building for their own grafting profit; and when the old residents protested the danger to the government credit in endorsing private enterprise they merely replied: "the credit of the State! What is the credit of the state to us?"[142] That those whom Leech and his fellows typify were men of no moderate talent in the wrecking of state finances is evidenced by the fact that Virginia entered the final stage of adjusting and paying her Reconstruction debt only in 1919.[143]

George W. Cable's *John March, Southerner* (1894) is a further depicting of the Reconstruction era and its evils:

"All corruptions bred by both sides in a gigantic war—and before it in all the crudeness of the country's first century—were pouring down and spouting up upon Dixie their rain of pitch and ashes. Negroes swarmed about the polls, elbowed their masters, and challenged their votes."[144]

The book is significant for its recognition that "the war . . . had not taken the slaves away. It could only redistribute them under a new bondage of wages instead of the old bondage of pure force. . . . Thousands must sink, thousands starve, for all were drunk with its cruel delusions".[145] The agricultural aspect of this readjustment—and the agriculture continued to the end of the century to be the most significant—is found in tenant system and the "crop lien". The great plantations were broken

---

140. *Ibid.*, p. 104.
141. Holland Thompson, *The New South*, Chronicles of America Series, 42: 185.
142. *Red Rock*, p. 210.
143. Holland Thompson, *The New South*, Chronicles of America Series, 42:233. See pages 227 to 233 in this volume for a concise survey of the funding and repudiation of state debts throughout the South—the background of the economic conditions pictured by Page and, to some extent, by Cable.
144. *John March, Southerner*, p. 55.
145. *Ibid.*, pp. 38-40.

up; but few of the landless whites and virtually none of the Negroes had sufficient money reserve to maintain themselves for a year and consequently no capital to apply to the land on which they were tenants. The country merchant assumed the office of banker to these tenant farmers, granting them supplies in advance, taking the crops when harvested, subtracting the accounts and turning over the surplus, if any, to the farmers.[146] Was this the freedom granted by the noble stroke of Lincoln's pen? Perhaps the Negroes were economically as well off under the old order. Perhaps there was truth in Major Garnet's words to Cornelius: "Food, clothing, shelter, you've never suffered a day's doubt about them! No other laboring class were ever so free of the cares of life".[147] The problem however, is not one of the past but of the future. And no member of either race, novelist or sociologist, has yet found a solution which seems satisfactory to all.[148]

THE IMMIGRANT

The way in which our novelists have viewed the Indian and the Negro as victims of racial prejudice has been pointed out. Free economic and social opportunities have been withheld, our fictionists have said. A wall of class consciousness has been erected against them. They surely are not our neighbors.

The Indian and Negro represent problems which have been wholly, or for many years strictly within our country. But the problem of race and nationality also has its external phase in the immigration to our shores of vast hordes from other nations, chiefly European. The immigration question, however, as a national economic problem is treated in our fiction before 1900 only slightly. The obvious reason, of course, is that not until the closing decades of the nineteenth century when the source of immigration shifted toward southern and eastern Europe,

---

146. Cf. Holland Thompson, *The New South*, Chronicles of America Series, 42:60-61.

147. *John March, Southerner*, p. 32.

148. Cf. Thomas Nelson Page, *The Negro: The Southerner's Problem* (1904), and George W. Cable, *The Negro Question* (1890), for serious essay studies by recognized novelists of the problems these novels treat—the after-the-war negro question. Several essays by John W. DeForest have been cited in earlier notes.

and when the free land of our western prairies had all been taken up, did the great influx of foreigners begin to assume the character of a definite economic problem. The immigrant with his interesting, varied racial traits had, of course, been treated in our fiction from the beginning, but any economic problem associated with him concerned his personal adjustment to the necessity of making a livelihood in the new land, rather than his effect as a body upon the country. Indeed until the last quarter of the nineteenth century immigration to America had received the unanimous approval of those already here. It had been encouraged both unofficially and officially. From the time of Richard Hakluyt, quaint chronicler of the English explorations of the sixteenth century, America had willingly, gladly, posed as the promised land. Hakluyt had told his countrymen that here could be found "golde, silver, copper, leade and pearles in aboundance," and every other object of man's desire—of quantity and quality never before known.[149]

Gilbert Imlay was only a little less extravagant in his attempt to entice immigrants to come to America. He insisted that there was no better place in the world for either surplus sons or surplus pounds seeking investment.[150]

As the new land began to develop commercially, railroad and canal companies, in great need of labor, imported workmen by the thousands, by advancing their passage money.[151] That it was almost universally believed until the time of the Civil War that the prosperity of the country depended largely upon a copious influx of population is evidenced by Lincoln's message to Congress in 1863 in which he called immigration a "source of national wealth and strength" and urged Congress to establish "a system for the encouragement of immigration". And Congress in conformity with the suggestion passed a law designed to aid the importation of labor under contract—a measure which was subsequently repealed.[152]

---

149. Cf. *Principal Navigations, Voyages and Discoveries*, v. 8, p. 89 ff.
150. Cf. *Topographical Description*, Appendix, 3rd edition (1797), p. 551.
151. Cf. Samuel P. Orth, *Our Foreigners*, Chronicles of America Series, 35:110.
152. Cf. *ibid.*, 35:110, p. 222.

As the nineteenth century moved into its final quarter the American land had become pretty well settled and the American character pretty well molded. To the fundamentally English elements of courage, order, self-respect, respect for law, instinct for rule, and a sense of racial integrity, had been added the Celtic contributions of loyalty, human sympathy, and political ingenuity, the German love of the fine arts and strong sense of family life, the French feeling for culture and appreciation of good manners, and the early Dutch and Swedish stolidity and respect for commercial integrity.[153] With all these elements integrated and developed by the democracy and individuality which were the very essence of pioneer life the American character had become a quite satisfactory achievement.[154] Further unrestricted and unselected immigration could but effect this character unfavorably, and create problems of economic support and adjustment in a now frontier-less country. It is here that the few novelists of the nineteenth century who treated immigration take up the story.

No one, perhaps, among our more reputable novelists has spoken more explicitly on this question than Henry B. Fuller. In *With the Procession* (1895) he depicted gangdom's growing control of government in Chicago and traced the evil in large measure to unrestricted and unselected immigration. "The last twenty years", says Tom Brower, speaking for his author, "have brought us elements that have never been in our national life before: a heavy immigration from southeastern Europe, for example". With these people has come the element of feudality, the essence of which is the "idea of personal loyalty". This may be all right in the land of their origin, "but it is not the right prop for a great republic".[155] The nation must see to it that it accepts only immigrants of independent will and intellect, and not such as will blindly follow ill-intentioned or incapable leaders.

---

153. Cf. Arthur Hobson Quinn, *The Soul of America*, pp. 4-18.

154. Cf. William Dean Howells, *Annie Kilburn* (1888), pp. 117-118, for a fictional description of the manner in which the different racial elements have been absorbed into American life.

155. *With The Procession*, pp. 246-248.

Frank Rosewater (*Utopia, a Romance of Today,* 1897) and John Bachelder (*A. D. 2050,* 1890) another utopian novelist, join Fuller in asking for more stringent immigration legislation. They feel not only that our immigrants should be more carefully selected but when admitted should be more systematically and intelligently distributed.[156]   Resuming his utopian perspective Bachelder declares that the trouble with the United States in the nineteenth century was that anarchists and communists of Europe "were permitted to promulgate their theories and inflame the passions of the ignorant masses, most of whom had been sent to the United States to relieve the crowded prisons and almshouses of Europe".[157]

The race angle in the labor market finds brief expression in Frank Norris' *McTeague* (1889), when Marcus Schouler comments: "Ah, the Chinese cigar-makers. . . . It's them as is ruining the cause of white labor. They are, they are for a fact. Ah, the rat-eaters!   Ah, the white-livered curs!"[158] This diatribe, however, is more a characterization of Marc than a serious Norris thought on oriental immigration.

But our novelists are far from putting all of the blame for the economic problems of immigration upon the foreigner and his government.   That evil ogre, the speculative capitalist, must bear the brunt here as elsewhere of the social critic's attack. Ignatius Donnelly, militant leader of American third-party movements, looking at the problem from the utopian perspective of *Caesar's Column* (1890) sees it in this light: "The silly ancestors of the Americans called it 'national development' when they imported millions of foreigners to take up the public lands, and left nothing for their own children".   Costello N. Holford joins the chorus of complaint in the introduction to *Aristopia* (1895) : ". . . This great republic of the new world, so long the hope of the the poor and oppressed of the old world, is fast becoming

---

156. Cf. *A. D.* 2050, p. 9, and *Utopia,* p. 138.
157. *A. D. 2050,* p. 41.   For evidence that this was no idle charge, see Samuel P. Orth, *Our Foreigners,* pp. 110-111, for a brief partial summary of "assisted" emigration from 1849 to 1885.   "In 1884 and 1885 over sixteen thousand persons were thus assisted from Galway and Mayo counties," Ireland, alone.   p. 111.
158. *McTeague,* p. 121.

like Europe socially, and threatens to become even worse than Europe."[159]

Boysesen (*Vagabond Tales*, 1889), Ford (*Which Wins?* 1891), Garland (*Jason Edwards*, 1897), and Dunne (*Mr. Dooley in Peace and War*, 1898), continue to attribute the economic problems of immigration not so much to the immigrants themselves as to the greedy capitalists who have made a mirage of the liberty and opportunity so happily envisioned in the promised land. Hjalmar Hjorth Boyesen, himself an immigrant in 1869, was perhaps the most able portrayer of immigrant psychology in his day, albeit an idealistic portrayal. Whenever his characters felt in their souls the longing for a State which has "the courage to disregard traditional routine and offer a free scope for individual development", they think of "but one such State in the world—the North American Republic. Thither [would they] hasten while [their] strength was yet unimpaired, while [their] spirit had yet wings to lift it above the sordid strife for bread".[160] They have faith that they can earn money and buy a homestead, or failing in that, that "the President will give me a farm".[161] They learn their error, however, as Hamlin Garland illustrates in the character of the German iron-worker, Berg: "I fly from dyrants, from work andt no pay, I reach a free landt where I am a slave under anoder name. I see eferywhere the march of feudalism. I lose hope. Ledt them beware! They squeeze me to de vall. I shall vight. I am a volf at pay. I haf reach my las' hope. If I fall now I trag somedings mit me."[162]

The only sound philosophy for the immigrant—but a very difficult one—is found in the attitude of Finley Peter Dunne's Mr. Dooley. Hearing the report of the discovery of gold in Alaska he observes: "Whin I was a young man in the 'ol counthry, we heerd th' same story about all America. . . . But faith, whin I'd been here a week, I seen that there was nawthin but mud

---

159. *Aristopia*, p. 5
160. "Liberty's Victim," in *Vagabond Tales*, p. 199.
161. Mary H. Ford, *Which Wins?* p. 17.
162. *Jason Edwards*, p. 55.

undher th' pavement . . . me experience with gold minin' is it's always in th' nex' county".[163]

In this brief survey of pre-twentieth century American fiction treating the economic and political problems of immigration no protest has been found against the social and economic obstacles thrown in a man's path because he is a 'Dago' or a 'Polak', as in our later fiction. In the novels of the late 1900's the immigrant is on the one hand condemned because of his unfitness and unwillingness to become in spirit a part of American institutions and on the other is sympathized with—despite the fact that he increases the acuteness of our problem—because greedy capitalists hold an oppressive monopoly of the milk and honey of the promised land.

II

Industry in Government as Represented in the Novel: The Invisible Empire

The relation between private economic units and public government is a subject which has received considerable attention from our social critics in fiction. Here as in many other phases of this study it must be noted that the problem reaches its fully developed significance only in the last quarter of the nineteenth century. *The Gilded Age,* in 1873, was our first really significant politico-economic novel. But history scarcely substantiates an inference that previous to that time economic forces made no effort to control government, for even the Constitution must be recognized as a document essentially dictated by property interests. We may only observe that comment on the relationship between business and government, and the corruption of legislators which that entails, was only incidental in our early fiction and never the main theme of a novel; from which we may conclude that the problems involved either did not seem to our novelists particularly acute, or that the writers of fiction felt the novel form inadequate to a developed analysis and criticism of the problems.

It would be inaccurate, however, to suppose that our earlier

---

163. *Mr. Dooley in Peace and War,* pp. 101-102.

fictionists did not make some very penetrating comments upon the economic phases of the practice of politics. Indeed they can be found with considerable emphasis as early as Hugh Henry Brackenridge (*Modern Chivalry*, 1792). Brackenridge proclaims a thesis which found later forceful echo in Cooper and has continued to our own day, that it is a mistake to elect legislators who are not capable of comprehending the country's economic interests. He protests against putting into office men to make laws requiring "a knowledge of commerce, of finance, and of an infinite variety of subjects" who know nothing about those subjects. "You are surely carrying the matter too far, in thinking to make a senator of this hostler", says Captain Farrago to the politicians who would boost Teague O'Regan into office; "to take him away from an employment to which he has been bred, and put him to another to which he has served no apprenticeship". Teague as a character is clearly intended as a satirization of the Old World peasant who strives to take advantage of American political equality to leap immediately to stations for which he is not fitted. The senator incident occurred in the Pennsylvania back-country. The aspect of things in Philadelphia is quite different. The Captain fearing that Teague will here be running for Congress is reassured by McDonald, a native of the city: . . . "There is na danger of Teague here, unless he had his scores o' shares in the bank, and was in league with the bankers, and had a brick house at his hurdies, or a ship or twa on the stocks".[165] How modern it sounds, too, to be told that Mr. Vapour, an eminent Philadelphian "had made a fortune by the purchase of public securities".[166] But in that day a more common method of making money, than getting inside tips on the granting of government franchises, was the practice of rounding up fake Indian chiefs— weavers and pedlars with peculiar haircuts served best—making treaties with them and getting monetary grants from the govern-

---

164. *Modern Chivalry*, v. I, pp. 30, 32.
165. *Ibid.*, v. I, p. 128.
166. *Ibid.*, v. I, p. 61.

ment in exchange.[167]   Here surely is one form of graft that has disappeared.

Washington Irving in the *Knickerbocker History* (1809) follows Brackenridge in demanding economically competent legislators.   The point is made through having Peter Stuyvesant give his big watch to a cobbler, who is setting himself up as a political critic, and forcing him to confess that he knows neither anything about fixing watches or governments.[168]   But Irving's most telling politico-economic criticism was aimed at those who desired to manipulate the national currency for their private profit:

"But the measure of the valiant Peter which produced the greatest agitation in the community was his laying his hand upon the currency. He had old-fashioned notions in favor of gold and silver, which he considered the true standards of wealth and mediums of commerce, and one of his first edicts was, that all duties to the government should be paid in those precious metals, and that seawant, or wampum, should no longer be a legal tender.

Here was a blow at public prosperity! all those who speculated on the rise and fall of this fluctuating currency, found their calling at an end: those, too, who had hoarded Indian money by barrels full, found their capital shrunk in amount: but above all, the Yankee traders, who were accustomed to flood the market with newly-coined oyster-shells, and to abstract Dutch merchandise in exchange, were loud-mouthed in decrying this 'tampering with the currency'. It was clipping the wings of commerce; it was checking the development of public prosperity; trade would be at an end; goods would moulder on the shelves; grain would rot in the grainaries; grass would grow in the market-place. In a word, no one who has not heard the outcries and howlings of a modern Tarshish, at any check upon 'paper money' can have any idea of the clamor against Peter the Headstrong, for checking the circulation of oyster-shells."[169]

In *Konigsmarke* (1823), his most interesting work, James Kirke Paulding satirizes the manner in which holders of public office, both before and since his time have used their official positions for private gain.   Of course at the time of which Paulding writes "political economy, or the science of starving on philosophical principles, was not much understood . . . but genius supplies the want of precept".[170]   Accordingly "Wolf-

---

167. Cf. *ibid.*, v. I, p. 75.
168. *Knickerbocker History*, p. 383.
169. *Ibid.*, pp. 266-267.
170. *Konigsmarke*, v. I, p. 97.

gang Langfanger [who had] brought his private affairs into great confusion by devoting too much of his time to the public good, began . . . to think it high time the public good should repay some part of its weighty obligations. He had accordingly invented and persuaded the Heer Piper to put into practice, a system of internal improvement which has been imitated, from time to time, in this country, ever since, with great success. The essence of his plan consisted in running in debt for the present, and living afterward upon the anticipation of future wealth".[171] He planned wharves for commerce that did not exist; he projected canals for barges whose timbers were still leafy in the forest. The right of eminent domain was to be callously applied to town and farm alike, for there must be new streets:

"But the masterpiece of Langfanger's policy was that of pulling down an old market, and building a new one in another part of the village, in the management of which business he is supposed to have laid down the first principles of the great and thriving science of political economy, or picking people's pockets on a grand scale. He caused the people living near the old market to pay roundly for its removal as a nuisance; and ·then caused the people that lived about where the new one was to be built, to pay roundly for the vast pleasure and advantage of its neighbourhood. Thus he pinched them through both ears, and got the reputation of a great financier."[172]

In the early days of the American Republic the control of society and government were in the hands of men of culture, breeding and wealth. But rule by a benevolent oligarchy, an unrecognized aristocracy, was not to continue far into the new century. French romantic theory in its American dress of Jeffersonian agrarianism supplemented by a practical equalitarian social philosophy born of ever-accelerated development along the frontier—even in 1797 "the emigrations from the settled to the unsettled parts of America [were] computed at forty or fifty thousand annually"—[173] was destined to reshape American society. Expressing itself both politically and economically the new spirit penetrated gradually through the whole social fiber forcing the simple eighteenth century temper of early republican life to retreat before its noisy journalism, its get-

---

171. *Ibid.*, v. I, p. 92.
172. *Ibid.*, v. II, p. 77.
173. Gilbert Imlay, *Topographical Description*, p. 198.

rich-quick speculation, and its aggressive social climbing. Leveling democracy driven by a current of pioneer energy was to determine the future course of the social stream.

The frontier spirit reacted less spectacularly on economic than on political life but quite as definitely. "In the first quarter of the century, the system of public land grants had been badly carried out. Most of the settlers were poor and owed the government for land. Those who defaulted payment through necessity were generally allowed to retain their land, thus suffering no penalty. Most successful settlers in turn refused to pay, even though they were able to do so. Commercial honesty suffered. Moreover, the pioneer distrusted the banks. When banks foreclosed mortgages (frequently to avoid bankruptcy), the pioneer naturally assumed the banks to be cruel and grasping. Thus the two stable financial agents in frontier life, the government and the banks, were regarded with distrust or contempt by the settlers: to be successful too often meant gaining wealth by getting the best of the banks or of the government. With the backwash of the frontier spirit on the older parts of America came commercial unscrupulousness and dishonesty"[174] and financial instability. It was the age of Andrew Jackson, and the ethical doctrine of Jacksonianism held that the good life lay in the pursuit of the American dollar.[175]

The equalitarian, non-individualistic, 'un-American' philosophy of the new age was particularly appalling to James Fenimore Cooper, eminent novelist-critic. He saw "the great moral postulate . . . Principle" nullified by "the great immoral postulate usually known as 'Interest', as 'Dollar-dollar-dollar'—nothing but 'dollar' . . . rang at the corners—in the public ways—at the exchange—in the drawing room—ay, even in churches".[176] But Cooper lays no specific charges of corruption at the doors of government, as do our later novelists. It was the tyranny of the many not the domination of the few that he assailed. No willful corruption but economic, intellectual, and moral inca-

---

174. John F. Ross, *Social Criticism of Fenimore Cooper*, pp. 63-64.
175. For the background of this analysis of the economic implications of the frontier see F. L. Paxson, *History of the American Frontier*, and F. J. Turner, *The Frontier in American History*.
176. *The Monikins*, pp. 379, 384.

pacity is the indictment he lodges against the government and the people. It is the old Brackenridge accusation. There is no individualism, no leadership: "men were accustomed to think, act, almost to eat and drink and sleep, in common".[177] Indeed "it is almost as great an offense for [an American] to know more than his neighbors, as it is for him to act on his own impulses. . . . We hold every citizen amenable to public opinion, in all he does, says, thinks, or wishes,"[178] and a man is condemned as 'proud' if he does not "neglect his teeth as the majority" do, and if he does not "blow his nose with his fingers".[179]

The Monikins (1835), an able satirical allegory, was Cooper's most thorough criticism of political practice. In picturing the personalities and institutions of Leaplow, a paradise of leveling democracy inhabited by monkeys, it holds the mirror up to America's monkey-like, log-cabin and hard-cider political campaigns, where the fitness of a candidate for office is the least of considerations. "The satire in *The Monikins* was Cooper's first reaction to politics in Jacksonian America; but as he watched the process of state and national affairs through the period of the compromises, through presidential elections, through the 'anti-Rent War' and the changing of the New York state constitution, he saw only confirmation of his theory of political degredation".[180] "America no longer seemed America": "in place of its ancient submission to law, its quick distinction between right and wrong, its sober and discriminating liberty, which equally avoided submission to the injustice of power, and the excesses of popular delusion, there had been substituted the rapacity of the plunderer, . . . interwoven with political machinery, and the truckling of the wretches entrusted with authority"[181] Government had "passed into the hands of sheer political emperics, whose ignorance and quackery were stimulated by the lowest passion for majorities";[182] Congress had

---

177. *Homeward Bound*, p. 47.
178. *The Monikins*, p. 249.
179. *The Crater*, p. 472.
180. John F. Ross: *Social Criticism of Fenimore Cooper*, p. 86.
181. *The Redskins*, p. 418.
182. *Sea Lions*, p. 453.

"degenerated into a mere electioneering machine".[183]   No more numerous and emphatic charges of economic and social incapability in government can be found in fiction than in the novels of James Fenimore Cooper; but there are no citations of large-scale political corruption, as in our later politico-economic novelists.

The Civil War shocked the country into a new national consciousness, rearranged the elements of economic life, and offered amazing new opportunities for cooperation between those so companionable vocations, business and politics.   Appomattox marked not alone the death of the Southern Confederacy but the birth of the Invisible Empire as well.   The feeling of security in the North caused by the success of the Union arms buoyed an unbounded optimism which made it easy to enlist capital in new enterprises, and liberal banking laws and a protective tariff stimulated industry.   In the decade following the war the production of pig-iron doubled, that of coal multiplied by five, and that of steel by one hundred.   Inventions and manufactures of all kinds flourished: from 1850 to 1860 manufacturing establishments had increased fourteen per cent; from 1860 to 1870 they increased seventy-nine per cent.

The Homestead Act of 1862 opened vast areas of public lands to a new migration.   Young men, and old—as well as women and children—went West, and the West called for communication with the East.   It was out of this demand that the great railroad systems were built: the Union Pacific, Central Pacific, Northern Pacific, Pennsylvania, Baltimore and Ohio, Erie.   What is of most significance to the student of economics and politics in our fiction is that prosperity at this time was organized on a new basis.   Compelled by the requirements of even greater capital the old business units of individual ownership or partnership gave way before a new mechanism of ownership, the corporation. As a trading unit it had existed for many years, but before 1860 the corporation was comparatively small and was generally based upon charters granted by special act of the legislature.

"No other event has had so practical a bearing on our

---

183. *Oak Openings*, pp. 486-487.

politics and our economic and social life as the advent of the
corporate device for owning and manipulating private business.
For it links the omnipotence of the State to the limitations of
private ownership; it thrusts the interests of private business
into every legislature that grants charters or passes regulating
acts; it diminishes on the other hand, that stimulus to honesty
and correct dealing which a private individual discerns to be his
greatest asset in trade, for it replaces individual responsiblity
with group responsibility and scatters ownership among so large
a number of persons that sinister manipulation is possible".[184]
And if quiet cooperation with the politician and his organization
is convenient for the general corporation, it is almost essential,
and terrifically profitable, to the quasi-public concerns like the
railroads.   During the twenty-one years between 1850 and 1871,
at which time the land grants were discontinued, the Federal
government placed more than 159,000,000 acres of land at the
disposal of the railroads, and the several state governments
55,000,000 acres more.   But more than this, the government
frankly and publicly subsidized the railroads, issuing bonds
dollar for dollar with the railroad issues.   It was an opportunity
not to be over-looked.   The inner ring of stockholders of the
Union Pacific organized themselves into a construction company
called the Credit Mobilier and awarded themselves contracts at
immensely profitable rates, paid essentially by the national
treasury.   The stock of the Crédit Mobilier, paying dividends of
three hundred forty per cent was in turn distributed where
effective among the senators and representatives for the purchase of additional favors.   The corruption was, of course,
eventually disclosed by three government investigating com-
mittees.   Oakes Ames of Massachusetts and James Brooks of
New York were recommended for expulsion from the House, and
Patterson of New Hampshire from the Senate; and among the
other most trusted congressmen drawn into the miasma of
suspicion were Garfield, Dawes, Scofield, Wilson, the newly
elected Vice-President, and Colfax, the retiring Vice-President.
   But the railroad scandal was not all.   In 1874 came the dis-

---

184. Samuel P. Orth, *The Boss and the Machine,* Chronicles of America,
v. 43, pp. 37-38.

closures of the Whiskey Ring, which had been defrauding the government of more than a million dollars a year. An exposure of even more startling humiliation revealed Secretary of War Belknap deeply involved in the division of fraudulent spoils at the government trading post of Fort Sill in the Indian Territory. General Schenck, representing the United States at the Court of St. James humiliated his country by dabbling in a fraudulent mining scheme.

What was true of the national government was true on a smaller scale in many of the states.[185] This is the now very adequate and definite background of the criticism in our politico-economic novels.

The Gilded Age (1873) by Mark Twain and Charles D. Warner was our first truly significant political novel. It is a picture of the political corruption of General Grant's administration. As Twain contemplated the common scoundrelism at Washington his spirit exuded scathing satire. The fictional disguise is slight enough to permit the identification of such leading legislators of the time as Ames and Butler. In Colonel Sellers is embodied the slackness of frontier political morals; he is quite frankly a Greenbacker and a public improvements advocate.

"The country is getting along very well, (he said) but our public men are too timid. What we want is more money. I've told Boutwell so. Talk of basing the currency on gold; you might as well base it on pork. Gold is only one product. Base it on everything! You've got to do something for the West. How am I to move my crops? We must have improvements. Grant's got the idea. We want a canal from the James River to the Mississippi. Government ought to build it."[186]

Laura Hawkins, the story's heroine is a western lobbyist who succeeds in twisting congressmen around her fingers in order to put through a profitable steal under pretense of founding an industrial school for the freedmen. Senator Dillworthy was probably "modeled upon Senator Pomeroy of Kansas, who had

---

185. This survey where not otherwise noted has been based on Orth, *The Boss and the Machine,* and Bogart, *Economic History of the United States.*
186. *The Gilded Age,* v. II, p. 141.

recently lost a reelection through an unlucky exposure of an attempt to bribe the Kansas legislature."[187]

But *The Gilded Age* is more representative of the general corruption of the time than literally analytic of the actual historical events. The Knobs University bill and the Goose Run, alias Columbia River, navigation project—schemes which do not touch the big robbers of the day—receive the emphasis. However, the railroad steal is not without representation. There is a glimpse of the financial machinations behind the construction of the Salt Lick Pacific Extension:". . . forty thousand dollars a mile over the prairie, with extra for hardpan—and it'll be pretty much all hardpan, I can tell you; besides every alternate section of land on this line. There's millions in the job".[188] We are given an intimation of "what 'seeing' a Pennsylvania legislature meant",[189] and a detailed memoranda of what a congressional appropriation costs.

"Just reflect, for instance. A majority of the House committee, say $10,-000 apiece—$40,000; a majority of the Senate committee, the same each—say $40,000; a little extra to one or two chairmen of one or two such committees, say $10,000 each—$20,000; and there's $100,000 of the money gone, to begin with. Then, seven male lobbyists, at $3,000 each—$21,000; one female lobbyist, $10,000; a high moral Congressman or Senator here and there—the high moral ones cost more, because they give tone to a measure —say ten of these at $3,000 is $30,000; then a lot of small-fry country members who won't vote for anything whatever without pay—say twenty at $500 apiece, is $10,000; a lot of dinners to members—say $10,000 altogether; lot of jimcracks for Congressmen's wives and children—those go a long way—you can't spend too much money in that line—well, those things cost in a lump, say $10,000—along there somewhere;—and then comes your printed documents—your maps, your tinted engravings, your pamphlets, your illuminated show cards, your advertisements in a hundred and fifty papers at ever so much a line—because you've got to keep the papers all right or you are gone up, you know. Oh, my dear sir, printing bills are destruction itself. Ours, so far amount to—let me see—10; 52; 22; 12;—and then there's 11; 14; 33—well, never mind the details, the total in clean numbers foots up $118,254.42 thus far!"[190]

The Gilded Age, has its picture of corrupt municipal government,

187. V. L. Parrington, *Main Currents,* III:169.
188. *The Gilded Age,* v. I, p. 149.
189. *Ibid.,* v. I, p. 168.
190. *Ibid.,* pp. 306-307.

too, in a brief tracing of the career of "the Hon. Patrique Oreille'
. . . a wealthy Frenchman from Cork,"[191] who assisted "the
great and good Wm. M. Weed himself" in stealing twenty million
dollars from New York City. To be sure "by and by the newspapers came out with exposures and called Weed and O'Riley
'thieves'—whereupon the people rose as one man (voting repeatedly) and elected the two gentlemen to their proper theater of
action, the New York legislature".[192]

In *The American Claimant* (1892) Twain touches again on the
corruptions and incapabilities of our national legislators; but
the treatment makes no attempt at the scope of *The Gilded Age*.
The fact that there is still an Office of Flint-Picker in the cellar
of the War Department years after "the flint-arm has gone out
and the forts have tumbled down"[193] is noted as a characteristic
example of Federal efficiency. Here too are revealed the important interests, the vast multitudes of acres and men, for whom
many of our congressmen stand: Washington Hawkins pretends
to represent the Cherokee Strip in Congress; he talks with
Sellers whose praise makes him modestly confess—"Why,
Colonel, there's nothing to it. That little, narrow, desolate,
unpeopled, oblong streak of grass and gravel, lost in the remote
wastes of the vast continent—why, it's like representing a
billiard table—a discarded one".[194] Here are glimpses of the
government of the world's greatest nation, as Twain sees it.

The second of our politico-economic novels to attack the Invisible Empire along a national front is *Honest John Vane* (1875)
by John W. DeForest. The Steam Navigation Company, which
distributed its stock almost openly in Congress, and the Subfluvial Tunnel Road project are the featured examples of the
corruption of government by private business interests. DeForest
also scored the economic incapability of our legislators, in the
character of Honest John Vane. He is described as being of
almost Eden-like nakedness and innocence,[195] and has never
read a line of Smith, Mill, or Bastiat. The Subfluvial Tunnel

191. *Ibid.*, v. II, p. 25.
192. *Ibid.*
193. *The American Claimant*, p. 21.
194. *Ibid.*, p. 24.
195. *Honest John Vane*, p. 41.

Road, a project in which Vane narrowly missed becoming disastrously enmeshed, was "meant to run through our country from north to south, under the Mississippi River, uniting Lake Superior with the Gulf of Mexico".[196] The enterprise was to be financed by government subsidy and loan. Essentially the road was to be built by the government at the expense of the Treasury for the benefit of directors and officers and boss stockholders, who would get the stock at fifty and sell it at par because of government backing[197] — a not inaccurate outline of the business methods and activities of the Crédit Mobilier. The palpable ridiculousness of a road to be built under the Mississippi River from Lake Superior to the Gulf of Mexico is DeForest's comment on the American frenzy of over-railroading, which led to the panics of 1873 and 1884, and to a less extent that of 1893 as well.[198]

In "An Inspired Lobbyist" (1872) DeForest had previously satirized the corruption of government by self-seeking commercial interests, in a more humorous and less fully developed short fictional work. The story is an outline of the career of Annias Pullwool the "most successful and famous lobbyist in Washington, and the most sought after by the most rascally and desperate claimants of unlawful millions".[199]

Democracy (1880) by Henry Adams is inferior to *The Gilded Age* in every way, and is less economically significant that *Honest John Vane;* its picture of political Washington, however, has none of the grotesquerie of the DeForest novel. The central character is Mrs. Madeline Lee, ultra-charming young widow; and, as Parrington points out, to essay "to penetrate the dark places of political jobbery through the eyes of a society woman, too high-bred to turn lobbyist and inveigle secrets out of ambitious politicians, is sufficiently absurd, yet not unchar-actertistic of the Henry Adams whose home was a distinguished salon and who in pottering about the political world of Washington deceived himself in thinking he had his finger on the

---

196. *Ibid.,* p. 86.
197. *Ibid.,* p. 94.
198. Cf. Bogart, *Economic History of the United States,* pp. 362, 390.
199. "An Inspired Lobbyist" in *Stories by American Authors,* p. 138.

web of intrigue."[200]   The commanding figure of Senator Silas P. Ratcliffe corresponds to Senator Dillworthy of the Twain-Warner novel, in mastery of political organization and ability to conceal official dishonesty beneath religious cant.   In his franker moments, though, he admits that "if virtue won't answer our purpose we must use vice, or our opponents will put us out of office. . . ."[201]   The book, however, touching only lightly on minor lobbies essentially ignores the fundamental economic problem of the strangle-hold big business had on government.   It is content to blame the evils of political corruption merely on the principle of democracy.

Thomas Stewart Dennison's *An Iron Crown* is a very comprehensive study of the manipulation of government by business. Dennison does not bother with the art of satire; his attack is direct and with a brass-knuckled fist.   Ophir, Ingledee, and Norwell are the chief characters in this novel, all able "fleecers of juvenile mutton"; but Dennison occasionally forgets that he has a fictional disguise for the black doings of the national drama, and dropping his narrative assails by name the Crédit Mobilier, Standard Oil, and Jay Gould.[202]   The story is supplemented, too, by, appendix notes from official documents and other reliable sources proving the truth of the fictional charges.

"The pirate of old boldly proclaimed his calling", Dennison points out.   But "the pirates of our own great republic plunder the people in the insidious disguise of public benefactors, under subsidies granted by subservient legislative bodies".[203]   In this fiction as in fact the railroad barons are represented as the blackest villains in the Gilded Age's pageant of corruption.   The Government promises to guarantee the railroad bonds; the organizers take their stock on a margin, and reap huge profits when their favorable bills go through—which they invariably, inevitably, do, for these dinosaurs of the age of big business know well the stuff which judges, juries, and legislatures are made of.   Here is the story of American railroad building:

---

200. *Main Currents,* III:170.
201. *Democracy,* p. 141.
202. *An Iron Crown,* p. 467-468.
203. *Ibid.,* p. 153.

"The Midland got its necessary legislation through Congress by joining forces with the Continental Pacific. Together these great corporations, through the lobby or 'Third House', moved on the national Legislature. There was unlimited wining and dining and trading of influence, and the smiles of fair women of amiable dispositions, and making of presents, and 'seeing' of Congressmen when all other means had failed. And so the railroads got what they asked, while a betrayed nation slept, only to awake covered with shame and disgraced by the men it had honored. In all history, even in the days of Romany infamy, there is no record of a greater grab. Of all the steals, rings, and rascalities which grew out of the Civil War, and the demoralization consequent upon it, these were the most unscrupulous in conception, daring in execution, and colossal in proportions. These companies built their roads out of the generous bounty of the government, which bounty was granted for the sole purpose of building a national highway for the benefit of the people. Their land grant was in itself an empire, and they scrupled not to take possession of it before they had fulfilled the conditions laid down in their charter. The unfortunate settlers on such lands were driven from their homes in some instances by bands of hired murderers, employed by these soulless money kings of the New World."[204]

In appendix notes Dennison quotes figures from the Report of the House Judiciary Committee which investigated the legislative activities of the Crédit Mobilier showing that the Crédit Mobilier stole from the Government above the cost of the Union Pacific railroad more than forty-three million dollars. In the construction of the Central Pacific C. P. Huntington, Leland Stanford, Charles Crocker, E. B. Hopkins, and Mark Hopkins defrauded the national treasury of more than sixty-nine millions. Counting in the value of lands at one to six dollars an acre "it is reasonable to estimate the entire Pacific railroad steal in all its crooked phases at two hundred and ten million dollars".[205] This is food for thought; and more:

"When four or five sewing-machine monopolies can wring from the women of the country one hundred millions in twenty years; when four or five railway kings can steal one hundred and sixty millions in twenty years; when an oil company can pile fabulous millions on millions in ten years; when a Wall-street pirate can steal from the American people one hundred millions in twenty years by wrecking railroads, seizing telegraphs, and endangering the business interests of the country; when three or four great coal monopolies can own the fuel of a continent, and charge extortionate prices for it; when the rich daily grow enormously rich and the poor daily grow poorer; when

---

204. *Ibid.*, pp. 76-77.
205. *Ibid.*, pp. 549, 584.

all these things can occur under the sanction of law, in a great republic, is it not time to stop and think? Having reflected, is it not time to act before our slavery is complete and irremediable?

What must we do? Join the ranks of the communist? No! Communism is a monster too vile to be tolerated for an instant. . . . What then? Purify politics. Elect honest men pledged to honest measures. If they betray their trust set them such an example as will make official corruption, bribery, and dishonesty a crime, sure to meet a swift, certain and righteous retribution."[206]

Among Dennison's more detailed criticisms are: corruption at the polls—the voting of one hundred men from Mrs. Whiff's boarding house where three men and two boys actually live;[207] the absorbing of all the profits of farms and mines by the railroads advancing their freight rates at will;[208] the railroads and telegraph lines doubling or trebling their capital (on paper) and "impudently demanding that the public shall pay an interest on this pretended capital which never existed";[209] the purchase of the courts by corporations;[210] and the granting of tax exemptions to great corporations whose franchises have been purchased from corrupted legislatures.[211]

Dennison's indictment of the ambassadors plentipotentiary of the Invisible Empire is probably the most specific, serious, and severe in our economic fiction. That his book should also be a good novel would perhaps be expecting too much.

"This craze of speculation, which seems to dominate everything of late years in our money-cursed country, is a very Juggernaut",[212] declares Edgar Braine the central character in George Cary Eggleston and Dolores Marbourg's *Juggernaut, A Veiled Record* (1891). Criticism of the railroads' corrupting invasion of municipal councils, state legislatures, and the national Congress is continued here. The Central Railroad wants a charter to run a line down the levee to the Point for a depot and a wharf. It is, says Edgar Braine, clearly "a trick to rob Thebes of her most fruitful source of revenue, by giving the

---

206. *Ibid.*, pp. 128, 129.
207. *Ibid.*, p. 61.
208. *Ibid.*, pp. 401, 418.
209. *Ibid.*, p. 438.
210. *Ibid.*, p. 464.
211. *An Iron Crown*, p. 464.
212. *Juggernaut, a Veiled Record*, p. 54.

levee, and with it the exclusive right to collect wharfage to this railroad crowd".[213] They easily buy the Thebes Aldermen over to their purpose, and eventually Braine, who as editor of "The Enterprise" has blocked their way. Having thus committed moral suicide, Braine writes and prints his obituary as a man, and becomes himself a very devil of a railroad manipulator. He buys his way to the United States Senate with his railroad power and then uses his position for the further enrichment of his private interests. In the struggle for money and power Braine has his wife, Helen, compromise herself with Everett, a member of the Cabinet, and the story thereafter loses its economic significance except as it traces the disintegrating effect of unscrupulous greed upon the human soul.

A Member of the Third House (1897) is Hamlin Garland's contribution to the literature depicting the ways of political Washington in the hands of corrupting business interests. The 'third house' is the sacred chamber of the representatives of the Invisible Empire, the national lobby—"a body of corrupt men who stand between the people and legislation".[214] Tom Brennan is the lawyer-lobbyist for Lawrence Davis' railway interests. His attitude is "The public be damned"![215] and his business 'suppressing' and 'inducing' legislators by the skillful use of liquor, money, and blackmail,[216] to the end that the railroad interests may be most efficiently served.

In his *Middle Border* stories Garland also occasionally criticizes the indirect control of government by great private forces. "The Return of the Private", for example, embodies a protest against the injustice of the control of the national currency during and after the Civil War by a small clique of New York bankers: "While the millionaire sent his money to England for safe-keeping, this man with his girl-wife and three babies, left his mortgaged farm and went away to fight for an idea. It was foolish, but it was sublime for all that".[217] If he had been paid for those fever-wracked days at the front, it

---

213. *Ibid.*, p. 48.
214. *A Member of the Third House*, p. 12.
215. *Ibid.*, p. 54.
216. Cf. *ibid.*, pp. 53-58.
217. *Main-Travelled Roads*, p. 189.

was in paper; his debt was now due in gold. Garland calls this injustice.

The Gilded Age, Honest John Vane, Democracy, An Iron Crown, Juggernaut, a Veiled Record, and *A Member of the Third House,* all dealt with the economic problem of private business in government on a national scale. The corrupting of government by private interests in state settings is the main theme of two other particularly able politico-economic novels— *John Andross* (1874), by Rebecca Harding Davis, and *The Octopus* (1901) by Frank Norris. But both Davis and Norris are too artistic to allow obvious and direct criticism to assume complete command of their novels. Their sense of art disciplines their theses.

John Andross is significant here for its protest against corruption in the Pennsylvania legislature. This part of the story is chiefly a recital of the activities of the National Transit Association, a corporation that "needed bills passed at Harrisburg sometimes, and was able to pay for the passage".[218] The 'Association' was controlled by the Whiskey Ring in Philadelphia. It is not unlikely that Mrs. Davis had in mind the St. Louis Whiskey Ring the exposure of which occurred the year this novel was published. There is no retribution, however, in *John Andross*: the Philadelphia 'Ring' was clever enough to make Colonel Latimer collector of revenue, and so to "strengthen the party in public estimation, beyond the power of any Citizen's Reform Party to damage it".[219] The book leaves only a moderately strong impression because the legislation which the 'Ring' is buying at Harrisburg is never very definitely described.

While Norris tried to hold himself to a non-propagandistic creed—indeed to a deterministic philosophy, the material which he presents in *The Octopus* is as definitely critical of the injustice of private business in government as that of any politico-economic novel in our fiction. Norris himself may not demand justice from the railroads, but his picture of their oppressive methods arouses us to demand it. He makes us see the rail-

---

218. *John Andross*, p. 72.
219. *Ibid.*, p. 154.

road as "the symbol of a vast power, huge, terrible, flinging
the echo of its thunder over all the reaches of the valley, leaving blood and destruction in its path; the leviathan with tentacles
of steel clutching into the soil, the soulless Force, the iron-
hearted Power, the monster, the Colossus, the Octopus".[220] There
is an understanding between the courts and the Railroad Commission and the railroads:[221] indeed "there never was and never
will be a California Railroad Commission not in the pay of the
Pacific and Southwestern". The Inter-state Commerce Commission is "the greatest Punch and Judy show on earth".[222]
The railroad had agreed to sell the alternate sections along
its route, granted by the government, for two dollars and fifty
cents an acre. But when the farmers of the San Joaquin Valley had leased and improved this land and then went to the
railroad land office to buy it the price was twenty-seven dollars
an acre, 'to anyone'.[223] With extortionate freight rates, secured
by complete control of legislature and courts, and with tyrannical holdings of land to be sold only at impossible prices the
railroad was supreme.

"Yes, the Railroad had prevailed. The ranches had been seized in the tentacles of the octopus; the iniquitous burden of extortionate freight rates had
been imposed like a yoke of iron. The monster had killed . . . beggared
. . . corrupted, driven to starvation and prostitution, widowed, killed the
very babe within its mother's womb."[224]

It is true that Norris tries to deny the propagandistic aspect of
this novel; at first by the deterministic conception of the railroads as the masters not the tools of men—the graphically portrayed death of S. Behrman in the hold of the wheat ship is
symbolic of the way in which the ultimate and fundamental
forces of life sweep over those who have seemed to govern
society rather than to be governed by it— and finally by a
declared belief in the moral order of the universe—in the permanency of the wheat, saving lives elsewhere in recompense
for those here destroyed. His conclusion is that "the larger

---

220. *The Octopus,* p. 51.
221. *Ibid.,* p. 11.
222. *Ibid.,* p. 105.
223. *Ibid.,* p. 271.
224. *Ibid.,* p. 650.

view always and through all shams, all wickedness, discovers the Truth that will, in the end prevail, and all things, surely, inevitable, resistlessly, work together for good".[225] But this we are tempted to discount for poetry, and keep as challenging criticism the picture of railroad oppression so powerfully painted.

These are the most significant novels in our fiction before 1900 in which the corrupting relation of business to government is the major theme. There are, of course, a large number of additional novels in which some comment is made on the economic problem inherent in a democratic form of government. Of these Robert Herrick's *The Gospel of Freedom* (1898) is one of the more important. The ease and completeness with which the Illinois government can be corrupted is the theme of criticism here. "The railroad companies have made a raid on the legislature to get a lot of privileges for nothing",[226] Theodore Jennings reports early in the novel. Another type of official dishonesty is revealed in the information that "Rensen's extra two millions came from a 'tip' on the sugar schedule of the Wilson Bill".[227] But the straight forward bribing of legislature and governor by Wren and his traction clique in order to get through their legislation is the political corruption matter that gets most emphasis in this novel. And supposedly more honest men—like John Wilbur—gambled on the success of the bribe by buying great blocks of traction stock. Of course, the Governor held a hearing on the bill—almost transparent even to those who did not know. "But what with false assessments and contributions to the city council, watered industrials, and tips on sugar . . ."[228] could you expect.

The principle of democracy, as it is being materialistically applied, is partly at fault. Herrick has his foreign critic, Simeon Erard, state an opinion that he with reservations personally shares: "The average man is your tin-god. When some day there are too many average men, and they all think stupidly

225. *Ibid.*, p. 652.
226. *The Gospel of Freedom*, p. 118.
227. *Ibid.*, p. 124.
228. *Ibid.*, p. 126.

that they have the same right to an average kind of easy living, why, you're going to have a portentous row, for a democracy is at the bottom irreligious and unidealistic".[229]

A considerable part of the narrative of Ellen Glasgow's *The Voice of the People* (1900) is concerned with shadows of corruption in the Virginia legislature. The book is not of great significance in this study because the shadows never focus into definite facts.

This is likewise true of Charles Dudley Warner's *A Little Journey in the World* (1889). The inference is that the congressional investigation "into land grants involved in Southwestern operations"[230] means that Rodney H. Henderson has employed the usual methods of railroad magnates with legislators. But the matter is dropped with only this reference.

Hjalmar Hjorth Boyesen is perhaps the most pointed commentator in our later fiction on the incapability of our legislators, and on our unidealistic methods of selecting them. In *The Light of Her Countenance* (1889) he has his hero Julian Burroughs declare: "Culture—nay, the possession of any talent or distinction beyond the average—is a disqualification for public life in a democracy . . . a democracy resents refinement, resents culture, and exalts only the average man".[231] The story reveals the revolt of Burroughs against the beer and whiskey treating, the saloon campaigning, necessary for election to Congress. Boyesen pays his respects, too, to those 'predatory societies' which "under the guise of some benevolent object bleed candidates, and with a beautiful impartiality accept bribes from all parties".[232] The charge of legislative incapability to grasp and solve the complex problems of modern life is continued in *The Mammon of Unrighteousness* (1891). Our representatives in government are not the great men we once had, Boyesen asserts. Compare faces.... "The average fool who formerly took pride in being represented by a wiser man, now prefers to be represented by as great a fool as himself. . . . In the modern

229. *Ibid.*, p. 156.
230. *A Little Journey in the World*, p. 270.
231. *The Light of Her Countenance*, pp. 68-69.
232. *Ibid.*, p. 74.

world tact is the accepted substitute for character. . . . It is no use quarreling with Fate; and in the United States the average man is the Fate that rules us and determines our place in the world".[233] Horace Larkin is given the post of minister at St. Petersburg solely because his wife and father-in-law have contributed liberally to the Republican campaign fund.[234] The 'Canal Ring' is cited as a powerful lobby in New York state legislature.[235]

A considerable number of our other critic-novelists have commented briefly on the various economic phases of politics. A chronological glance at some of these comments will serve to show the place of the problem in our fictionists' thought.

Edward Eggleston was a sufficiently penetrating observer to know that what he said historically of the 1840 campaign was at least partially true of his own time: "The Whig leaders of 1840 roasted beeves in order to persuade the independent voters to listen to arguments on the tariff; they washed down abstruse reasonings about the United States Bank with hard cider; and and by good feeding persuaded the citizens to believe in internal improvements.[236]

Henry Francis Keenan: "I saw Congressmen selling their votes daily. I saw confidants of the Cabinet trafficking on their relations; I saw Senators bartering almost openly in the lobby".[237]

Edward Everett Hale: The railroads are "not dealing fairly by the people of the State, who have given them their charters".[238]

Albert Chavannes: "If you inquire into the vast fortunes which exist in your country, you will find that most of them are due to the investments of profits made in certain lines of business carried on for the benefit of the Community".[239]

Henry B. Fuller: Brainard's "manipulation of city councils and state legislatures had been freely charged".[240]

233. *The Mammon of Unrighteousness,* pp. 7, 8, 304.
234. *Ibid.,* p. 382 ff.
235. *Ibid.,* p. 332.
236. *Roxy* (1878), p. 10.
237. *The Money-Makers* (1885), p. 40.
238. *Sybil Knox* (1892), p. 269.
239. *The Future Commonwealth* (1892), p. 27.
240. *The Cliff-Dwellers* (1893), p. 35.

Caroline C. Walch: "... wholesale robbery of state and nation".[241]

Finley Peter Dunne: "Willum J. undherstands that there's a few hundhreds iv thousands iv people livin in a part iv th' town that looks like nawthin' but smoke fr'm th' roof iv th' Onion League Club that have on'y two pleasures in life, to wurruk an' to vote, both iv which they do at th' uniform rate iv wan dollar an' a half a day. That's why William J. O'Brien is now a sinitor. ... "[242]

Albert Adams Merrill: From the utopian perspective of 2199— under the 1900 system "the only man represented was the one capable of buying a representative".[243]

Theodore Dreiser: Hurstwood, in New York soon "discovered the influence of Tammany Hall and the value of standing in with the police. The most profitable and flourishing places he found to be those which conducted anything but a legitimate business".[244]

Alcanoan O. Grigsby: After the Civil War the legal tender debt was funded into bonds payable in legal tender, interest in gold. Then "a law was enacted resuming specie payments, and the bonds were made payable in coin, now the people who had taken paper dollars for their services in saving the Union, were taxed to pay gold dollars to the money kings for the paper dollars they had received . . . a barefaced, legalized robbery" which continued for thirty years.[245]

In their attack upon the Invisible Empire our knights in critical fiction have pointed out that no large and oppressive monopoly can exist without the consent and support of law; that if industry makes money through being in government it does so by the co-operation of government, either unknowingly or through conscious, paid purpose. There are three major charges running through this fiction from 1792 to 1900. First, that a great number of our legislators are economically incapable; they are unable to comprehend the country's problems, and so are subject un-

---

241. *Doctor Sphinx* (1898), p. 340.
242. *Mr. Dooley in Peace and War* (1898), pp. 112-113.
243. *The Great Awakening* (1899), p. 63.
244. *Sister Carrie* (1900), p. 325.
245. *Nequa, or the Problem of the Ages* (1900), p. 262.

knowingly to the influence and fraud of great private interests. Brackenridge, Irving, Cooper, DeForest, Adams, Boyesen, and Herrick have been particularly emphatic in this indictment. Second, that travesty has been made of government through the buying of political office either directly or by lavish treating and multitudinous favors. It is obvious, of course, that when a man makes a financial outlay to secure an office he does so with the belief and intention that the office shall somehow reimburse him. The fictionists who have treated this form of governmental corruption are Brackenridge, Cooper, Twain and Warner, Dennison, Boyesen, Eggleston, and Dunne. ˙ Third, that municipal councils, state legislatures, and the national Congress, and courts of all degree are bribed to pass legislation and render decisions favorable and profitable to special private interests—subsidation, tax-exempt franchises, monopoly privileges, public improvements subject to graft. A particular phase of this third general article of indictment is the manipulation of the national currency by private banking cliques to the detriment of the public — written upon by Irving, Garland, and Grigsby. Virtually all of our politico-economic novelists treat this third charge in its general scope. The more important ones may be named in this approximately chronological order: Brackenridge, Paulding, Twain and Warner, DeForest, Dennison, Eggleston and Marbourg, Garland, Davis, Keenan, Warner, Fuller, Herrick, Walch, Merrill, Glasgow, and Dreiser. Strong forces to the fight, here; but the Invisible Empire as they well know is a subtle and powerful foe.

III

General Economic Injustice and Unhappiness as Treated in the Novel: The Whole Truth

Like Matthew Arnold the writers of economic criticism in American fiction see

> The complaining millions of men
> Darken in labor and pain.

There had always been unhappiness in the world, they point out, but the industrial age brought a new kind of misery. The weak it bound with insidious fetters, mockingly calling them freemen; the strong it mailed with a "callous insensibility to social wrongs and individual sorrows".[246] The tremendous concentration of economic power in the hands of the few which the industrial age has wrought is only realized when one computes the productive capacity of machines in terms of the productive power of men. "You look around you and you see a nation of sixty millions—apparently; but secreted in their hands and brains, and invisible to your eyes, is the true population of this Republic and it numbers forty billions"![247] This vast multitude of men— the seen millions and the unseen billions—is dominated by a handful of 'Masters of Bread' who scruple not to lay up at the expense of their suffering servants untold treasures susceptible to the corruption of moth and rust. Theirs is the greedy power— an impersonal force, perhaps, but still the power—that has piled up the world's population in great seething cities, any one of which might be described as Robert Herrick has described Chicago: ". . . a stupendous piece of blasphemy against nature. Once within its circle the heart must forget that the earth is beautiful".[248] The spirit of bigness and be-damnness is the governing force. The fever of life has metamorphosed what should have been men into commercial dinosaurs. There is no limit to their aggrandizing ambition. They look ever forward, as they tell you frankly and callously: "We don't take account of yesterday's news in Chicago. We take today's and grumble because we can't get tomorrow's"[249]—"for he that loveth silver shall not be satisfied with silver; nor he that loveth abundance with increase". Meanwhile, driven by gnawing bellies, labor

> A Thousand men in troubles wide and dark;
> Half-ignorant, they turn an easy wheel,
> That sets sharp wracks at work, to pinch and peel,

and no one raises a hand to distill the saltness out of human tears.

The problems of moral integrity and social justice which

---

246. H. H. Boyesen, *Social Strugglers* (1893), p. 84.
247. Mark Twain, *The American Claimant* (1892), pp. 81, 83.
248. *The Gospel of Freedom*, p. 104.
249. Ellen Glasgow, *The Descendant* (1897), p. 237.

became constantly more acute as Big Business grew to maturity were strikingly foreseen by Timothy Flint in the first quarter of the nineteenth century. He had spent a decade along the Mississippi Valley frontier and returned to New England to find such towns as Salem, Waltham, Pawtucket, and Dover, which he had known before as pleasant villages—almost open country— now amazingly industrialized. Their new order of life struck him with its possible danger:

"There is not a doubt in my mind, that this new development of the resources of the facilities of travelling, the argumented calls for expenditure, and temptations to it, the greater value of money in procuring what was but luxury at first, but which has now become necessary, have furnished new excitements to avarice. You can perceive in New England, that the wits of the people are doubly sharpened in all the arts of money-getting. Have we not to fear, that this rage for travelling, this manufacturing and money-getting impulse, and the new methods of reasoning and acting, will overturn our puritan institutions? New England founded her empire of industry and opinion, not in natural but moral resources, in her ancient habits, and her ancient strictness, her schools, her economy and industry, her stable and perennial habits of worship. Should these be changed as I much fear this new order of things is changing them, it will be written upon the table of her forsaken temples, "the glory is departed".[250]

Flint's fear was amply justified. The age of the machine had arrived. In 1838 Kay had invented the flying shuttle, multiplying the capacity of the loom; in 1767 Hargreaves completed the spinning-jenny; in 1771 Arkwright perfected his roller spinning machine. A few years later Crompton combined the roller and the jenny, and after the application of steam to spinning in 1785—it had already been effectively used in the mining industries—the power loom replaced the hand loom. Within the course of a few decades the whole economic order was changed. Centuries had been required for the slow development of the medieval system of feudalism, the guild system, and the handicrafts, but now came changes so sudden and profound that even today society has not yet learned to adjust itself to the myriad needs and possibilities which the union of man's mind with nature's forces has produced. The industrial revolution took the workman from the land and crowded him into the towns; it

---

250. Timothy Flint, *Recollections of the Last Ten Years* (1826). Quoted from Knopf reprint (1932), pp. 375-76.

took the loom from his cottage and placed it in the factory; it took the tool from his hand and harnessed it to a shaft. It robbed him of his personal skill and joined his arm of flesh to an arm of iron; it reduced him from a craftsman to a specialist: from a maker of shoes to a mere stitcher of soles. From this it took at a single sweep his interest in the workmanship of his task, his ownership of the tools, his garden, his wholesome environment, and even his family. All were swallowed by the black maw of the ugly new mill town. The hardships of the old life were forgotten in the horrors of the new; for the transition was rapid enough to make the contrast striking. Indeed it was so rapid that the new class of employers, the capitalists, found little time to think of anything but increasing their profits, and the new class of employees, now merely wage-earners, found that their long hours of monotonous toil gave them little leisure and no interest.[251]

Here was born the economic class consciousness that constitutes the most basic problem of democracy. The "rich and successful formed a kind of secret society, pledged to advance any member, to keep the others out by indifference. When the others manage to get in, for any reason, they lend them aid to the exclusion of those left outside".[252] Of course many did get in while there continued to be free land in the West to aid the disaffected or disappointed artisan in achieving economic independence. The development of the frontier served to keep the demand for labor constant, except during the rare intervals of financial stagnation, and the door of opportunity open to the energetic and able artisan. The chronicles of American industry are replete with names of prominent leaders who began at the apprentice's bench. But these like their lesser fictional counterparts, Gerrish, in William Dean Howells' *Annie Kilburn* (1888) and the *Quality of Mercy* (1892), Jimmy Debber in J. W. Sullivan's *So the World Goes* (1898), Charles Millard in Edward Eggleston's *The Faith Doctor* (1891), having achieved a higher economic

---

251. For this summary of the change of life entailed by the Industrial Revolution, see Samuel P. Orth, *The Armies of Labor*, pp. 1-8, and Ernest L. Bogart, *Economic History of the United States*, Chapter XI, pp. 148-159.

252. Robert Herrick, *The Web of Life*, p. 133.

rank themselves forgot their brother's relation to the lowly with whom they had formerly labored. "For it is a rule of good society that as soon as you arrive you effect to have always been there".[253]

It was natural that the class divisions of the new industrial civilization marked on the one hand by the concentration of wealth in the hands of the few and their apparently closed conspiracy to exploit the many to the maximum degree should be combatted on the other by the organization of labor to fight for its rights and its life. The first strike had occurred in the United States in 1741. From the last decade of the eighteenth century on they occurred intermittently in most of the chief cities of our Atlantic seaboard. They were, however, local agitations and never reached the scope of a labor movement. The fundamental idea of fighting organization with organization was there nevertheless. "What we want to know", said Albert Brisbane, disciple of Fourier's associationism and author of *The Social Destiny of Man* (1840) "is how to change, peacefully, the system of today. The first great principle is combination." As the growth of manufacturing and commerce became greatly accelerated after the Civil War, so the labor organization movement reacting to the growing ills of industry spread swiftly. Strikes swept the country in successive waves in the late seventies, the eighties, and the nineties. Strike statistics tabulated by the United States Bureau of Labor for the twenty-five year period from 1881 to 1905 disclose the fact that 38,303 strikes and lockouts occurred, involving 199,954 establishments and 7,444,279 employees.[254]

It is obvious of course that these strikes represent the workers' reaction to what they considered oppressive conditions of labor and life. They were a human protest against the inhumanity of the capitalistic order. The novels of economic criticism in American fiction, particularly from 1860 to 1900, picture the industrial and social injustices out of which these protests grew, and seek by specific avowal or implication to accomplish the reforms for which labor organizations were striving by direct

253. Edward Eggleston, *The Faith Doctor*, p. 56.
254. Cf. Ernest L. Bogart, *Economic History of the United States*, pp. 158-159 and Samuel P. Orth, *The Armies of Labor*, pp. 45-86, 172.

action. Neither American workmen nor American economic novelists were content to sit quietly and observe with Charles Dudley Warner: "It is the penalty that we pay for the freedom of republican opportunity that some must be very rich."[255] They insist rather that capitalistic monopoly, the essence of the industrial age, "is the great enemy of the human race".[256]

It must be apparent that the development of trusts and the greed of men for unlimited wealth which they signify was more than a chance matter. It was the logical outgrowth of a national philosophy which had as its summum bonum the American dollar—the mercenary philistine philosophy of Jacksonian democracy. The commercial depravity and the baneful influence of that depravity upon every other aspect of life in the Jacksonian era marked a decline in traditional American idealism that left our subsequent national life without a challenging spiritual standard. There was probably no greater critic of these times—in fiction or out—than James Fenimore Cooper. The society of the republic which passed from Federalism to Jeffersonianism and then transformed itself into Jacksonian democracy was, as a recent scholar has pointed out,[257] the background of Cooper's life. The nation's changing culture came to be his chief interest, and his critical reactions, both strongly felt and strongly expressed, were an acute commentary on the process of American development. Often they were more—a prophetic insight which told him a hundred years ago the direction democracy in the United States was taking—the road toward the sordid materialism of the age of big business. Evils Van Wyck Brooks and Sinclair Lewis point out after the fact, Cooper saw at their inception.

Cooper's critical fiction falls into two chief periods. In Europe from 1826 to 1833 he wrote three novels *The Bravo* (1831), *The Heidenmauer* (1832), and *The Headsman* (1833)

---

255. *A Little Journey in the World* (1889), p. 125.
256. Henry Olerich, *A Cityless and Countryless World* (1893), p. 92. See also S. Byron Welcome, *From Earth's Center* (1894), p. 213; B. J. Wellman, *The Legal Revolution of 1902* (1898), p. 119; D. L. Stump, *From World to World* (1896), p. 36 and other utopian novelists for bitter assailments of the trust, the ultimate expression of an individualistic economy.
257. John F. Ross, *The Social Criticism of Fenimore Cooper* (1933), p. 29.

interpreting American democracy for an international audience
—or rather upholding the democratic ideal by contrasting the
United States with earlier professedly democratic governments.
At home again after 1833 he wrote for an American audience
critical fiction scoring the political, social, and economic evils
of Jacksonian democracy: *The Monikins* (1835), *Homeward
Bound* (1838), *Home as Found* (1838), *Stanstoe* (1845), *The
Chainbearer* (1846), *The Redskins* (1846) and *The Crater*
(1847). Cooper's last novels *The Oak Openings* (1848), *The Sea
Lions* (1849) and *The Ways of the Hour* (1850) also contain
social and political criticsm.

It is an interesting fact that the novels which Cooper wrote
abroad supposedly justifying and lauding America were in the
course of things a criticism of the America which he found when
he returned home. The thought of *The Heidenmauer, The Bravo*
and *The Headsman* is therefore of essentially one piece with his
later specific indictments of Jacksonian philistinism and materialism. In the first of these novels Cooper had portrayed the
plight of the lower classes oppressed in the "conflict between
monk and baron". The setting of *The Bravo* is Venice, of *The
Headsman*, Switzerland. Cooper points out that in both of
these so-called republics the government was really by the strong
and the few, and therefore wrong and weak. His pronounce-
ment on this issue has many counterparts in our later fictionists
of economic criticism, especially the utopian novelists of the last
quarter of the nineteenth century.

"It may be taken [he wrote] as a governing principle, in all civil relations,
that the strong will grow stronger and the feeble more weak, until the first
become unfit to rule or the last unable to endure. In this important truth
is contained the secret of the downfall of all those states which have crumbled
beneath the weight of their own abuses. It teaches the necessity of widening
the foundations of society until the base shall have a breadth of securing
the just representation of every interest."[258]

The theme of Cooper's later criticism was that the America
of the Jacksonian era had become degraded from the level of
society which prevailed under the Federalistic regime of the
earlier years of the republic. It was against the tyranny of the

---

258. *The Bravo*, p. 157.

bourgeois unidealistic majority, really dominated by skillful, insidious demagogues who cared for nothing but power that Cooper chiefly protested.[259] *The Monikins, Homeward Bound* and *Home as Found* are the most forceful expressions of this criticism. "Since Cooper held that the political equalitarianism of the nation never implied herd life and herd thought, and since the tyranny of the majority meant the extinction of individualism, this tyranny was for him the prime social evil in the new democracy".[260] *Stanstoe, The Chainbearer,* and *The Redskins,* comprising the "anti-Rent trilogy" are Cooper's defense of the sanctity of property rights.

Cooper's specific comments on money worship, speculation, and commercial depravity, while not so extensive as his account of politics were nevertheless significant—and equally unfavorable. Looking on the buying and selling in Wall Street, Effingham in *Home as Found* saw a very mania of stock speculation and real estate gambling. There were beautifully drawn and colored maps of newly constructed townsites; ". . . scores were eagerly bidding against each other. . . . One was purchasing ragged rocks, another the bottom of rivers, a third, a bog, and all on the credit maps".[261] The story of "the farm of old Volkert Van Brunt" was typical of these operations: the land was bought as a farm for five thousand dollars; it was subsequently subdivided and mapped into lots; it passed through the hands of numerous dealers and speculators and brought finally the sum of three hundred thousand dollars.[262] Pervasive inflation—extravagant issues of paper money, false appraisals of all kinds of property were daily occurrences. The entire country was like "a man who is in the incipient stages of exhilarating intoxication, and who keeps pouring down glass after glass, in the idle notion that he is merely sustaining nature in her ordinary func-

259. It is obvious that the issues involved, here are largely political and social rather than economic, no effort has been made to treat their full ramifications in this study. But see John F. Ross, *The Social Criticism of Fenimore Cooper.*

260. John F. Ross, *The Social Criticism of Fenimore Cooper,* p. 81.
261. *Home as Found,* p. 114.
262. *Ibid.,* p. 113.

tions".[263]   This was the uninspiring drama of the Jacksonian dollar-chase.[264]

The nation had sown a wind, and it was to reap a whirlwind. The petty mercenary creed of the Jacksonian Era was to become the super-materialistic philosophy of the Age of Big Business.

Two pre-Civil War novels which stand in interesting contrast to the works of later writers treating the same themes and scenes are *Richard Edney and the Governor's Family* (1850) by Sylvester Judd, and Alice B. Haven's *Loss and Gain* (1860).   The first of these depicts the New England town of Woodylin.   The capital and labor relationship is represented in Richard Edney's contacts with Captain Creamer, owner of Green Mill.   The effect of factory toil is suggested in this story by the brief picture of Violet, who never strong, is afflicted by tuberculosis through her work in the mill.   There is, however, in Captain Creamer, representing capital, a sympathy and humanity that contrasts sharply with later New England mill life pictures—as, for example, in Elizabeth Stuart Phelps.   The effect of Judd's work as a whole is one of romance rather than realism.

Loss and Gain depicts the "systematic household oppression" of young girls.[265]   Conditions of similar character and implied protests against them are found also in Susan Warner's *The Wide Wide World* (1850), Maria Cummins' *The Lamplighter* (1854), Mary E. Wilkins Freman's *A Humble Romance* (1887) and Kate Douglass Wiggin's *Timothy's Quest* (1890).   Alice Haven's novel is chiefly interesting here, however, for its picture of the department-store from the working girl's point of view.   The hours, from seven to seven, are difficult more because of the conditions Margaret has to face at home than because of the arduousness of toil which they require.   The movement of the story is based on a false accusation of theft rather than a protesting representation of the way in which killing wages affect the lives of the sales-girls.   A definite and interesting later

---

263.   *Ibid.*, p. 115.
264.   Cf. John F. Ross, *Social Criticism of Fenimore Cooper*, pp. 87-88.
265.   *Loss and Gain*, p. 9.

contrast is found in Margaret Sherwood's *Henry Worthington, Idealist* (1899).

It was Rebecca Harding Davis who first brought fiction importantly into the service of the social conscience as it pondered the growing evils of large scale industrialism. Writing of the harsh and brutal exploitation of labor in the Pennsylvania iron district Mrs. Davis utters a criticism the argument of which is merely the picturing of truth. Her appeal is candid, personal: "I want you to hide your disgust, take no heed of your clean clothes, and come right down with me—here, into the thickest of the fog and mud and foul effluvia". You shall know the truth, Rebecca Harding Davis is saying in *Life in the Iron Mills* (1861), that the truth may, perhaps, help to make free those slaves "red-faced and pale—whiskey-bloated and heavy brained, Irish, Dutch, black," who are in reality feeding the great furnaces with their own bodies.

A Story of Today (1862)[266] continues Mrs. Davis' effective presentation of sordid industrialism. The setting is an Indiana woolen mill. The operatives are mostly women, and it is against their exploitation that the novelist protests, "My story is coarse", Mrs. Davis concludes her novel; "it is meant as a mere groping hint. It has no conduit of God's justice running through it, awarding good and ill". Mrs. Davis felt much as Hamlin Garland did later: "I do not understand the problem, but it must be solved".[267]

It was with "The Tenth of January" published in the *Atlantic Monthly* for March, 1868, that Elizabeth Stuart Phelps first gained recognition as a critic of conditions in the New England mills. What she said of the particular town she was describing was equally true of hundreds of others: "Of the twenty-five thousand souls who inhabit that city, ten thousand are prisoners,—prisoners of factories. . . . Of these ten thousand, two-thirds are girls: voluntary captives indeed: but what is the practical difference? It is an old story, that of going to jail for want of

---

266. Later, *Margaret Howth*.
267. *Jason Edwards* (1891), p. 43.

bread".[268] "The Tenth of January", however does not embody the sordidness nor the comprehensiveness of criticism of Miss Phelps' later economic fiction.

The Silent Partner appearing in 1871, was a dithyrambic plea for justice for the mill-hands. It was one of the earliest, if not the first New England novel of industrialism. The Phelps economic protest is made on a moral basis. As she says in her preface: "Had Christian ingenuity been generally synonymous with the conduct of manufacturing corporations, I should have found no occasion for the writing of this book".[269] Reports of the Massachusetts Bureau of Statistics of Labor, the testimony of friends and personal observation are the professed bases of this Phelps tract. There is some weakness in realistic grasp of materials, but there are also episodes of great power between the blind, deaf and dumb Catty and her often unconvincingly drawn sister. The *Silent Partner* is the story of a young woman brought up in luxury, daughter of a manufacturer, who on her father's death wishes to join in the management of the factory, but on being politely rejected by her partners she engages in personnel work among her employees. There she encounters poverty as a sordid fact, and that discovery works a moral change in her life. She sees ill-fed men and women working eleven hours and more, often at temperatures of 115 to 125 degrees; she becomes intimately acquainted with Bub, typifying child-labor, an old man at eight years of age, caught and killed in the weaving machinery while trying to steal chewing tobacco from a fellow laborer. This is what goes on behind the scenes as the Capitalist promenades his heroic way through the national pageant of Big Business.

The story of Capital's inhumanity to Labor is a continued one —with merely new authors taking up the theme. J. G. Holland is the writer of the next installment. His novel *Sevenoaks* (1874) was a picture of a mill town which "may have been, or may be, in Maine, or New Hampshire, or Vermont, or New

---

268. "The Tenth of January" in *Atlantic Monthly,* March, 1868, pp. 345-346.

269. Phelps, Elizabeth S., *The Silent Partner,* p. v.

York",[270] and of "a lot of human beings that are treated like brutes—sold every year to the lowest bidder to be kept. . . . They go hungry, and naked, and cold . . . and we pretend to be Christians".[271] Robert Belcher, the owner of "the great mill", the soul and center" of Sevenoaks, "was not a gentleman. He supposed himself to be one, but he was mistaken".[272] He does not scruple even to steal the inventions of Paul Benedict, one of his workmen, and allow him to starve and fret himself into virtual insanity. Not content even with the exploitative mill business which capitalistic law calls legitimate, Belcher sponsors a fake oil speculation selling to poor clients stock he knows is worthless, and buys the Crooked Valley Railroad that he may issue bonds "for the purposes of stealing"—because: "I must have excitement".[273] This idea of the capitalist's satisfying some whim or desire of his own whatever the cost to others found further forceful denouncement in Henry B. Fuller's conclusion to *The Cliff-Dwellers* (1893): "It is for such a woman (as Cecelia Ingles) that one man builds a Clifton and that a hundred others are martyred in it".[274]

Edward Bellamy's *The Duke of Stockbridge* (1900)[275] represents the clash of class interests in an historical setting. It is the story of Shay's Rebellion in western Massachusetts, the "revolt of debtor-farmers in 1786 against their harsh creditors and the oppressive State government."[276] As Parrington points out, "it was a hasty piece of work that falls off greatly in the latter part; yet in its sympathy for the agrarian rebels and its probing of the economic sources of the post-Revolutionary unrest, it was far removed from the temper of Federalist historians".[277] It is an account of the tyranny of property rule—of the exploitation of the debtor farmer by the creditor gentleman in the period of economic maladjustment following the Revolu-

---

270. *Sevenoaks*, p. 2.
271. *Ibid.*, p. 17.
272. *Ibid.*, p. 4.
273. *Ibid.*, p. 334.
274. *The Cliff-Dwellers*, p. 324.
275. Written and published serially in 1879. Cf. Francis Bellamy's introduction to 1900 edition.
276. *The Duke of Stockbridge*, p. v.
277. V. L. Parrington, *Main Currents* III:303.

tionary War: "During these years the annual tax in Massachusetts amounted to $200 per family—more money than the average farmer or mechanic saw in two years. The chief industry therefore was the law; the courts were concerned in emptying farmers' houses under foreclosures, and filling the jails with good men who could not pay their debts. . . ."[278] The essence of Bellamy's analysis of the social struggle is suggested by a few paragraphs:

"I use ter think ez there wuzn't no sech varmint ez a tory; but I didn't know nothin' 'bout lawyers and sheriffs them times. I calc'late ye could cut five tories aout o' one lawyer an' make a dozen skunks aout o' what wuz left over."[279]

Thus felt the agrarian. But note the gentleman:

"That is the trouble nowadays, . . . these numskulls must needs have matters of government explained to them, and pass their own judgment on public affairs. And when they cannot understand them then, forsooth, comes a rebellion. I think none can deny seeing in these late troubles the first fruits of those pestilent notions of equality, whereof we heard so much from certain quarters, during the late war of independence."[280]

Francis Bellamy's reference to *Looking Backward* and *Equality* in the introduction to the 1900 edition of *The Duke of Stockbridge* indicates that despite the book's emphasis upon historical accuracy its author was not unmindful of the criticism of his own day that might be inferred from it.[281] It is chiefly from this point of view that *The Duke of Stockbridge* merits consideration in this study.

Helen Campbell's *Mrs Herndon's Income* (1886) resumes the complaint against conditions of mill labor. She has an unnamed character, a member of the Ultimates, paint the picture in its darkest hue.

"I've been in every print and cotton mill in New England. I know, and you know that they're child-killers, women-killers! The best of them are hells. I've come from one of the best this week,—a factory eight hundred feet long, and swarming with children from eight to twelve. They were paid ten to fifteen cents a day, and they worked twelve hours to get it! In the next town the pay was the same, but the time eleven hours instead of twelve . . . the fathers could make sometimes a dollar a day . . .

---

278. *The Duke of Stockbridge*, p. vii.
279. *Ibid.*, pp. 22, 28.
280. *Ibid.*, p. 349.

but averaged eighty-seven cents . . . there were hundreds to take their places if they struck for less hours and more pay . . . all over this cursed land you call free, they are bond-slaves and no hope for soul and body. . . . I want a chance for every working man, woman and child to own themselves."[282]

Mrs. Campbell's drawing of the character of Mr. Longshore is intended at once to modify the militant socialistic outlook of labor upon this situation and to persuade mill owners to be more considerate and less selfish. Longshore confers with a protesting committee from his workmen and agrees to restore the wage scale in force before the depression suggested a cut, and to make up back pay.

"My men [he says] owners and capitalists are not all rascals. They have only followed old ways without thinking. . . . Times are hard, and workmen are more plenty than work; but as long as I live hereafter I take my share of losses, and deal by you as I hope to be dealt by when my own account is handed in."[283]

He has nothing but scorn for the model village idea which Harness, a rival mill-owner, suggests. "The feudal system did its work in feudal times" but he has "yet to see natural republican life in one of these model villages".[284] Mrs. Campbell's desire is that "the poor shall be placed in such a situation as will enable them to create new wealth for themselves".[285]

The Silent Workman (1886) by Clinton Ross treats the capital-labor relationship from a largely unbiased point of view. It depicts briefly a strike in Philip Twickenham's iron works at Middlewood in southern New York. There is no effort to secure sympathy for either side, and the terms on which the strike is settled are not recorded. However the picture of Eb Randall, the 'Silent Workman', seems to relate itself to Millet's and Markam's "The Man with the Hoe" and to the plea for labor there embodied.

Dan Beard, the author of *Moonblight and Six Feet of Romance* (1892) looked out from his hotel window and saw a host of

---

281. This seems to be Parrington's opinion also; Cf. *Main Currents*, III: 303.
282. *Mrs. Herndon's Income*, p. 214.
283. *Ibid.*, p. 371.
284. *Ibid.*, p. 416.
285. *Ibid.*, p. 417.

"black slaves in a Pennsylvania town". They were, however, only a group of miners who had begged for work and had taken what was thrown to them. Sam, the bar-keeper comments: "The South was full of just such freedom before I enlisted and fought through the war to free the black slaves, and never tumbled to the fact that my own arms and legs were soon to have shackles made for 'em".[286] Beard introduces into his story charts showing how miners are enslaved by their forced expenditures for equipment and by unnecessary 'dockage'. They receive forty-two and one-half cents for cutting and loading the ton of coal that sells for five dollars.[287] Beard describes the strike through which the miners are seeking a more living wage as "the last feeble effort of manhood to save itself from hopeless and degrading slavery".[288] He protests strenuously against railroad combines controlling coal mining conditions and against the importation of foreign labor to force strikers back, or starve them. The government can and should do something to remedy these conditions. "Show me a tyrannical and unjust government", Professor Follium challenges, "and I will show you vice, squalor, poverty and crime, because the atmosphere and surroundings produce them".[289]

Agnes Maule Machar's *Roland Graeme: Knight* (1892) does not picture industrial conditions directly but reflects them in its pages exuding Christian Socialist teaching. Trusts are assailed as the oppressors of labor, and the strike defended as a right of the workingman. There is vehement denouncement of the underpayment of laboring men of whom "the one-half are not even able to earn enough for their daily bread, and have to depend on the labor of women and children to eke out their miserable existence".[290]

In *The Wisdom of Fools* (1897) Margaret Deland resumes the criticism Rebecca Harding Davis had hurled thirty-five years before at labor exploitation in the Pennsylvania iron district. The old evils have not been done away, have not even been

---

286. *Moonblight and Six Feet of Romance*, p. 35.
287. *Ibid.*, pp. 110-112.
288. *Ibid.*, p. 148.
289. *Ibid.*, p. 76.
290. *Roland Graeme: Knight*, p. 184.

mitigated. The mill-slaves are still "gaunt and stunted creatures, hollow-eyed with bleared and sodden faces, whose inces-
sant toil to keep alive had crushed out the look of manhood, and
left them silent, hopeless, brutish, with only one certainty in
their stupefied souls: 'men don't grow old in the mills'."[291]
Their wives and children still seek refuge from the biting winter frosts by coming to the only really warm place they know,
the great pile of hot slag. Mrs. Deland emphatically nominates
Robert Blair, iron magnate, for a place in the rogues gallery
of fictional and factual capitalists who have "ground the face
of the poor".[292] Blair's defense of his getting labor as cheaply
as possible is that everybody else does so. He thinks to justify
his uncurbed acquisitiveness by building a hospital for Mercer,
by founding a night school, by giving to colleges; but Mrs.
Deland rebukes him and his like, pointing out that such false
charity is a delusion and a snare. "We have got to consider
moral economics; we have no business to gratify our selfish
sentimentalism at the expense of society".[293]

Margaret Sherwood's *Henry Worthington, Idealist* (1899)
presents a picture of "the big cheap department stores where
they advertise great bargains that aren't there at all, and mal-
treat their clerks, and underpay their women. . . ."[294] It is a
condemnation, too, of the "gigantic trusts [that] are every day
swallowing up the money of the poor",[295] and of the false self-
satisfying charity that Mrs. Deland had scored: "A man thinks
after he has made a fortune by inventing a patent poison, or
selling whiskey, or gambling in stocks, or running a dishonest
dry-goods shop, that if he only endows a theological seminary,
or sends his money to the heathen he is doing a lot of good".[296]
The Gordon fortune has been made selling 'bargain' dry-goods,
with 'cash girls' paid as low as a dollar a week and clerks subject to a system of severe fines—as much as a dollar, on a dollar-
and-a-quarter-a-week's salary. The goods, of course, were made

---

291. *The Wisdom of Fools,* p. 96.
292. *Ibid.,* p. 100.
293. *Ibid.,* p. 247.
294. *Henry Worthington, Idealist,* p. 23.
295. *Ibid.,* p. 59.
296. *Ibid.,* p. 60.

at two of the worst sweater-dens in the city.[297]   Knowing these things Annice Gordon knew that her father "was responsible for the criminal element in the conditions under which work was done for him".   Henry Worthington voices his author's appeal to the public to remedy these conditions: "All I ask is for people with consciences to set a standard by refusing to have anything to do with money obtained by unfair means".[298]

The slavish circumstances under which women are forced to labor receive further condemnation in Theodore Dreiser's *Sister Carrie* (1900).   Caroline Meeber comes down from Columbia City, Wisconsin, to pay Chicago board to her sister and brother-in-law Minnie and Sven Hansum.   A shop girl was the destiny Minnie had in mind for Carrie;[299] but utterly without experience of any kind Carrie soon found that she had no chance of securing employment of any but the lowest kind.   She is offered three dollars and fifty cents a week as a cap stitcher and takes the desperate chance of refusing the position.   She later gets a shoe job, sewing uppers at four dollars and a half a week.   The conditions of labor are sordid and unhealthful, utterly blighting. So in the course of things, Carrie being as physically attractive as she is, becomes the mistress of Drouet and of Hurstwood. Except that she sold herself for a very much better price Carrie might well have said with Rose Haggerty, a character in one of Helen Campbell's true stories of the New York slums: "But let God Almighty judge who's to blame most—I that was driven, or them that drove me to the pass I'm in".[300]   The cause behind our social ills and injustices is a subtle one.   "The true meaning of money", Dreiser declares, "yet remains to be popularly explained and comprehended.   When each individual realizes for himself that this thing primarily stands for and should only be accepted as a moral due—that it should be paid out as honestly stored energy, and not as usurped privilege—many of our social, religious, and political troubles will have permanently passed".[301]

Robert Herrick's *The Web of Life* (1900) analyzes the capital-

---

297. *Ibid.*, p. 97, 117, 118, 119.
298. *Ibid.*, p. 104.
299. *Sister Carrie*, p. 16.
300. *Prisoners of Poverty* (1887), p. 29.
301. *Sister Carrie*, p. 70.

labor relationship against the background of the great Pullman strike in Chicago. Being an able novel by a skillful novelist it reflects the strike through its effect upon individuals as representative of the clashing groups rather than treats the trouble through direct picturization. "The poor had come lean and hungry out of the terrible winter that followed the World's Fair. In that beautiful enterprise the prodigal city had put forth her utmost strength, and, having shown the world the supreme flower of her energy, collapsed".[302] Of course it was only labor that suffered. Capital represented by Brome Porter, best conceived of as "brute force, padded superficially by civilization",[303] smugly refused to arbitrate or compromise, saying: "We are making money by having 'em quit".[304] For Capital life is based on the cruel creed of "getting something others haven't—as much of it as you can and as fast as you can".[305] As Labor, specifically the members of the American Railway Union pondered their grievances they realized that "this prodigal country of theirs had been exploited—shamefully, rapaciously, swinishly; . . . and now that the first signs of exhaustion were showing themselves, the people's eyes were opening to the story of greed. Democracy! Say, rather, Plutocracy, the most unblushing the world had ever seen—the aristocracy of the those who have. . . .[306]

Herrick is quite as bitter against the false prophets who lead labor movements as against the capitalists themselves. Dr. Howard Sommers forecasts the outcome of the strike: ". . . this row will be ended on the old terms—the rich will buy out the leaders. Better times will come, and we shall settle down to the same old game of grab, on the same old basis". Sommers' old acquaintance Dresser has been a leader in the American Railway Union. It is "people like you", Sommers tells him, who "are the real curse".[307] Nor was Sommers' prediction an idle one. When it became again profitable for the Pullman Company to resume operations, one of the strike leaders took

---

302. *The Web of Life*, p. 135.
303. *Ibid.*, p. 24.
304. *Ibid.*, p. 33.
305. *Ibid.*, p. 40.
306. *Ibid.*, p. 138.
307. *Ibid.*, p. 140.

his bribe and bought "the finest little ranch you ever saw out in Montana" and Dresser took his and bought a profitable interest in a Chicago financial journal.[308]   The old human impulse of selfishness is no respecter of persons; the leaders of labor are as greedy as the behemoths of capital.   "Men fought and gambled today in the factories, the shops, the railroads, as they fought in the dark ages, for the same ends—for sensual pleasures, gross love of power, barbaric show.   They would fight on glorifying their petty deeds of personal gain; but not always. . . . The barbarians of trade would give way, as had the barbarians of feudal war".[309]   But Herrick proves himself wrong in the impression which this conclusion leaves.   New players have been substituted, new plays have been devised, but the game itself has never been changed.

Mary E. Wilkins Freeman believes the true reward of labor is and should be the growth in character of the laborer.[310]   *The Portion of Labor* (1901) argues, however, in its picture of mill conditions for a more humanitarian attitude on the part of capitalist-owners toward their employees.   Andrew Brewster states the position of the workman: "I ain't a toady to no rich folks . . . and I don't want any favors of 'em—all I want is pay for my honest work, and that's an even swap, and I ain't beholden. . . ."[311]   Robert Lloyd's action in drastically cutting the wage scale of his hands at the first drop in the demand for shoes Mrs. Freeman looks upon as unnecessary and unjust.   The complaint is voiced through Mrs. Brewster, mother of the strike-leading Ellen: "For a man worth half a million to cut down the wages of poor, hard-working folks in midwinter is cruelty.   I don't care who does it".[312]   The right to work for a fair wage with growth in character as the major reward is Mrs. Freeman's program for labor.

Among the more specialized themes of criticism in the novels treating the economic injustice and unhappiness that has grown up with the development of the industrial age are those of finan-

---

308. *Ibid.*, p. 257.
309. *Ibid.*, p. 168.
310. *The Portion of Labor*, p. 563.
311. *Ibid.*, p. 104.
312. *Ibid.*, p. 470.

cial chicanery and unsatisfactory living conditions in both city and country. Both are further specific phases of the oppression of the weak by the strong under the heartless philosophy of an individualistic economy.

The complaint against speculation is an old one in our literature. The problem finds its most succinct early statement in James Kirke Paulding's *Letters from the South* in 1835. "It is a shame to tempt the people," Paulding declared, "from the wholesome labors of the field, and the enjoyment of a moderate independence, by putting faith in the speculative advantages of some little nook or corner along the river-side, where a town is founded—upon speculation—grows for a little while with inauspicious rapidity — then lingers awhile between life and death, and then sinks into a modern ruin. . . ."[313]

An excellent fictional satirization of early speculative dealings in land was written by Royall Tyler in *The Algerine Captive* (1797). A group of 'Hertford' gentlemen are represented as wanting to buy Underhill's New York lands, originally granted by the Dutch. Underhill's record of his reaction to the circumstances of the proposal is done in fine irony.

"I candidly confessed that I was not possessed of the title, and knew not the particular spot where the land lay, and consequently was unwilling to sell land without title or boundaries. To my surprise they laughed at my scruples, and observed that they wanted the land to speculate upon; to sell, and not to settle. Titles and boundaries, in such cases, I understood were indifferent matters, mere trifles".[314]

However the problem of speculation did not reach its greatest acuteness until the last quarter of the nineteenth century. And it is in this period that it receives its most important treatment in our fiction. After the Civil War immigration into the West and Northwest became more rapid than ever before: demobilized soldiers, unemployed and oppressed eastern factory hands, and a horde of immigrants flocked to the Middle Border. They believed the glamorous pictures[315] of railway promoters and land speculators drawn from life, and anxious for homes of their

---

313. Letters from the South, v. II, p. 52.
314. *The Algerine Captive*, p. 21. See also James Fenimore Cooper's satirization of similar land speculations already cited in this study.
315. Cf. Hamlin Garland, *Jason Edwards*, p. 62.

own they staked out claims and planted their wheat and their corn. "Hope embroidered their dreams." But the life so beautifully envisioned was only a mirage; philanthropy had not been the motive of the railroads and the speculators—they had not lured these settlers West for nothing. "Freight rates were pushed sky high on them, almost at once; it became cheaper, with corn selling at ten cents a bushel, to use it for fuel than to ship it anywhere; and down in Kansas they were saying that it was about time to "stop raising corn and start raising hell". Many of the homesteads had to be rented from absentee landlords in Europe and New York, who had 'sneaked in on the ground floor' and secured huge chunks of western America from the government (by fraud or favor) which they in turn leased out to tenants. By 1900 over a third of all farms in the United States were being tilled in this way, and mortgages on rural property amounted to more than a billion dollars. As the economic value of the frontier rose under cultivation, an 'unearned increment' flowed into the bulging pockets of a few men in silk hats, either in the form of rents or interests on loans".[316]

Edward Eggleston's *The Mystery of Metropolisville* was written in 1873. Literally it was a "retrospective tale" but its criticism of speculation whatever the time or place is palpable. It pictures a speculative frenzy with "everybody frantically trying to swindle everybody else."[317]

"The village grew, as hundreds of other frontier villages had grown, in the flush times; it died, as so many others died, of the financial crash which was the inevitable sequel and retribution of speculative madness . . . The plowshare remorselessly turns over the earth in places where corner lots were once sold for a hundred dollars the front foot. . . ."[318]

Eggleston discloses some of the fraudulent methods by which large holdings of land were obtained—such as the building of a house on wheels and hauling it from place to place, swearing it in on each claim as a house on that claim. Men also were known to swear that there was glass in the window of a house when there was only a whiskey bottle sitting on the sill.[319]

316. Harry Hartwick, *The Foreground of American Fiction,* p. 206.
317. *The Mystery of Metropolisville,* p. 13.
318. *Ibid.,* p. 11-12.
319. *Ibid.,* p. 90.

Squire Plausaby in *The Mystery of Metropolisville* is a graphic and fairly typical picture of the speculation promoter and small-town swindler. He is essentially of the same stuff as the great railroad robbers who invaded the halls Congress itself—of smaller capacity, more petty nature, of course—but able to cover his infractions of moral and legal statutes with glib religious cant and the appearance of integrity.

Eggleston's satirization of the manner in which development promoters undermine the economic stability of a community is nowhere done with better point than in his recording of a joint resolution introduced into the Senate and House of the Indiana Territorial Legislature providing "that not more than two-thirds of the area of this territory shall be laid out in town-sites and territorial roads, the remaining one-third to be sacredly reserved for agricultural use".[320]

H. H. Boyesen moves the scene to Minnesota but his picture of over-development through speculation is essentially like Eggleston's. His criticism is not so apparent, but its implications are the same. Hardanger, he tells us, "was a typical western town; it modestly regarded itself as a prodigy of intellectual and commercial enterprise . . . and could demonstrate by incontrovertible figures that if the village continued to grow at the present rate (and there was no conceivable reason why it should not) it would within twenty years become the natural metropolis of the West".[321]

Development projects by land speculators in the East are criticized by Amanda M. Douglass in *Hope Mills* (1880). The novel reveals how speculators quietly bought up the immediately out-lying farms of a likely industrial center and then sent abroad a great cry of "come to the mills and factories". With skillful enticements shouted in their ears the people came. Depression inevitably resulted from this artificial urbanization and everybody suffered but the speculators.

Clinton Ross' *The Speculator* (1891) is a far less significant book than one might expect from its title. There is but little complaint against speculation; the fact of its existence, the

---

320. *Ibid.*, p. 215.
321. *Falconberg* (1879), p. 117.

part it is playing in modern life, is only observed. There is no
talk of "unearned increment", no advocacy of the single tax.
There is some feeling of injustice, however, in Ross' noting that
the Jarvis family "for almost a hundred years have controlled
properties that have increased as marvelously as the development
of the new continent."[322] But the speculation in this novel is
concerned chiefly with stocks rather than land. Samuel Chester,
the story's central figure, is a manipulator of railroads. The
wretchedness brought to many people by his "failure to carry
through the Wyoming-Pacific" is an implied criticism of speculative methods.

Although his thought runs largely to more restricted industrial
problems Dan Beard voices occasional pertinent complaint
against speculation in *Moonblight and Six Feet of Romance*
(1892). He holds that all wealth comes from the earth, and
that all who do not own ground are essentially slaves.[323] Those
therefore who grab up great holdings for speculative purposes
are enemies of the best interests of the people.

Henry B. Fuller's *The Cliff-Dwellers* (1893) is a representation of the vast speculations that went into the making of
Chicago and its spirit of "bigness and be-damnness". The real-
estate angle of its artificial development is pictured through
the enterprises of McDowell. Inherently dishonest even with
his own family he scrupled not to fleece his clients at any opportunity. The shabby falseness of his development projects
would be disclosed by heavy rains: "His plank walks would
float off in sections; the trees along his avenues would sag
deeply into the slush . . . and the cellars of the three or four
unfinished houses that he had artfully scattered through this
promising tract would show odds and ends of carpenter's refuse
floating around in muddy water a foot deep".[324]

Erastus M. Brainard is Fuller's representation of the stock
speculator and manipulator who was such a significant factor
behind the growing pains of Chicago and our other cities. He
advised the investments of his clients, sold them stock, forced

---

322. *The Speculator*, pp. 8-9.
323. *Moonblight and Six Feet of Romance*, p. 89.
324. *The Cliff-Dwellers*, p. 103.

its decline and brought it back at a half or two-thirds of the former quotation.[325] Fuller's protest is that those machinations which gave more wealth and power to McDowell, and Brainard, and Ingles meant misery and -wretchedness to hundreds of others.[326]

Hamlin Garland's most developed protest against the oppressive speculative holding of western farm land by great mortgage syndicates, the railroads, and such other "land gobblers" as the Standard Oil Company[327] is to be found in *Jason Edwards* (1891). Edwards, a Boston iron worker, gradually "squeezed into one of the worst places in the city, simply because rents are so high and wages so low",[328] determines to go West and "get a piece of free land". It was the glamorous picture on a railroad circular that finally crystallized his resolution:

"The farmer himself in the foreground was seated on a self-binding reaper holding the reins over an abnormally sleek and prancing pair of horses. He wore a fine Kossuth hat and a standing collar, and his shirt was immaculate. A deer was looking out at him (with pardonable curiosity) from a neighboring woodlot. It was the ideal farmer, and the farm of the land-boomer and the self-glorifying American newspaper".[329]

It is to Boomtown in western Minnesota that Edwards takes his family. To their utter and disillusioning dismay the only free land obtainable is forty miles from the railroad. The land syndicate represented by Judge Balser controls every nearer acre. Crops could not be raised that would justify forty miles of hauling to reach the railroad; the only alternative was to purchase land from the Balser syndicate at ten dollars an acre—entailing a heavy mortgage with oppressive interest. The appalling over-building of railroads which lies at the basis of western land speculation schemes is revealed in Balser's observation that Boomtown already has seven lines of road, "and a new one being graded, will be ironed before the snow flies".[330] It is a striking fact that a timber claim as Judge Balser sells it "is not a claim with trees on it, but a claim on which the

---

325. *Ibid.*, p. 37.
326. *Ibid.*, p. 324.
327. *Jason Edwards*, p. 120.
328. *Ibid.*, p. 58.
329. *Ibid.*, p. 62.
330. *Ibid.*, p. 123.

government wants trees put."[331]   It is against the fundamental dishonesty and the blighting oppression of Judge Balser and his tribe that Garland pours out his bitterness.

The evil of speculation as exemplified in the dishonest or unfair manipulation of stocks values finds further criticism in J. G. Holland, H. H. Boyesen Caroline Walch, Randal I. Tyler, Henry Francis Keenan, and Robert Herrick.   The substance of their attack is essentially like that of Fuller and Ross, already cited.   The loathsome picture of Robert Belcher in *Sevenoaks* (1875) embodies Holland's chief criticism on this point.   Even Mrs. Belcher realizes "that the poor would have been better off if Mr. Belcher had never lived".[332]   He promotes an oil speculation taking the money of innocent investors for what he knows is worthless stock;[333] he buys up the Crooked Valley Railroad and issues bonds "for the purpose of stealing".[334] Such is Holland's denunciation of the fraud that is practised through the issue of false securities.

In *A Daughter of the Philistines* (1883) H. H. Boyesen treats the evil of stock speculation in its stricter sense. Boyesen's protest is expressed through Harold Wellingford, the central character of the novel; whose disapproval of stock speculation is uncompromising.   Despite his thorough knowledge of the market and exchange he prefers to live by his "own labor, and not by gambling with the results of other people's work".[335]   The dishonest manner in which stock is manipulated to drive out small-holders when something valuable develops is disclosed by the Maid of Athens gold mine incident.[336]   The outlook of Boyesen upon this problem—and most of the other novelists cited share it—is revealed in Wellingford's telling his wife, Alma, that she is wrong in thinking that

"speculation supports the majority of the American people.   If that were the case the days of the republic would be numbered.   A state can only grow securely upon a foundation of quiet, orderly labor.   The mere negative

331. *Ibid*, p. 123.
332. *Sevenoaks*, p. 176.
333. *Ibid.*, p. 142.
334. *Ibid.*, p. 265.
335. *A Daughter of the Philistines*, p. 132.
336. *Ibid.*, p. 248.

activity of artificially inflicting and contracting values is in no sense productive, and is a constant check and discouragement to legitimate commerce.
It is inevitable, I suppose, that in a country of such vast productive power
the gambling passion should be stimulated in many, but let it be well understood that these many do a positive injury to the rest of the community. . . .
They unsettle values and by iniquitous combinations raise the price of the
necessaries of life . . . make the public morals constantly more lax, and by
needlessly increasing the element of chance corrupt our politics, retard civilization, and insult the logic of creation".[337]

Calleen Mayner in Caroline C. Walch's *Doctor Sphinx* (1898)
was expressing the same thought in an ironical form when she
observed: "In order to become a great financier, then, one
must learn how to endanger the honest savings of hardworking
men. . . ."[338]

Randal Irving Tyler's *"Four Months After Date"* (1898)
describes itself as a "business romance". It is, however, an
enlightening picture of the financial maze behind great money
operations. The railroad stock manipulations depicted here
while not specifically criticized as dishonest are clearly a part
of the great game of speculation at which others point an accusing finger for its disruption of our economic stability.

Henry Francis Keenan's *The Money-Makers* (1884) sketches
a very similar scene. It however, expresses its protest against
speculation and the juggling of values much more emphatically.[339]

"Chicago", declares Robert Herrick, "is an instance of a successful, contemptuous disregard of nature by man!"[340] Basic
in that 'contemptuous disregard' is the speculation already described by Henry B. Fuller in *The Cliff-Dwellers* (1893)
Herrick's *The Gospel of Freedom* (1898) continues the protest
as it applies to stock manipulations. The point is illustrated
most aptly by Adela Wilbur's protest when her husband wants
to take the way of the controlling capitalist in the decline of
the Water-Hoister Company. She declares that "to step out
and let other people bear the burden of its hard days would

337. *Ibid.*, pp. 220-221.
338. *Doctor Sphinx*, p. 345.
339. *Cf. The Money-Makers*, p. 62 ff.
340. *The Gospel of Freedom*, p. 101.

be "if not dishonesty, cowardice".[341]   But John Wilbur is at heart the conscienceless speculator who scruples not to ruin others so long as his own position can be maintained secure. He is not so corrupt as to help the Wren traction clique bribe the Illinois legislature and governor, but he hesitates not at all to speculate on the success of their bribe by buying great blocks of traction stock. When Adela Wilbur asserts that John "was not a bad man", Theodore Jennings significantly replies that "the good people of Chicago are running things on a wrong basis".[342]

A summary of the criticism of financial chicanery in the fiction of the last quarter of the century should not overlook a protest, brief and casual, against loose banking methods outside of the field of speculation. The novels most significant for this criticism are William Dean Howells' *The Quality of Mercy* (1892) and Charles Dudley Warner's *The Golden House* (1894). Their analyses of the effects of defalcations upon the community implies a demand that stricter systems of accounting should make such things less probable. Edward Everett Hale's *Sybil Knox* (1892) should also be mentioned in this connection for its criticism of the loose handling of trust funds.[343]

The problems of speculation and the juggling of stock values are seen to have claimed considerable attention from the novelists cited. On the whole, however, these questions are more adequately treated in our utopian fiction.[344]

It was natural that our critics in fiction examining the evils of industrialized society should voice particular protest against the living conditions entailed by the fierce struggle for subsistence in large urban centers. Where men were measured by multitudes rather than individuals it was so easy for the strong to become callous to the conditions of the weak. "Having solemnly resolved that all men are created equal and have certain inalienable rights, among them life, liberty, and the pursuit of happiness, we shut our eyes and waited for the formula to

---

341. *Ibid.*, p. 120.
342. *Ibid.*, pp. 126, 129.
343. *Sybil Knox*, p. 226.
344. Cf. Chapter II of this study.

work. . . . When after a hundred years we opened our eyes . . . our country had grown great and rich; through our ports was poured food for the millions of Europe. But in the back streets multitudes huddled in ignorance and want. The foreign op-pressor had been vanquished, the fetters stricken from the black man at home; but his white brother, in his bitter plight, sent up a cry of distress . . . the problem of helpless poverty, grown vast with the added off-scourings of the Old World, mocked us, unsolved. Liberty at sixty cents a day set presently its stamp upon the government of our cities, and it became the scandal and the peril of our political system".[345] "One may find for the asking an Italian, a German, a French, African, Spanish, Bohemian, Russian, Scandinavian, Jewish, and Chinese colony. Even the Arab . . . has his preserves at the lower end of Washington Street. The one thing you shall ask mainly for in the chief city of America is a distinctively American com-munity".[346]

The racial characteristics of many of the inhabitants of the slums of New York and other cities are a factor in their manner of life, but the protest of our novelists is launched against the heartless severity of economic competition that has forced these people to overwork and under-eat each other into constantly more crowded depressing, and unhealthful conditions of life.[347] Mark Twain was probably thinking of the environs of the Brooklyn span when he wrote of London Bridge that "children were born on the Bridge, were reared there, grew to old age and finally died there without ever having set foot on any other part of the world but London Bridge alone."[348] So they live, and finally "in the common trench of the Poor Bury-ing Ground they lie packed three stories deep, shoulder to shoulder, crowded in death as they were in life, to 'save space'. . . . The nameless ones buried here equal the nameless babes picked up on the street—a virtual balance, year after year".[349] It is against this kind of life, lived in the "depths of want,

---

345. Jacob A. Riis, *A Ten Year's War* (1900), pp. 3-4.
346. Jacob A. Riis, *How the Other Half Lives* (1890), p. 21.
347. Cf. Finley Peter Dunne, *Mr. Dooley in Peace and War* (1899), p. viii.
348. *The Prince and the Pauper* (1881), p. 77.
349. Jacob A. Riis, *How the Other Half Lives*, p. 178.

wretchedness and degredation", against this kind of nameless death in our "cultured, palace-decked, church-jewelled"[350] cities that a number of our citric-novelists have forcefully protested.

Among the novels of the late 1880's that most strongly embodied this criticism were Helen Campbell's *Miss Melinda's Opportunity* (1886),[351] Joaquin Miller's *Destruction of Gotham* (1886) and Kate Douglass Wiggin's *The Story of Patsy* (1889). Edward Eggleston's *The Faith Doctor* (1891) was apparently written with an inadequate knowledge of the slum conditions which it describes. Eggleston's picture is fairly sombre, drawn as it is from the point of view of Charles Millard, but he feels that the conditions of tenement-house living are only uncomfortable and miserable to those accustomed to something else, those who look in from the outside.

Jacob A. Riis' stories of the sweaters' slaves in Mulberry Street "are from the daily grist of the police hopper", serious and accurate studies of slum life. The whole tragedy of industrialized society is suggested in *Nibsy's Christmas* (1893) when it is pointed out that for the undernourished, ill-fed inhabitants of the tenements Christmas was "but the name for persecution and suffering, reminder of lost kindred and liberty, of the slavery of eighteen hundred years, freedom from which was purchased only with gold".[352] Riis' pictures of New York's slums in the stories comprising *Out of Mulberry Street* (1897) are even more graphic than in his earlier work. Outside: "the street has the appearance of a deep black canon with cliff-dwellers living in tiers all the way up, their watch-fires showing like so many dull red eyes through the night."[353] Inside: "there are only three chairs, a box, and a bedstead in the room. . . . The bed hides the broken plaster in the wall through which the wind came in; each chair-leg stands over a rat-hole, at once to hide it and to keep the rats out. One is left; the box is for that. . . ."[354]

---

350. B. O. Flower, *Civilization's Inferno* (1893), p. 3.
351. For the full implications of Mrs. Campbell's fiction see her essay studies, *Prisoners of Poverty* (1886) and *Darkness and Daylight* (1891).
352. *Nibsy's Christmas*, p. 9.
353. *Out of Mulberry Street*, p. 154.
354. *Ibid.*, p. 7.

Stephen Crane is a naturalist in fiction rather than a sociologist. The criticism of slum conditions embodied in *Maggie* (1893) and *George's Mother* (1896) is objective rather than subjective: it consists in our reaction to the material presented rather than in Crane's reaction to it. Most of the homes within blocks of The Bend are like the Johnson's 'reg-lar livin' hells'. "Why do I come an' drin' whisk' here thish way?", asks Maggie's father. " 'Cause home reg'lar livin' hell"![355] Maggie goes to work in a collar and cuff factory but soon yields to the entice-ments of illicit sexual intercourse. "When a girl is bringed up d' way I bringed up Maggie, how can she go teh d' devil"? wonders Mrs. Johnson. But given her environment we wonder only that she could have been expected to go anywhere else. The picture and theme remain the same in *George's Mother,* as we watch George Kelcey, a good-natured country boy suc-cumb to the economically-decreed ill conditions of slum life and go likewise "teh d' devil".

J. W. Sullivan's *Tenement Tales of New York* (1895) are much less sordid than many of these pictures of slum life. In-deed Sullivan often becomes unrealistically sentimental, as, for example, when he has Tom King, professional gambler, ask Minnie Kelsey to marry him without trying any other method of getting her.

Alvan F. Sanborn's *Meg McIntyre's Raffle* (1896) is very much in the vein of Sullivan's stories. Many of its characters are Irish and have something of poetry in their souls whatever the depth of their economic conditions. Sentiment rather than sharp, stinging indictment of our economic order is the conspicu-ous element in Sanborn's stories.

"The great question of the tenement-house is the one of the children it produces", declares Ellen Glasgow in *Phases of an Inferior Planet* (1898).[356] It is the environment of today be-coming the heredity of tomorrow. Father Algercife through whom the slum conditions are chiefly pictured in this novel holds that the improvement in tenement living conditions de-pends as much upon cleanliness as Godliness: "I have per-

---

355. *Maggie*, p. 148.
356. *Ibid.*, p. 197.

suaded ten converts to take the pledge of a daily bath. It was tough work".[357]

Differences (1899) by Hervey White is a romance against the background of a Chicago settlement house, and its relation to the poor. Its picture is squalid but not bitter.

The heaviness with which the hand of fate rests upon the lives of the iron workers of Pennsylvania and the mill hands of New England, the utter drabness of life entailed by the industrial organization of those communities is best depicted in our fiction by Rebecca Harding Davis and Margaret Deland, Elizabeth Stuart Phelps and Mary E. Wilkins Freeman. What meaning has the word 'home' for such people as the Wolfes, father, Hugh, and Deborah, central characters in Mrs. Davis' "Life in the Iron Mills" (1861). They live in a damp, dark cellar, significant background for their neurotic temperaments and broken bodies — Deborah's deformed back, Hugh's tubercular lungs. Nor are the other workers in this harshly exploited community a whit better off; some even live on the warm ash in the mills. Who then can reply to the challenge of Margaret Houth, in *A Story of Today* (1862): "The world's a failure. All the great old dreams are dead. Your own phantom, your Republic, your experiment to prove that all men are born free and equal—what is it today?" The question is repeated thirty-five years later in Margaret Deland's *The Wisdom of Fools* (1897). The barons of iron still ignore the houseless bodies and seared souls of their workers. Mothers and children must still seek refuge from the winds of winter by going to the slag piles for warmth—climbing far up where it is hot.[358]

In *The Silent Partner* (1871) Elizabeth Stuart Phelps has her heroine scrutinize closely the abject living conditions which heartless exploitation of New England mill workers has brought about: she sees the mill girls in the company boarding house living six in a room, often sick, always cold, fed by a cook who wipes her sweating dirty face on the dish towel; she visits another laborer who must keep his consumptive wife and eleven children in two small, dirty rooms above a cellar that is flooded

357. *Ibid.*, p. 196.
358. *The Wisdom of Fools*, p. 100.

all the year round by the offal, the stench, from the mills. The routine of mill life is a depressingly vivid picture: the girl operative breakfasts on bread and molasses, eating while she dresses, she forgets her shawl, turns back for it, throws it over one shoulder, and steps out into sudden, raw air and the moonlight. She hangs up shawl and crinoline, and by gas-light goes shivering to the looms, chilled to heart; the carelessness about her shawl means a few less winters she will require shawling. She thinks of experimenting with death and a wadded coffin. But by the time the gas is out she is less inclined to the wadded coffin; she chats with her neighbor across the alley. Her neighbor is of either sex and any description.[359]

Hedged In had preceded *The Silent Partner* by a year. In its early chapters it protests against the living conditions in the milltown of South Atlas. Thicket street "had the proportions, to say nothing of the qualities of a rainspout". There were four persons to four families in a room, twisted children, wharves and whale-oil, staggering houses, shops for grog. The central theme of the novel is, however, a protest against the manner in which an unforgiving society hedges in the individual who has once sinned, no matter how completely she has rehabilitated herself in the meantime.

Mrs. Freeman's *The Portion of Labor* (1901) is markedly less drab in its picture of the mill operative's life than the works of Elizabeth Phelps. The characters of Maria and Abby Atkins show us, however, that the conditions against which the earlier protest was made still exist.[360]

If the life in the tenements of our great cities and in our centers of industry is sordid and oppressive and opportunityless, so too is life on the American farm. Capitalistic exploitation plays no favorites. The drabness and slackness of rural poverty began to appear in our fiction with Edward Eggleston's *The Hoosier Schoolmaster* (1871) and *The Mystery of Metropolis* (1873). These earlier studies, however, merely reflect the western farm life as it visibly is; there is "no brooding sense of social injustice, of the wrongs done the Middle Border by unjust laws,

---

359. Cf. *The Silent Partner*, p. 72.
360. Cf. *The Portion of Labor*, pp. 449, 514-515.

of the hardships that are increased by the favoritism of government".[361]

Two other significant predecessors of Hamlin Garland in
realistic protest fiction of the Middle Border are E. W. Howe
and Joseph Kirkland. Howe's *The Story of a Country Town*
appeared in 1882. Fairview and the surrounding Kansas country
were but typical of the whole of inland America." . . . Towns
sprang up on credit, and farms were opened with borrowed
money . . . men mortgaged their possessions at full value,
and thought themselves rich, notwithstanding".[362] There is
an unrelieved sombreness about *The Story of a Country Town*
that subtly and effectively accomplishes the air of utter, depressing drabness in the life it describes. Even the religion of
the people added to their discomforts, for "it was hard and
unforgiving".[363] There is a strong complaint against the injustice of rural child labor in the dramatic portrayal of Ned West-
lock's youth being harshly wrung from him by hard work.
Much of Howe's protest against the emptiness of this life is
embodied in the character of Jo Erring. "I don't want to be
like the people here", he declares, "for noιe of them are contented or happy; but I intend to be like the people I am certain
live in other countries. I cannot believe but there is a better
way to live than that accepted at Fairview. . . . Therefore
I shall begin differently, and work harder, and to more purpose
than the people here have done, to the end that I may be a
different man".[364]

Joseph Kirkland's *Zury: The Meanest Man in Spring County*
(1887) is a picture of Illinois farm life rather than a protest.
Life is revealed with considerable sordidness for the most part
but there is no economic futility. Hard work and a sharp mind
bring their rewards even if they do entail a soul-searing meanness pounded into a man's soul by the forces against which he
fights. The struggle-shortened life of Mrs. Peddicomb in this
novel is typical of the women of the Middle Border: "She died

361. Vernon Louis Parrington: *Main Currents*, III:288.
362. *The Story of a Country Town*, p. 2.
363. *Ibid.*, p. 4.
364. *Ibid.*, p. 100.

(as was and is common among farmers' wives) at not much over thirty years of age, just when her life ought to have been in its prime".[365] In *The McVeys* (1888), a sequel to *Zury*, Kirkland turns from the depicting of farm life to a description of life in the small town of the Middle West. The picture is brighter and more hopeful, less mean and empty.

It is Hamlin Garland, of course, who is the most important writer of economic criticism fiction treating the problems of rural America. He is a prophet saddened by the plight of his people. His stories are burdened with the protest of one oppressed with the meanness of a world that takes such heavy toll of human happiness. Garland declares that he presents farm life "not as the summer boarder or the young lady novelist see it—but as the working farmer endures it".

Main-Travelled Roads (1891) is a collection of six short stories dealing with life as Garland knew it along the Middle Border. Several of these stories protest vehemently against the injustices which weigh so heavily upon the struggling farmer; but their protest is in the truthful depicting of conditions—Garland rarely intrudes his own character upon a story. In "Under the Lion's Paw" The Son of the Middle Border relates the story of a farm mortgage, teaches a lesson in political economy, paints a tragedy of darkest cast; "No slave in the Roman galleys, could have toiled so frightfully [as Haskins] and lived, for this man thought himself a free man".[366] And after he had rehabilitated a run-down farm, the mortgage holder, Butler, doubled the rent and the selling price. Typical this was of the practice of the railroads and eastern mortgage companies; and against it Garland is most bitter. "The Return of the Private" is the story of a soldier who comes from the war broken by fever, with no recognition and with no stake among those he has helped to make rich. "While the millionaire sent his money to England for safe-keeping, this man with a girl-wife and three babies, left his mortgaged farm, and went away to fight for an idea. It was foolish, but it was sublime for all that".[367]

---

365. *Zury: The Meanest Man in Spring Country*, p. 74.
366. Garland, Hamlin, Dedication to *Main-Travelled Roads*.
367. *Ibid.*, p. 223.

"Up the Coule" is a pitiless accusation of our vaunted conditions that give every man the chance to rise above his brother. Good-natured selfishness and indifference are represented as the favorite ideals of our system. "A Branch Road", "Among the Corn-Rows", and "Mrs. Ripley's Trip" complete the volume without adding any new elements to the Garland protest.

In *Prairie Folks* a year later, 1892, Garland continued in the pattern his first volume had set. There is deadening drabness in the life he portrays. He writes of the typical farmer:

"Back of him were generations of men like himself, whose main business had been to work hard, live miserably, and beget children to take their places when they died. He had long since ceased to kiss his wife, or even speak kindly to her. There was no longer any sanctity to life or love."[368]

Garland describes Sim Burns as characteristic of the average prairie farmer. "His whole surrounding was typical of the time. He had a quarter-section of fine level land, bought with incredible toil, but his house was a little box-like structure, costing perhaps, five hundred dollars. It had three rooms and the ever-present summer kitchen attached to the back. It was unpainted and had no touch of beauty, a mere box."[369]

Mrs. Bacon in "Elder Pill, Preacher" is Garland's picture of the woman produced by the hard life of the Middle Border. She "was still muscular in her age and shapelessness. Unlovely at her best, when about her work in her faded calico gown and flat shoes, hair wisped into a slovenly knot, she was depressing".[370]

"The poor of the Western prairies", Garland reveals, "lie almost as unhealthily close together as do the poor of the city tenements. In the small hut of the peasant there is as little chance to escape close and tainting contact as in the coops and dens of the North End of proud Boston".[371] He had already illustrated this indictment with *Jason Edwards* (1891), disclosing the oppression wrought upon the aspiring western farmer by the railroads and mortgage syndicates.

In *Rose of Dutcher's Coolly* (1895) Garland drew a full-length

---

368. *Ibid.,* p. 189.
369. *Prairie Folks,* p. 108.
370. *Ibid.,* p. 37.
371. *Ibid.,* p. 114.

portrait of an idealist in revolt against the narrowness of farm life. The secondary thesis of the novel is a criticism of the difference between nature and law in regard to the sex life. This novel does not have the air of inevitability that pervades many of Garland's early short-stories; for Rose does escape from the depressing emptiness of the Middle Border farm life. The escape, however, is strictly an individual experience. There is no mistaking the drab and hopeless condition of those who were left behind. *A Little Norsk* (1892) is in broad outline a very similar story; as protest, however, it has no real significance.

A Spoil of Office, appearing in 1897, is social tract rather than a work of art despite Garland's prefatory apology:

"The three great movements of the American farm herein used as background—the Grange, the Alliance, the Peoples' party—seem to me to be as legitimate subjects of fiction as any war or crusade. They came in impulses with mightiest enthusiasm; they died out like waves upon the beach; but the power which originated them did not die; it will return in different forms again and again, so long as the love of liberty and the hatred of injustice live in the hearts of men and women".[372]

The familiar Iowa backgrounds are in the story—the harsh lives and bent weary figures of men and women—but there is also an idealized heroine who suggests what life may become when injustice is done away and the blighting toil lessened. "The heart and center of this movement", says Ida Wilbur, "is a demand for justice, not for ourselves alone, but for the toiling poor wherever found. It is no longer a question of legislating for the farmer, it is a question of the abolition of industrial slavery."[373]

Although they make no pretense at a comprehensive picture of the drab emptiness of western farm life there are a number of other novelists who definitely protest against the oppression of the farmer by the railroads and mortgage syndicates. Among these H. H. Boyesen ("Liberty's Victim", in *Vagabond Tales,* 1889), Thomas Stewart Dennison (*An Iron Crown,* 1885), Mary H. Ford, (*Which Wins?,* 1891), Samuel Crocker (*That Island,*

---

372. Garland, Hamlin, *A Spoil of Office,* p. viii.
373. *Ibid.,* p. 245.

1892), and Frank Norris (*The Octopus*, 1901) are the most important.

Complaint against the empty narrowness of farm and village life is however, not restricted to fiction of the West. Harold Frederic's *Seth's Brother's Wife* is a drab story of farm life in upper New York state. There is not, however, any protest against economic forces that seem to willfully drain the life's blood from the community. Frederic's criticism is merely of the sour, bitter, petty lives of the farming people unrelieved by any grace or beauty. It is in the city that he sees opportunity and hope for the starved minds and dwarfed souls of the farm. In *The Copperhead* (1893) Frederic turned his pen to a description of farm life in Illinois. This story has none of the bitterness of his earlier novel but merits mention for its brief picture of farmers "flying westward before the locust-like cloud of mortgages".[374]

There is much of the idyllic in Sarah Orne Jewett's picture of New England life, but she could not overlook the pathetic poverty of which her section offered abundant examples. "The Town Poor" in *Tales of New England* (1879) is perhaps Miss Jewett's most effective treatment of the pitiful hopelessness that can be found in village life. The story is a protest against Hampden's ill consideration of the Misses Bray, and against individual shirking of responsibility by those who could help. "They give their consent", we are told, "to goin' on the town because they knew they'd got to be dependent, an' so they felt 't would be easier for all than for a few to help 'em."[375] They were accordingly "bid off for five dollars a month" to Mr. James who took them to his isolated farm and consigned them to a dark, little, upper back room with little wood or food.[376] It is against the hopeless outlook of the soul that Sara Orne Jewett protests in these *Tales of New England*.

The same mood and purpose are to be found in Mary E. Wilkins Freeman's *Pembroke* (1891). The novel's intent is to "portray a typical New England village of some sixty years ago

---

374. *The Copperhead*, p. 13.
375. *Tales of New England*, v. 4, p. 281.
376. *Ibid.*, p. 287.

. . . but villages of a similar description have existed in New England at a much later date, and they exist, today in a very considerable degree".[377]   The narrowess of rural New England life, however, is appreciable only by the outside observer. There is no dissatisfaction and unhappiness among these people because of their restricted view of life, but "it may be that the lack of unhappiness constitutes the real tragedy".[378]

"Two Old Lovers" in *A Humble Romance and Other Stories* (1887) is interesting in the blithe contrast of its picture of the little mill town of Leyden with Elizabeth Stuart Phelps' earlier pictures of similar scenes.

"The Revolt of Mother"[379] is a protest against the suppressed state of the New England farm wife.   Sarah Penn sorely needs a new house; Adoniram is well able to afford it.   He builds a barn instead—much better than the house in which they have lived for forty years.

Kate Sanborn's *Adopting an Abandoned Farm* (1892) offers a succinct summary of the arduous, profitless toil of New England farm life: "It's all work, with no play and no proper pay, for Western competition now prevents all chance of decent profits.   Little can be laid up for old age, except by the most painful economy and daily scrimping; and how can the children consent to stay on, starving body and soul?   That explains the 3,318 abandoned farms in Maine at present.   And the farmers' wives!   What monotonous, treadmill lives!   Constant toil with no wages, no allowance, no pocket money, no vacations, no pleasure trips to the city nearest them. . . .   Some say their only chance for social life is in going to some insane asylum. . . . In general, it is all one steady rush of work from March to November; increasing uncomplaining activity for the barest support, followed by three months of hibernation and caring for the cattle. . . .   It may have been true long years ago that no shares,

---

377. *Pembroke*, p. v.

378. *Ibid.*, p. vii.

379. In *A New England Nun and Other Stories* (1891).

factory, bank, or railroad paid better dividends than the plow-share, but it is the veriest nonsense now".[380]

Among the novelists who present a brief on the capitalistic side of the capital and labor question, C. M. Cornwall, Thomas Bailey Aldrich, John Hay, and F. Hopkinson Smith are particularly notable. They show us the other side of the slate, and the picture is very different.

Cornwall's *Free Yet Forging Their Own Chains* (1876) depicts conditions attending a strike by the Pennsylvania coal miners at Scranton and Cedar Ridge. A ten percent reduction in wages had been put in force because there was plenty of stock on hand and no demand. Even with the reduction the mines were still running at a considerable loss; the owners preferred this to turning the men out in midwinter. It is against the strike which the miner's union decreed under these circumstances that Cornwall protests. Union leaders and agitators are characterized as "lazy scamps".[381] Ned Malcome, who wears the hero's mantle in this novel, refuses to join the union, continues to work under adverse and dangerous circumstances, and condemns the 'walking delegates' who have brought on the strike:

"I'm a truer friend to my comrades than you rascally lot of hypocrites and assassins who shoot or stab your victims in the dark, and try to blow up men and children with gun powder, simply to keep them from an honest living, while such as you and Sam Walker filch from them the hard savings you are too lazy to earn for yourselves."[382]

Cornwall's contention is that the unions are greater oppressors of labor than the capitalists. Why then have both?

The same thought is the basic theme of Thomas Bailey Aldrich's *The Stillwater Tragedy* (1880). The Marble Workers' Association, the novel reveals, has attempted more and more to dominate Slocum's business. He may take only two apprentices a year when he could use several times that number. Wages are kept up. "So his business instead of naturally spreading and becoming a benefit to many, was kept carefully pruned

380. *Adopting an Abandoned Farm,* pp. 109-111.
381. *Free Yet Forging Their Own Chains,* p. 37.
382. *Ibid.,* p. 310.

down for the benefit of the few".[383]   The leaders of agitation in
Stillwater are an Italian, Torrini, and two or three others with
"foreign grievances" who squander a quarter of their week's
wages at the tavern and make windy speeches.   "These men
get three times the pay they ever received in their own land,
and are treated like human beings for the first time in their
lives", and yet they organize a strike for twenty-five cents a day
more and one hour earlier off, Saturdays.   Aldrich's philosophy
of industry is stated by Denyven a non-union marble-worker:
"every soul of us has the privilege of bettering our condition
if we have the brain and the industry to do it".[385]   "The trades-
unions will discover their error some day", Aldrich insists,
"when they have succeeded in forcing manufacturers to import
skilled labor by the wholesale".[386]   "Strikes are", at the best,
"terrible mistakes.   Even when they succeed, what pays for
the lost time and the money squandered over the tavern bar?
What makes up for the days or weeks when the fire was out
on the hearth and the children had no bread"?[387]   The question,
of course, has two sides.   "Every man has the right to set a
price on his own labor, and to refuse to work for less; the
wisdom of it is another matter".[388]   The idea of a sympathetic
strike is particularly scored by Aldrich.   For members of a trade
to strike when no grievance exists in their trade, is like a man
in sound health committing suicide because someone with a
nervous breakdown has done so.   In *The Stillwater Tragedy* as
in other defenses of the present order of capitalistic business,
the 'walking delegate' is the black villain of the piece—"a glib
person disguised as the Workingman's Friend, no workingman
himself, mind you, but a ghoul that lives upon subscriptions and
sucks the senses of innocent human beings".[389]

John Hay's *The Breadwinners* (1884) is also clearly a "partisan defense of economic individualism", "an attack upon the

---

383. *The Stillwater Tragedy,* p. 64.
384. *Ibid.,* p. 138.
385. *Ibid.,* p. 139.
386. *Ibid.,* p. 165-166.
387. *Ibid.,* p. 166.
388. *Ibid.,* p. 167.
389. *Ibid.,* p. 171.

rising labor movement", a "defense of vested interests", a satire
exuding an "odor of property-morality".[390]   Labor agitation is
attributed to the very scum of the social group.   Hay in drawing his picture of a mid-western industrial city tells us that shops
began striking without orders.   The officers of the labor unions
"seemed to be losing their control of the workingmen; and a
few tonguey vagrants and convicts from the city and neighboring towns, who had come to the surface from nobody knew
where, were, beginning to exercise wholly unexpected authority.
They were going from place to place, harranguing the workmen,
preaching what they called socialism, but what was merely riot
and plunder".[391]   The grotesqueness of the satire comes to light
when the strike is broken by the women's boxing their hus-
bands' ears, and chasing them back to work.   There is truth,
however, in Hay's charge that the officers of labor organizations
often profit financially at the expense of those they allegedly
represent.   The effect of strikes and labor movements of whatever sort is always bad, asserts Hay.   Sam Sleeny for example,
"was not the quiet, contented workman he had been.   He was
sour, sullen, and discontented.   He nourished a dull grudge
against the world."[392]

In *Tom Grogan* (1896) F. Hopkinson Smith tells the story of
the attempt of the Staten Island stevedores' union to dictate to
contractor (Mrs.!) Tom Grogan—particularly as to wage and
contract rates per hour.   "They discussed several plans by which
she could be compelled either to restore rates for unloading, or
be forced out of business altogether".[393]   But right, capitalistic
right, prevails, and Tom Grogan continues her draying business
uninterrupted.   The union dues, she charges go to "yer dirty
loafers—the officers and walking delegates."   "Ye'd be a ridin'
delegate if ye could", she denounces Crimmins; "but there's one
thing ye'll niver be, an' that's a workin' delegate, as long as

---

390.   V. L. Parrington, *Main Currents* III:174.
391.   John Hay, *The Breadwinners*, p. 215.
392.   *Ibid.*, p. 246.
393.   *Tom Grogan*, p. 61.
394.   *Ibid.*, p. 76.

ye kin find fools to pay ye wages for bummin' around day 'n' night".[394]

The picture of tenement life as lived by Tom Grogan and her dependents is very pleasant. There is no mention of squalor. Everything has a clean look and sweet smell; there is kindliness, there is love.[395]

An exceedingly significant book in relation to these fictional defenses of the capitalistic order in the United States is Walter A. Wyckoff's *The Workers* (1897). It is a two-volume diary of the experiences of a Princeton professor of political economy who set forth entirely without money to work his way across America by securing manual labor of every sort. He entered upon his "experiment in reality" with "no theories to establish and no conscious preconceptions to maintain".[396] His object was to learn the real truth about conditions of labor. Volume one of his book treats conditions in the East, volume two in the West. Wyckoff finds working conditions in urban America sufficiently drab and difficult, but his picture of farm life in the Middle Border bears considerable contrast to Hamlin Garland's well-known sketches of the same period—the 1890's. Work was easy to find among the middle western farmers, and no one offered to pay less than five dollars a week and board. With few exceptions these people were of kindly, pleasant disposition, and had a cheerful outlook upon life.[397] Writing in Denver a review of his experiences up to that time Wyckoff records the salient conclusions of his first hand investigations.

"I have found many jobs thus far, and in scarcely one of them have I failed to see the means of winning promotion and improved position, while not a few have seemed to me to open a way to considerable business success to a man shrewd enough to seize it and persistent enough to develop it. Often, as I look back upon two thousand miles of country crossed—apart from the splendor of it—the almost overwhelming impression that it leaves of boundless empire wherein a growing, intelligent, industrious, God-fearing people are slowly working out great ends in industrial achievement and personal character and in national life, an impression which thrills one with a new-found knowledge and love of one's country, with her "glorious might of

---

395. For further citation of the content of this novel see Chapter III of this study.
396. *The Workers*, v. I, p. ix.
397. *Ibid.*, v. II, p. 290 ff.

heaven-born freedom" and the resistless resurgence of her boundless ener-
gies, and notwithstanding all waywardness, a deep-seated, unalterable consciousness of national responsibility to the most high God; apart from all
this, the strongest sense which possesses one in any retrospect of a long,
laborious expedition like mine, is that of a wide land, which teems with opportunities open to energy and patient toil. Local labor markets there are
which are terribly crowded, as I found in Chicago to my cost. Awful suffering there is among workers who are in the clutch of illness, or, bound by
ties which they cannot break, are unable to move to more favorable regions;
pitiful degradation there is among many who lack imagination to see a way
and the energy to pursue it, and who, without the congenital qualities which
make for successful struggle, sink into the slough of purposeless idleness; deep
depravity and unutterable misery there are in the great congested labor-cen-
tres, many of whose conditions are in the price which we pay for our economic freedom. But the broad fact remains, that the sun never shone upon
a race of civilized men whose responsibilities were greater and whose problems were more charged with the welfare of mankind, among whom energy and
thrift and perseverance and ability were surer of their just rewards, and
where there were so many and such various chances of successful and hon-
orable career." [398]

---

398. *Ibid.*, v. II, pp. 319-321.

CHAPTER TWO

THE ANSWER AS THE NOVELISTS GIVE IT: SIGNPOSTS TO UTOPIA

I

Reforms Suggested by the General Novelist

The economic problems of civilization are old, old problems, and the solutions suggested for them have been many. It is a striking fact that virtually all of these solutions have been tried at one time or another, at least on a limited scale—that is all except one: a changing of the fundamental impulses of human nature. Does the continuance of injustice and inhumanity, greed and oppression, in our society mean that the preaching of all the prophets of the past has been wholly vain? The cynic may say yes; but the more rational answer is that the present is no worse than it is because there have always been idealists who vehemently challenged their fellowmen to the good life. Today's world is only as good as it is because of the unrealized utopian dreams of yesterday.

It must be obvious that no social critic need be taken seriously who does not believe that society can in some way be improved. And those who believe in the possibility of social improvement generally have some idea of how it can be brought about. However, he who reads the economic critical fiction of America will find that the social betterment program set forth in it is often a negative one, appreciable only by inference. Only a few of the twenty-odd novelists from Brockden Brown to Florence Converse—treated in section one of the preceding chapter—who particularly complain of economic class consciousness in America, of the sixteen fictionists from Brackenridge to Norris—section two of Chapter One—who most conspicuously criticize the corruption of government by greedy private interests, of the forty fictional denouncers of general social injustice and inhumanity from Cooper to Herrick—as analyzed in section three of Chapter One—have a definite, fully developed program for the eradication of the evils they assail. It may be implied, however, that those who criticize class distinctions believe their removal desirable; that those who see vast evil in the manipulation of government by great business interests would remove business from government; and that those who hold urbanized industrialization undesirable, who look upon the underpayment of labor as both economically unsound and humanly unjust, and who see in the oppressive living conditions of the lowly gradually greater degredation of the race, would decentralize industry, pay labor a higher wage, and insist upon better living conditions for the masses. The spirit of reform is definitely in all of this fiction.

A positive, constructive program for social betterment is, however, specifically outlined by only a limited number of our regular economic novelists. This of course, is not true among the utopian fictionists; they assume the evils of society to be obvious and place their major emphasis upon definite remedial measures. Those, too, who have treated the problem of the Indian, the negro, and the immigrant are more uniformly specific in what they propose to do about the conditions depicted than the novelists who have treated more general problems. Helen Jackson, for example, saw the granting of full citizenship with all property rights as the thing that must be done for the Indians. John W. De Forest, Albion Tourgée, Mrs. Walworth, Thomas Nelson Page, and George W. Cabale advocate a program of education for the negro, taking cognizance of his opportunityless background and adapted to his race temperament and economic needs. It remained for a utopian novelist, Edward A. Caswell, to suggest at the beginning of the twentieth century that the race problem might be solved by the intermarriage of whites and blacks promoted by a 'bounty' payable to every such union.[1] In examining the immigration problem Henry B. Fuller, Frank Rosewater, and John Bachelder think the future good of America can be promoted by more careful restriction, selection, and distribution of immigrants; they never, however, become so definite as to advocate, let us say, national quotas based on a particular census and selection at the source by American consuls.

Much of the reform desired by our economic critics in fiction

---

1. *Toil and Self*, p. 64.

can however, only be inferred. If a definite course of action is difficult or impossible to outline we may assume that an author's criticism of a condition means that he advocates the converse of that condition as desirable for American society. When Washington Irving frowned on the "dozen paniers full of sage laws usually heaped on the backs of young cities", and commended the decree of William the Testy that every man who proposed a new law should do so with a halter about his neck, we may safely and soundly conclude that he is advocating the simplification of the American judicial code.[2] When James K. Paulding declared that ". . . to us it seems that the very beau ideal of human happiness would consist in this imaginary union (if such a one were possible) of all the simplicity of rural innocence, all the mild excitements of rural amusements and rural occupations, with gentle manners and intellectual refinement",[3] we may infer that he was arguing for the revival of dying Jeffersonian agrarianism to prevent the encroachments of a growing industrial economy. When Mark Twain had Colonel Sellers talk himself into a belief that he could 'materialize' the ten thousand soldiers from the victorious legions of history who would chase the Indians as effectively as the twenty-five thousand American soldiers employed in that commendable service he probably meant to advocate saving the tax-payer money by reducing our military expenditures;[4] when he had his Yankee lecture to the 'freemen' of King Arthur's realm he was really pleading for American loyalty to our country not "to its institutions or its office-holders"—for "institutions are extraneous, they are its [the country's] mere clothing, and clothing can wear out, become ragged, cease to be comfortable, cease to protect the body from winter, disease and death. . . ."[5]—was apparently arguing for some modification of the Constitution more favorable to the masses of people; when he had the restored Edward VI say to the dignitaries of his government: "What dost thou know of suffering

2. Cf. *Knickerbocker History* (1809), pp. 129, 219.

3. *Westward Ho!* (1832), v. II, p. 10.

4. *The American Claimant* (1892), p. 33.

5. *A Connecticut Yankee in King Arthur's Court* (1899), p. 105.

and oppression? I and my people know, but not thou", he was undoubtedly challenging the men who sit so smugly in the halls of Congress accepting retainers for looking after the legal business of the Invisible Empire to get out into the by-ways of American life and learn the needs of the people.[6] When Elizabeth Phelps[7] or Margaret Sherwood[8] or Theodore Dreiser[9] criticized the oppressive wage-scale that drives women to under-nourished death or prostitution, advocacy of reform providing more adequate reward for labor is implied. When Twain and Warner[10] or Robert Herrick[11] depicted the corruption in gov-ernment that piles up huge profits for the few at the expense of the many, we may be sure that they were in spirit recom-mending more stringent penalties for malfeasance in office. When Edward Eggleston[12] or Henry B. Fuller[13] pictured the dishonest methods of development promoters who take the money of "widows and unprotected women . . . whose five thousand" becomes "so much less than five thousand",[14] their intent was obviously to recommend legislation that would make such speculative dishonesty impossible. Or, looking at the other side of the shield, when C. M. Cornwall,[15] Thomas Bailey Aldrich,[16] John Hay,[17] and F. Hopkinson Smith[18] scathingly satirized labor union methods they really meant to recommend the abolition of unions for the best interests of all concerned.

It is not necessary, however, to depend upon inference for the purport of all the reforms which our economic critics in fiction would bring about. Some have been quite explicit in the programs by which they would alleviate the ills of earth and direct men on the way to the good life. An individual

---

6. *The Prince and the Pauper* (1881), p. 274.
7. *The Silent Partner* (1871) and *Hedged In* (1870).
8. *Henry Worthington, Idealist* (1899).
9. *Sister Carrie* (1900).
10. *The Gilded Age* (1873).
11. *The Gospel of Freedom* (1898).
12. *The Mystery of Metropolisville* (1873).
13. *The Cliff-Dwellers* (1893).
14. *Ibid.*, p. 37.
15. *Free Yet Forging Their Own Chains* (1876).
16. *The Stillwater Tragedy* (1880).
17. *The Breadwinners* (1884).
18. *Tom Grogan* (1896).

survey of the most important of these critics in the last quarter of the nineteenth century will clarify a comprehensive summary of the remedial measures which they recommend.

J. G. Holland's *Nicholas Minturn* (1877) is a denouncement of the pauperizing spirit of mission churches and professional charity organizations. It charges that these make no effort to rehabilitate but are simply content to keep their poor dependent upon themselves. Holland feels sure "that if three-quarters of the money that has been expended upon food and clothing, and Sunday-schools and preaching, had been devoted to the enterprise of placing the pauper population in better conditions,—to giving them better tenements, better furniture, instructions in the facts and possibilities of common life, entertaining books, suggestive pictures, and training in household arts,—the good results of religion itself would be ten-fold greater than they are".[19] Carrying out the reform ideas of his author Nicholas Minturn organizes a lecture course for the poor at The Atheneum. "Bread" was the first of a series of subjects which were chosen both from the fields of the necessary and the ornamental. These lectures allegedly improved the people: "A degree of self-respect came back to them. They were more industrious, more frugal, less intemperate".[20] Holland believes that there need not be more than a thousand paupers in New York City;[21] his plan for rehabilitating the falling and the fallen in the economic race is set forth in a speech of Minturn to the representatives of the city's several charity organizations:

"I would like to see every charitable organization existing in the city, including my own enterprise, swept out of existence. I would like to see established in their place a single organization whose grand purpose it is to work a radical cure of pauperism. I would like to see the city government, which is directly responsible for more than half the pauperism we have, united in administration with the chosen representatives of the benevolence of the city, in the working out of this grand cure. I would like to see the city divided into districts so small that one man can hold in each, not only a registry of every family living in it, but obtain and preserve a knowledge

19. *Nicholas Minturn*, p. 270.
20. *Ibid.*, p. 294.
21. *Ibid.*, p. 340.

of each family's circumstances and character. I would have a labor bureau in every district, in connection with this local superintendent's office. I would have the record of every man and woman even more complete than any which has ever been made up by your mercantile agencies. I would have such vagrancy as we find illustrated by the tramps and dead-beats who swarm about the city, a sufficient crime for condemnation to hard labor in prisons and factories built for that purpose. I would make beggary on the street a misdemeanor punishable by imprisonment. I would have every helpless person understand where help in emergencies can always be had by a representation, subject to immediate and competent examination. I would see the matter so arranged that a premium would be put upon truth, and a ban upon falsehood. Temperance and intemperance should always be considerations in dealing with the poor. There is no limit to the benefits which such an organization as this would have the power to inaugurate and perpetuate, and, gentlemen I verily believe that under its intelligent and faithful administration we could banish beggars from the streets, introduce a new era of prosperity and virtue among all the suffering poor, and save ourselves forever from the terrible pauperization that curses and almost kills the cities of the old world."[22]

The assembled representatives of charity respond with no offer of approval and cooperation. A popular speaker from among them rises and recommends the religion of Christ as the solution to the social problem, but Minturn in refutation referring to the Parable of the Sower declares: ". . . the seed is thrown away, where the fowls of the air pick it up, unless a soil is prepared in advance . . . I believe in Christianity, but before I undertake to plant it, I would like something to plant it in."[23]

Advocacy of a cooperative plan of industry is the salient feature of Amanda M. Douglass' *Hope Mills* (1880). Yewbury is pictured as a solid, conservative, prosperous New England town; but over-production has brought on a new low-wage scale and in its wake a strike in the clothing mills of Lawrence, Eastman, and Minor. Not being a Marxian, Miss Douglass thinks that some capitalists are decent and human and so represents David Lawrence. He declares to his partners: "It has always seemed to me that a liberal wage policy with workmen brought its own reward. They are large consumers. Cut them down to mere food and shelter, and clothes are the first

22. *Ibid.*, p. 342.
23. *Nicholas Minturn*, pp. 344-345.

to go".[24]   Eastman and Minor, however have no consciences;
nor can they see the soundness of Lawrence's economics in not
oppressing the poor.   The strike goes on.   The Yewbury Bank
is closed—by reason of the mismanagement and defalcations of
George Eastman — and David Lawrence, trying to revive it
without loss to poor depositors, dies.

Jack Darcy, the story's hero, a young hand in the now tightly
closed Hope Mills, "poured over pages of Adam Smith, he
turned to Ruskin for comfort, he picked up Brassey's figures
and experience, and Stuart Mill's strong, kindly reasoning . . ."[25]
With Yewbury in the throes of depression he determined to
organize the "Hope Mills Cooperative Association" and take
over the Lawrence mill for operation on a cooperative basis.
Using his wide influence among the men he marshalled all of
their financial forces, and then with his sterling character for
collateral borrowed the remainder of the money necessary to
get the enterprise under way.   "Then the company's agreement
was put in lawful, legal shape.   The managing board of five men
were to have sole charge of buying, selling, and manufacturing.
They were to give all their time and ability, to watch the state
of the market, and conduct everything for the benefit of the
whole corporation.   Darcy was to prepare a balance-sheet semi-
annually, showing profit and loss; and this was to be open to
the inspection of the firm.

The parties to the second part, the workmen, were to work
ten hours a day, six days in the week, under the supervision of
Hurd and Yardley.   The wages of the men and the salaries of
the managers were to be put at the minimum rate, and both
parties were to draw two-thirds of this sum weekly.   At the end
of the year, the profits on labor and capital were to be evenly
divided; one-half apportioned to the capital, the other half
divided pro rata; but only half of this sum to be drawn out
yearly the other turned over to the capital stock, and placed
to each man's credit.   If any operative should become dissatis-
fied, and leave, his share of the profits was to be forfeited to a
fund for sick and disabled workmen. . . . Shares of capital as

24. *Hope Mills*, p. 78.
25. *Ibid.*, p. 115.

low as fifty dollars would be within reach of the workmen. . . .
Each man was to use his best endeavors to promote the interests
of the firm. At the end of five years, the agreement was to cease,
and the profits to be divided."[26]

Through Darcy's ability, of course, the venture proves successful. At the end of five years the accrued capital stock was
over a hundred thousand dollars, which was "divided in the
pro rata of each man's share, the larger amounts making the most
of course." There had been "steady work for the whole five
years the people now saw the object of saving"; their passwords
were "honesty, industry, and fidelity".[27]

Henry Francis Keenan's "social parable", *The Money-Makers*
(1885) argues that labor is the sole producer of wealth, and
ought so to be recognized in the distribution of rewards. Keenan
holds that "the primal and enduring capital of the human family
is human labor (for without human labor there would be no
values) and that the duty of enlightened men is to safeguard
that most precious of all capital".[28] His program of reform is
not outlined in detail, but like Howells, Bellamy and most of
the other utopian novelists, he sees a stronger, purer, more socialized government as the answer to the problem of man's inhumanity to man. He calls upon Congress to legislate for the millions not the millionaires.[29]

As has been pointed out previously in this study *An Iron
Crown* (1885) by Thomas Stewart Dennison is the most directly
severe indictment of the robbery of the people by great business interests—through their corruption of legislators—in our
economic fiction. Nor has anyone offered a more specific chart
of recommendations for the correction of the evils assailed than
Dennison. The measures proposed are these:

1. Provide by law for a careful government supervision of all transportation by common carriers, and for government control of inter-state commerce.

2. Make stringent laws for the protection of the purity of the ballot box,
and enforce severe penalties for their violation.

---

26. *Ibid.*, p. 164.
27. *Ibid.*, pp. 368-369.
28. *The Money-Makers*, p. 246.
29. *Ibid.*, p. 330.

3. In the case of the rising generation and future immigrants, deprive the illiterate of the right of franchise.

4. Reform the jury system so that juries will not so frequently consist of blockheads and knaves. Then there will be at least grounds for hope that all offenders against the law may be punished regardless of wealth or social standing.

5. Public opinion must make bribe-taking as odious and dangerous as horse-stealing once was. Then corruption in official life will diminish.

6. All intelligent citizens must take an active part in politics, and see that honest, intelligent legislators and incorruptible judges are chosen to manage the machinery of the State.[30]

Living conditions in the slums of a great city have been most effectively pictured by Helen Campbell and Jacob Riis. J. G. Holland,[31] Kate Douglass Wiggin,[32] Joaquin Miller,[33] H. H. Boyesen[34] and others have, however, also treated the problem. That all desire to remedy the conditions depicted may, of course, be obviously inferred; but Holland, whose program of rehabilitation in *Nicholas Minturn* has just been cited, Campbell, and Riis are the ones who have most definitely outlined remedial measures.

Mrs. Campbell's story is an old, old tale she tells us:

"Since the Church first began to misinterpret the words of its Founder, since men who built hospitals first made the poor to fill them, the "thou shalt not" of the priest has stood in the way of a human development that, if allowed free play, had long ago made its own code, and found in natural spiritual law the key to the overcoming of that formulated by men to whom the divine in man was forever unrecognized and unrecognizable."[35]

But it is hopeless, Mrs. Campbell avers, to talk rashly as some do, threatening that "your owners will be shot down like dogs if they won't hear reason".[36] A program of gradually extended economic education is the fundamental solution; otherwise the same old drama of injustice will go on with only different persons in the parts. To those who would arise in immediate Marxian war Mrs. Campbell declares: "You delay what you

---

30. *An Iron Crown*, pp. 467-468.
31. *Nicholas Minturn* (1877).
32. *The Story of Patsy* (1899) and *Timothy's Quest* (1890).
33. *Destruction of Gotham* (1886).
34. *Social Strugglers* (1893).
35. *Prisoners of Poverty* (1887), p. 78.
36. *Mrs. Herndon's Income* (1886), p. 214.

would hasten. What good to these masses is your equal division, if they know not what money can do? Destruction must come. We wait for that, but not till our masses have learned what they need. Emancipation begins for the few. It is for them to react on the remainder. It is the rich who must be reached and taught that through them is the sole emancipation for those through whom their riches have come. It is the incapables who have hoisted up the capables."[37]   It is through increasing the percentage of capables that permanent improvement can be made.

In attacking one phase of the problem immediately Mrs. Campbell would solve the question of decent yet economical living quarters for the shop girls of a great city by organizing house-keeping units. *Miss Melinda's Opportunity* (1886) sets forth this feature of the Campbell reform program. Because one of them reminds her of an old friend, Miss Melinda Van Zenden helps Polly, Milly, and Amy, working girls—clerks, to furnish a small apartment and set up housekeeping for themselves. An itemized list of expense, quoted by Mrs. Campbell, demonstrates the practicability of the scheme. Miss Melinda is pleased and uses the money intended for foreign missions to purchase other houses where more girls may establish themselves on a cooperative housekeeping basis. She also founds a club for shop-girls—providing magazines, varied classes, and a wholesome social life. Mrs. Campbell feels that much can be done at the shop-girl level of the social scale. If philanthropic persons and organizations will but take example from Miss Melinda's so successful experiment, effective work can be accomplished toward maintaining and increasing the self-respect and social worth of a class of society which too much ignored in the past has often slipped to a lower level.

There is no definite program of reform in the fictions of Jacob A. Riis, *Nibsy's Christmas* (1893) and *Out of Mulberry Street* (1898), unless one interprets them in the light of Riis' essay studies. The latter make clear the fact that the conditions Riis describes in his narratives are intended as an emphatic argument for better housing conditions and better educational and

---

37. *Ibid.*, p. 216.

economic opportunities for the lower tenth. Like Holland, Riis condemns charity that makes no effort to rehabilitate its recipients. "It is money scattered without judgment—not poverty—that makes the pauper".[38] "Neither legislation nor charity can cover the ground", can correct the ills which have grown up in the social life of the Other Half, he declares. "The greed of capital that wrought the evil must itself undo it, as far as it can be undone. Homes must be built for the working masses by those who employ their labor; tenements must cease to be 'good property' in the old heartless sense. 'Philanthropy and five per cent' is the penance exacted".[39] ". . . Half the miseries of society" are due "to the sundering of the home-ties in childhood",[40] and the remedy for those miseries is the maintenance of home-ties through a humanitarian building program. In 1890 one hundred thousand persons in New York lived in 'rear tenements' built at the backs of the old brown-stone Knickerbocker houses on crowded plots intended for small yards.[41] It is the complete razing of these that Riis strenuously urged. More light, water, closed sewers, these were improvements which he said must be made. The need was for closer, more intelligent superintendence in better tenements.[42] Riis urged the founding of "industrial schools, coordinate with public schools, in authority" in the slum districts. He joined with Mrs. Campbell in insisting that the child labor laws applicable to factories should be extended to include tenement work. Something must be done because the bad environment of one generation becomes the heredity of the next. "Society exists for the purpose of securing justice to its members, appearances to the contrary notwithstanding. When it fails in this, the item is carried on the ledger with interest and compound interest toward a day of reckoning that comes surely with the paymaster".[43]

George Thomas Dowling in *The Wreckers* (1886) urges the practical application of the teachings of Christ as the program

---

38. *The Children of the Poor* (1892), p. 277.
39. *How the Other Half Lives* (1890), pp. 4-5.
40. *The Children of the Poor*, p. 277.
41. *A Ten Year's War* (1900), p. 140.
42. *Ibid.*, p. 133.
43. *Ibid.*, p. 140.

to be followed in renovating society. The world can never for-
give itself, he declares, that it failed to hear and heed the cry
that fell from the lips of a poor peasant in Gethsemane over
eighteen hundred years ago.[44] We must put emphasis upon
the things human beings have in common, instead of dwelling always upon the points in which we differ; then all classes
will understand one another so much better, and understanding will do justice.[45]

The point of the *Gentle Breadwinners* (1888) by Helen Alice
Nitsch is that daughters should be taught some form of self-
support, of domestic character at least, lest an unforeseen
exigency of economic circumstances should force self-respecting
control of their life's course from their hands. Left
penniless by the death of their father in the midst of a speculation that had swept away all of his money, Dorothy and May
Fortescue cast about for some means of support. Dorothy, the
enterprising one of the sisters, takes up fancy cooking, learns
with astounding rapidity and accomplishes an amazing financial
success. Whereupon Mrs. Nitsch quotes innumerous recipes,
and the story becomes a glorified cook-book.

Cooperative industry as the key which will unlock the door
to a new social order is advocated again in Edward Everett
Hale's *How They Lived in Hampton* (1888). Hale contends
that there are three factors in production: "capital, work, and
the directing skill which should enable capital to use the workman's industry".[46] This story was written to suggest a more
equitable arrangement of their several interests, to demonstrate
"the Christian relations of capital to workmen". The scheme
described began as a five-year plan.[47] There were three parties
to the corporation: Thankful Nourse, who invested $72,500,
John Workman, who put in $500, and William Spinner, who
contributed $2000 to the enterprise. Each member had the
right to sell his stock at any time. Workman and Spinner,
were to be the working managers "for the benefit of all parties

44. *The Wreckers,* p. 66.
45. *Ibid.,* p. 133.
46. *How They Lived in Hampton,* p. 34.
47. *Ibid.,* p. 25 ff.

concerned". The profits were to be divided one-third to the owners, one-third to the managers, one-third to the workmen—after deducting the expense claims of each party: 4% on $75,000, $600 for each manager, and three-fourths of a standard wage for each workman. If the mills should not earn four per cent after paying the other expenses the owners should receive only the amount which it did earn. The record should be open to any stock-holder—and any workman should be able to buy stock—or to any person commissioned by one-third of the workmen in the mill "who are to be regarded as having the rights of partners in the concern". In the event of the death of any workman, or of his leaving the mill, his representative in Hampton should receive his share of the profits, as if he had remained in the employ of the corporation. At the end of seven years the enterprise had proved a tremendous success. Nourse's shares had all been "taken off his hands by purchase" of the workmen, who "were more and more interested in the plan. . . . It cultivated their self-respect. . . . It proved profitable to them". A cooperative store supplemented the benefits which a cooperative mill had brought to Hampton.[48]

Hale also suggests that capital ought to be paid at two different rates: "one by which I am paid for my money when I do not take care of it, and take no risks; this is a much lower rate than the rate to be paid me when I take care of it myself, and when I do take some risk" — an 'idiot rate' and a 'working rate'.[49]

William Dean Howells was the first regular novelist in American literature—as distinguished from the writers of utopian fiction—to advocate complete national socialism as the solution for the country's economic problems. This doctrine had, however, not reached its fully developed scope in the first of Howells' economic novels, *Annie Kilburn* in 1888. But the seriousness of the problem is already fully grasped. Howells sees even such fine-spirited enterprises as the Peck Social Union, which Annie eventually gets organized, as merely palliative and not at all curative of the real ill. It is in the Reverend Peck's analysis

---

48. *Ibid.*, p. 74.
49. *Ibid.*, p. 6.

of the labor-capital situation that we have a forecast of the later Howells' socialistic doctrine: "Yet in the labor organizations, which have their bad side, their weak side, through which the forces of hell enter, I see evidence of the fact that the poor have at last had pity upon the poor, and will no more betray and underbid and desert one another, but will stand and fall together as brothers".[50] Monopolies in labor as well as capital "prophesy the end of competition; they eliminate one element of strife. . . ."[51] They look forward to a collective control of industry securing social justice for all men.

The Quality of Mercy (1892) contains little positive economic philosophy. It is a significant book, however, in its further revealing of Howells' growing disposition to think in collective and social terms. In tracing out the way in which Northwick's defalcation effects an ever-widening circle of characters the novelist emphasizes his conception of the interdependence of all the cogs of the social machine. Lawyer Putney in this story, and also in *Annie Kilburn,* is Howells' most outstanding example of a character advocating the Henry George single-tax doctrine. Howells' personal wavering attraction toward this idea had been set forth in a letter to Hamlin Garland dated January 15, 1888.

"I'm interested in what you say of the drama. . . . But I'm still more interested by what I will call your appeal to me. . . . Your land tenure idea is one of the good things which we must hope for and strive for by all the good means at our hands. But I don't know that it's the first step to be taken; and I can't yet bring myself to look upon confiscation in any direction as a good thing. The new commonwealth must be founded in justice even to the unjust rather than anything less than justice. Besides, the land idea arrays against progress the vast farmer class who might favor national control of telegraphs, railways, and mines, postal savings-bank and life-insurance, a national labor bureau for bringing work and workmen together without cost to the workman, and other schemes by which it is hoped to lessen the sum of wrong in the world, and insure to every man the food and shelter which the gift of life implies the right to. Understand, I don't argue against you; I don't know yet what is best; but I am reading and thinking about questions that carry me beyond myself and my miserable literary idolatries of the past; perhaps you'll find that I've been writing about them. I

---

50. *Annie Kilburn,* p. 241.
51. *Ibid.,* p. 241.

am still the slave of selfishness, but I am no longer content to be so. That's as far as I can honestly say I've got."[52]

Mrs. Camp in *A Traveller from Altruria* (1894) is identified as another Georgite among Howells' characters when she says: "Perhaps no one has a right to own any portion of the earth".[53]

It is in *The World of Chance* (1893) and through the patriarchal Hughes that Howells most definitely espouses the collectivist organization of society. The new order can and must be attained by an active campaign of the people. "Tolstoi is mistaken", Hughes declares; "in quitting he would have us withdraw from the world, as if, where any man was, the world was not there in the midst of him". "We shall never redeem the world by eschewing it. . . . The body politic is to be healed politically. The way to have the golden age is to elect it by the Australian ballot. The people must vote themselves into possession of their own business, and intrust their economic affairs to the same faculty that makes war and peace, that frames laws, and that does justice".[54] Cooperative organization within individual industries or individual communities is not enough Hughes insists:

"I have had enough of communities. The family we hope to found must include all men who are willing to work; it must recognize no aliens except the drones, and the drones must not be suffered to continue. They must either cease to exist by going to work, or by starving to death. But this great family—the real human family—must be no agglutinated structure, no mere federation of trades-unions; it must be a natural growth from indigenous stock, which will gradually displace individual and corporate enterprises by pushing its roots and branches out under and over them, till they have no longer earth or air to live in. It will then slowly possess itself of the whole field of production and distribution."[55]

This is the kind of world Howells would substitute for the "World of Chance"—a world in which the weak grow strong only by accident, and in which not even the strong are secure. Howells had stated the same idea in *A Hazard of New Fortunes* (1889).

"What I object to [says Basil March] in this economic chance-world in

---

52. Mildred Howells, *The Life in Letters of William Dean Howells*, v. I, pp. 407-408.

53. *A Traveller from Altruria*, p. 124 (edition of 1908).

54. *The World of Chance*, p. 90.

55. *Ibid.*, p. 122.

which we live, and which we men seem to have created. It ought to be a law as inflexible in human affairs as the order of day and night in the physical world, that if a man will work he shall both rest and eat, and shall not be harassed with any question as to how his repose and his provision shall come. Nothing less ideal than this satisfied the reason. But in our state of affairs no one is sure of this. No one is sure of finding work; no one is sure of not losing it."[56]

The problem of technological unemployment "makes its first appearance in the American novel with the story of Denton, lithographer and inventor, in *The World of Chance*".[57] Denton has devised an invention which he knows will replace a considerable number of workmen. He hesitates about making it available for use, torn between his family's need for money and his sympathy with the doomed craftsmen. His pondering upon the dilemma eventually drives him to insanity. Howells' solution for the problem of technological unemployment, as for the other ills of the "World of Chance" is the substituting of a controlled monopoly, a national socialism for the competitive industrial order. His belief that no less comprehensive solution would be practical or effective finds reiteration in *New Leaf Mills* (1913). Owen and Felix Powell, their wives and Owen's children are the central figures of the story. They propose to, and do, buy a mill property in rural Ohio, intending to found a communistic colony, controlled by them at first, but gradually extended to include others who should see "that the new-comers did not wish merely to make money for themselves, but to benefit all by improvements that would increase the price of their land and give employment to their children". They propose "turning over quite a new leaf".

After Felix dies Owen is induced by the aspect of things to give up the mill and colony scheme and return to the city— taking up a church-book business. "He did not relinquish the ideal of a true state of things which he and his brothers had hoped to realize at New Leaf Mills, but he was inclined to regard the communistic form as defective. The communities of Robert Owen had everywhere failed as signally as that of New

56. *A Hazard of New Fortunes*, v. II, pp. 252-253.
57. Walter Fuller Taylor, "William Dean Howells and the Economic Novel" in *American Literature* IV:111, May, 1932.

Leaf Mills, which indeed could scarcely be said to have passed the embryonic stage. But he argued, . . . that if some conception of society could possess the entire State, a higher type of civilization would undoubtedly eventuate".[58]

The economic creed of William Dean Howells has been summed up with conspicuous clarity by Walter Fuller Taylor: "The system of competitive capitalism, with its accompanying ideal of individual success, is no longer satisfactory. It produces only a heartless struggle for survival, governed largely by chance, in which no life is secure; in which even invention, fruit of man's ingenuity, only adds to the misery of the unemployed. It produces, contrary to the equalitarian ideals of America, insuperable class distinctions between the rich and the poor. Competitive capitalism should therefore be replaced by socialism; the machinery of government should be employed to control production in the interest of all rather than in the interest of the exploiting few. This socialism should not be the effect or agent of class conflict, but should represent the will of the majority, peaceably expressed by suffrage."[59]

Christian socialism is the solution Albion W. Tourgée offers in *Murvale Eastman* (1890) for the problem of man's inhumanity to man. "It is no longer a defensible theory", he contends "that 'what is good for the hive is good for the bee'; the converse rather, is the measure of policy. The welfare of the governed is acknowledged to be the supreme function of government. . . ."[60] The government must guarantee freedom for every man—not for the strongest only; total wealth is no index of national well-being if the masses of the country suffer under the oppressive "control of opportunity" by the few. Tourgée puts his emphasis upon the Christian rather than the socialistic part of his program. Murvale Eastman has studied all the proposed systems of government from Plato's time until the present and has become increasingly convinced of the superiority of the Christian idea, "its wisdom and simplicity in dealing not with

---

58. *New Leaf Mills,* pp. 6, 154.
59. "William Dean Howells and the Economic Novel" in *American Literature,* IV:113, May, 1932.
60. *Murvale Eastman,* pp. iv-v.

methods but with men; not with theories but with individuals; not with conditions but with motives".[61]   The golden rule is the only possible basis for the good life.

Mary H. Ford (*Which Wins?*, 1891) is in essential agreement with Tourgée's religious solution of economic problems. She feels that the conditions which exist are not the will of the majority, that "if you can plainly tell one half of the world how the other half lives, how it suffers, how it strangles and dies daily under the exactions of injustice, humanity will rise as one man, and strike down its oppressions, and. never rest until it stands free under heaven".[62]

There is also much of the Christian Socialist atmosphere about Agnes Maule Machar's *Roland Graeme, Knight* (1892); more definite and more economic reforms are, however, suggested. Of these the most significant is government regulation of "railway companies and joint stock companies".[63]   It is also proposed that all unappropriated land should be preserved for the use of the community.[64]   Henry George's single-tax idea is tentatively accepted.   "Public measures" are advocated to prevent what is customarily described as overproduction.   This, however, is really under-consumption, the result of unequal and "frequently unjust distribution of wealth".   Giving to Labor, therefore, a larger portion of the profits of industry would react to promote the progress of the country as a whole.[65]   Women should receive equal wages for equal work.[66]

Edward Fuller, author of *The Complaining Millions of Men* (1893) has his hero, Frank Baretta, propose a great national labor union including every workman in the United States.[67] The implications of such a suggestion are definitely socialistic. But after thus beginning as a serious study the book degenerates into a fantastic and foolish romance.

Hamlin Garland has already been cited as the most important

---

61. *Ibid.*, p. 86.
62. *Which Wins?* p. 250.
63. *Roland Graeme, Knight*, p. 188.
64. *Ibid.*, p. 188.
65. *Ibid.*, p. 186.
66. *Ibid.*, p. 190.
67. *The Complaining Millions of Men*, p. 120.

prophet of the mortgage-oppressed western farmers. And it is he who has the most definitely outlined program for the relief of his people. "Writers and orators", Douglass Radbourn tells Lily Graham in "Lucretia Burns", one of the stories in *Prairie Folks* (1892) "have lied so long about 'the idyllic' in farm life, and said so much about the 'independent American farmer' that he himself has remained blind to the fact that he is one of the hardest-working and poorest-paid men in America. . . . It ain't so much the grime that I abhor, not the labor that crooks their backs and makes their hands bludgeons; it's the horrible waste of life involved in it all. . . . The worst of it is, these people live lives approaching automata. They become machines to serve others more lucky or more unscrupulous than themselves".[68] It is through Radbourn in this story that Hamlin Garland most explicitly sets forth his proposals for economic reform. He would abolish all indirect taxes; provide for the State control of all privileges the private ownership of which interferes with the equal rights of all. He would utterly destroy speculative holdings of the earth. He would have land everywhere brought to its best use, by appropriating all ground rents to the use of the State.[69] It is this single-tax doctrine, derived from Henry George, that is the core of Garland's reform program. It finds further explicit espousal through Reeves in *Jason Edwards* (1897),[70] and is implied frequently in Garland's other fiction, especially in *A Spoil of Office* (1892).

The single-tax is also advocated by Dan Beard in *Moonblight and Six Feet of Romance* (1892). All wealth comes from the earth, he asserts; if, therefore, "any one wants to use the earth let him pay the rest for the privilege at market rate".[71]

A program of social and industrial education for the "submerged tenth" in the slums of our great cities finds further advocacy in H. H. Boyesen[72] and Margaret Sherwood.[73] Both picture settlement house projects in which a spirit of help and

---

68. *Prairie Folks*, pp. 125-126.
69. *Ibid.*, p. 128.
70. p. 83.
71. *Moonblight and Six Feet of Romance*, p. 91.
72. *Social Strugglers* (1893).
73. *An Experiment in Altruism* (1895).

rehabilitation is doing much for those who have found the obstacle-race of life too difficult. Margaret Sherwood leans decidedly toward socialism as the ultimate solution to the economic problems of our individualistic civilization. She has a resident of Barnet House tell the trend of her mind.

"It is an economic fact that Socialism is inevitable. Whether we will or no, it is coming as surely as the days are moving on. It is equally true that it, as a system, offers to the individual a justice that no other form of government can offer. Under the centralizing system of socialism, with land and forces of production in the collective ownership of the people, and monopolies done away, will come at last that granting of equal rights to all that democracy has failed to realize."[74]

Ellen Glasgow's *The Descendant* (1897) advocates a much modified socialism as the answer to the economic ills of society. Michael Ackershem states Miss Glasgow's serious outlook upon the situation. Thus far, Ackershem declares, schemes of socialism have "failed in the essential principle—that is, in reaching an equilibrium of moral restraint and moral liberty. Socialism and individualism need to coalesce to give the surest protection to the rights of man with the widest personal liberty. . . . Centralization and individualism need to be reconciled, and can be. . . ."[75] This is apparently the Glasgow economic philosophy, but the methods of applying it to life are nowhere explicitly given.

Caroline F. Walch's *Doctor Sphinx* (1898) deserves mention among the novels advocating definite economic measures for its scathing denunciation of the low tariff.[76] The welfare of the workingman, it holds, is dependent upon a strong protective policy. The novel also embodies a plea for the practical education of girls, lest their only escapes from a parasitic dependence be prostitution or death.[77]

Differences (1899) by Hervey White is a romance written against the background of settlement house relations to the poor. It proposes substituting rehabilitation for the usual pauperizing charity, but not so emphatically as some of the novels

---

74. *Ibid.*, p. 118.
75. *The Descendant*, p. 80.
76. *Doctor Sphinx*, p. 341.
77. *Ibid.*, p. 346.

already cited. A public works program of municipal improvement is also suggested, both for its contribution to the beauty and health of our cities and for its employment at respectable wages of those who might otherwise go hungry.[78]

David Lubin's *Let There Be Light* (1900) sees "money and liberty" as "largely equal and synonymous terms". Lubin leans toward the belief that "collectivism or, as it is more generally denominated, socialism, will give to each man, woman, and child, what the present system will not or cannot give . . . each his or her proper due".[79] He feels, however, that the weakness inherent in human nature is too deeply rooted for the ideal social equality to be brought about at once by nominal collectivism.[80] The spirit of socialism is more necessary and more effective than the letter of socialism. Christ is the "sure rule and sure guide",[81] Lubin declares. The book resolves itself into a hope that theoretical Christianity can be made practical, and the economic ramifications of its program become less definite as the story progresses.

The Burden of Christopher (1900) by Florence Converse exudes the air of Christian Socialism but specifically advocates cooperative industry as the solution to the problem of a fairer distribution of the profits of production. Christopher Kenyon is vehemently opposed to any scheme of social organization that does not recognize the inherent equality of the workingman with any other member of society. "I don't believe in charity!", he declares; "I won't build hospitals, I won't found workingmen's homes! Let the sick rot, and the poor starve, let misery increase till the world understands why!"[82] Kenyon places his shoe factory of twelve hundred employees on a profit-sharing basis, hoping to work gradually towards cooperation. In his failure he realizes that he should have introduced the cooperative principle and its attendant equality at once.[83] Miss Converse

---

78. *Differences*, p. 54.
79. *Let There Be Light*, p. 91.
80. *Ibid.*, p. 97.
81. *Ibid.*, p. 183.
82. *The Burden of Christopher*, p. 59.
83. *Ibid.*, p. 42.

also advocates equal wages for the equal work of women,[84] and government ownership and operation of the railroads.[85]

Examining these novelists for points of similarity in their programs of reform we find considerable agreement on a number of the matters at issue. All the fictionists who treat living conditions in the slums of our large cities agree that a spirit of rehabilitation must be substituted for the usual pauperizing attitude of charity. There must be an intelligent, rigorously carried out program of industrial and social education. Those who have advocated measures of this kind are Holland, Campbell, Riis, Boyesen, Sherwood, and White. Holland would develop a complete integration of all the charity organizations of a city with the municipal government; he would divide the city into districts small enough to enable the superintendent of rehabilitation in that district to know personally every individual in his territory. Campbell and Riis also advocate a systematic rehousing campaign for slum sections.

More comprehensive in scope is the program of Christian socialism advocated by Dowling, Tourgée, Ford, Machar, and Lubin. This doctrine stemming from the English clergyman and novelist, Charles Kingsley, proposes to accomplish brotherhood and equality in the economic relations of life through the practical application of the teaching of Jesus. Socialism in its technical economic form is advocated unqualifiedly only by Howells, although Sherwood subscribes tentative support to it. Ellen Glasgow also has socialistic leanings but would modify the syndicalistic program to preserve as much as possible of individual initiative. Cooperative industry within individual units is advocated by Douglas, Hale, and Converse. Dennison, Machar, Garland, and Converse urge government ownership and operation of public utilities.

The single-tax idea of Henry George receives support from Howells, Machar, tentatively, Garland, and Beard. Garland would also abolish all indirect taxes and destroy speculation in land. Equal wages for women doing the same work as men is advocated by Machar and Converse. Campbell and Riis would

84. *Ibid.*, p. 41.
85. *Ibid.*, p. 14.

extend the child labor statutes applicable to factory labor to include tenement work as well. Practical education for girls is urged by Nitsch and Walch. The latter also advocates a high protective tariff policy in the interests of better living conditions for American workmen. Edward Fuller believes that much can be done for the benefit of labor through a great national union embracing every workman in the 'United States —a plan socialistic in its implications. Dennison would reform the jury system, pass more stringent laws guarding the purity of the ballot box, provide severer penalties for malfeasance in office, and deny the franchise to the illiterate. It is through these measures that the critics in our regular fiction think much may be done in achieving the ideals of equality and fraternity.

II

The Program of the Utopian Novelists

The amount of utopian fiction in American literature is not very widely known. There are, however, some sixty odd novels —novels by courtesy, for many of them are quite short and few have literary merit—in our fiction before 1900 that picture the ideal nowhere. The purpose of this type of writing is the two-fold one of arraigning capitalism before the bar of contemporary opinion and of elucidating the socialistic theory of life. It is most adequately understood as a satirization of existing conditions rather than an advocacy of the literal application of the schemes set forth: often a novelist writes of his utopian title or his utopian framework that it "recognizes the visionary character of the utopian scheme and protects the author from any charge of light-headedness; while into this visionary fabric of a state he is able to work a solid and valuable criticism of the social world about him".[86] One may say, then, that fundamentally these utopian fictions do not differ from the regular novel of economic criticism. But even if the ultimately communistic programs which they advocate are discounted their story mechanism still sets these utopian novels apart from our regular critical

---

86. David Hilton Wheeler, *Our Industrial Utopia and Its Unhappy Citizens,* p. 7.

fiction and makes clarity in this study best served by their treatment as a separate group. Emphasis is placed upon the elements of their program of reform rather than upon the criticism of existing conditions which may be implied from it.

The world is too much with us, hold these utopian novelists; and they take us off on glamorous journeys through ideal no-wheres, the realms of heart's desire. They stand on the Mt. Nebo of idealism and describe for us their vision of the promised land, extended wide in circuit, undetermined square or round, with opal towers and battlements adorn'd of living sapphire.

But fascinated by the new machinery these writers too often focus their attention upon industry rather than upon society as a whole; they see in reorganization and redistribution all that is necessary for the good life. They fail to comprehend that the true Utopia can only be realized through the substitution of creative for possessive impulses; that man's nature must in some inexplicable way be changed from selfishness to unselfish-ness. But there is merit even in a program of temporary redis-tribution, for as Plato and every subsequent utopian has pointed out, wealth and poverty are both bad—one is the parent of luxury and indolence, and the other of meanness and viscious-ness, and both, therefore, of discontent and unhappiness. In preaching "a large liberty" the utopian fictionists maintain that "there can be no real freedom until the necessaries of life are first made free and accessible to all, for while the neces-saries of life are left to competition, the smartest will get the most and the weakest will get nothing. . . ."[87]

The manner in which the economic problems of our national life increased in proportion to the ever-growing industrialism of the nineteenth century has already been referred to. Despite the fact that the first labor union in America was organized at least as early as 1648,[88] that our first significant strike occurred in New York in 1741, and that by 1834 strikes were so preva-lent that the New York *Daily Advertiser* declared them to be "all the fashion",[89] the relations between capital and labor

---

87. Crawford S. Griffin, *Nationalism*, p. 3.
88. Samuel P. Orth, *The Armies of Labor*, p. 21.
89. *Ibid.*, p. 172.

became in the decade after the Civil War critical in a way that had never before been known. Through the Knights of Labor (organized 1869) and its successor the American Federation of Labor (established 1886), as well a considerable number of smaller organizations which either disintegrated or merged themselves with this by direct affiliation,[90] the working classes began to show a startling degree of class consciousness and a determination to secure a betterment of their conditions. The increasing militancy of their movement was met with little conciliation or tact and as a consequence there resulted literally thousands of strikes attended by considerable bloodshed and property destruction.[91]

And industrial labor was not alone in distress: from the West came persistent clamors for relief. Citing on the one hand steadily falling prices and on the other accumulating debts, the farmers demanded a thorough revision of the monetary system, producing an inflation that should insure better selling prices and facilitate the meeting of their obligations. Closely associated with these two major issues, the industrial and the agricultural, was a host of reform projects which, in the large commanded a considerable following. Notable among these were the single-tax movement led by Henry George and the anti-monopoly agitation which culminated in the Interstate Commerce and the Sherman Anti-trust acts.[92]

Because of the profound disquiet and dissatisfaction of the last quarter of the nineteenth century, "it followed, not unnaturally, that it was a period marked by numerous attempts to discover an escape from the conditions that existed. Such an explanation accounts for whatever hold Socialism was able to get in this country. Alien as the Marxian principles have always been to the distinctively American temperament, they proved to be not wholly without appeal when transplanted to this country after the Civil War. From 1877 on, the Socialist Labor Party played a part in American politics, while throughout the rest of the

90. Cf. *Ibid.*, pp. 63-167.-
91. *Ibid.*, p. 172.
92. Cf. Allyn B. Forbes, "The Literary Quest for Utopia 1880-1900", *Social Forces* VI:179 ff, December, 1927.

century Socialist leaders attempted to secure control of the new working-class movement. A similar explanation underlies the series of agrarian movements culminating in Populism, which had such a profound influence upon the course of nineteenth century American politics".[93]

Doubtless less practical but possessing an immense attraction as a means of fleeing from reality, if not accomplishing needed reform, was literature. And the expression of American idealists in economic and social fiction during the last quarter of the century gains additional significance when it is borne in mind that this was not the first time that the United States had come into close contact with a utopian movement. The three decades before the Civil War had seen the rise and decline of an applied utopianism that had in its course attracted a considerable number of the American people. Its inspiration, however, was European. The factory system and its attendant evils had developed much more rapidly abroad than here. The reflection of these in the thought and writings of Owen, Fourier, and Cabet, is the background of the numerous attempts to establish utopian colonies. The United States was chosen as the site for many of these projects because its vast extent of cheap land afforded ideal conditions for carrying out the foreign theories.[94] For the utopian aspirations of the last quarter of the century, however, there was little free or cheap land to serve as an outlet. Moreover the rapidly increasing industrialization and urbanization had destroyed the degree of isolation which made the organization of the earliest communities seem feasible. Indeed by the end of the Civil War virtually all of the communities except those distinctly religious had disappeared.[95] They had failed partly because the idealism of their founders was

---

93. *Ibid.*, VI:180-181.

94. The Owen and Fourier movements produced nearly all the significant non-religious communistic colonies in America; the former eleven colonies, the latter thirty-four. The Owen epoch was at its height in 1826, the Fourier in 1843. Cf. John Humphrey Noyes, *History of American Socialisms*, pp. 14-20.

95. Cf. John Humphrey Noyes, *History of American Socialisms* (1870) p. 655. Over fifty idealistic communities have been founded in the United States since the Civil War, largely under American auspices. But none have been of any great size or significance. Cf. Samuel P. Orth, *Our Foreigners*, p. 102.

not inherited in sufficient measure by their successors, partly because they attracted and too often accepted persons who came with selfish personal motives rather than with the purpose of contributing to the success of the community, but even more because they had been compelled to make contacts with the outside world and to adopt its competitive methods.[96]

In the failure of the earlier utopian colonies, for the causes just cited, is the negative reason why utopian teaching changed its form of expression from the applied example of an actual community, to a literary picturization and exposition. The positive reason is the great growth in the popularity of the novel— the tremendous increase in the number of readers, and the possibility, therefore of reaching a larger audience.

It must be borne in mind that while most of our utopian novels before 1900 were written during the last fifteen years of the century there were occasional examples of utopian fiction almost from the beginning of the novel in America. Apparently the first utopian novel published in America was *Memoirs of the Year Two Thousand Five Hundred,* which came from the press of Thomas Dobson in Philadelphia in 1795. It was apparently hard for the author of these Memoirs to kick against the pricks, for try as he will to picture for us a new way of life he cannot escape from the old order. What is the form of government? "Is it monarchial, democratic, or aristocratic? It is neither of them; it is rational and made for man." "Our citizens are all equal; the only distinctions we know are those which naturally arise among men from their virtue, their genius, and industry".[97] "That extreme inequality of rank and fortune, the most destructive vice in every political society, is here no longer seen; the meanest citizen has no reason to blush at his condition; he associates with the highest, who disdains not his connection. The law has equalled mankind to the greatest degree in its power; instead of creating those injurious distinctions, that produce nothing but pride on one side, and hatred on the other it has been solicitous to destroy all those obstacles that

---

96. Cf. Allyn B. Forbes, "Literary Quest' for Utopia, 1880-1900", *Social Forces* VI:181, December, 1927.
97. Louis Sebastian Mercier, *Memoirs of the Year 2500,* p. 256

might divide the children of the same mother". The people
pay in taxes one fiftieth part of their annual income. "He that
has no property, or what is only just sufficient for his maintenance, is exempt". There is a coffer, too, for "free gifts". These
furnish "the means of accomplishing every important project
. . . the free gifts frequently amount to more than the tribute".[98]

There is no prostitution. There is free state medicine. All
public officials are prohibited the use of money: it is high treason,
indeed, for them to use it in any way. Everything they need,
"their lodgings, their tables, their diversions, are all charged to
the state", and paid only over the king's signature. The possibility of graft is thereby avoided. The state is "founded
principally on agriculture" and cultivates "interior commerce
only", for "foreign traffic was the real father of that destructive
luxury, which produced in its turn that horrid inequality of
fortunes, which caused all the wealth of the nation to pass into
a few hands".[99] "The most considerable persons in the nation
employ their opulence in discovering the secrets of nature; and
gold, formerly the source of vice and the wages of sloth, rewards
those labours that are subservient to humanity".[100] A creative
instinct has apparently been substituted for the acquisitive in
human nature. How this was done is not made clear.[101]

Charles Brockden Brown was our first native Utopian in
American fiction, and his works, *Alcuin* (1798) and the unfinished
Memoirs of Carwin the Biloquist. But Brown is nowhere very
definite in his program for the new order. He does little more
than hope "that the tasks now assigned to a few might be
divided among the whole; and what now degenerates into cease-
less and brutalizing toil, might by an equitable distribution, be
changed into an agreeable and useful exercise". He is not sure
however but that "this inequality is incurable".[102] The 'Isle'
which serves as the utopian setting of the second part of *Alcuin*
(i. e. parts 3 and 4) is a place of exceedingly indefinite location.

---

98. Louis Sebastian Mercier, *Memoirs of the Year 2500*, p. 286, 300-304.
99. *Ibid.*, p. 307, 311-312.
100. *Ibid.*, p. 214.
101. For further details regarding this book and the other utopian novels
in America see Chapter III of this study.
102. *Alcuin*, p. 25.

The general picture is one of ideality: there is the feeling of complete economic equality, but Alcuin under Mrs. Carter's insistence goes quickly to a specific discussion of the place of women in the society, leaving the general economic order without detailed description.[103]

Carwin of the *Memoirs* is also a character in *Wieland*. Taken to Europe by the mysterious Englishman, Ludloe, he is later sent to Spain to study man and human institutions. On his return to England Ludloe tells him of a political association engaged in a great and arduous design. The details are not divulged but Carwin discovering an atlas with a map of an unknown island country perceives that Ludloe's hope must be to found a new civilization.[104] "This dream of an ideal commonwealth beyond the sea was the most persistent result of Brown's early political speculations. It appears again in *Ormond*".[105] According to Dunlap further evidence of Brown's utopian thought may be found in the fragmentary *Sketches of the History of Carsol*, and *Sketches of the History of the Carrils and Ormes*. These were intended as part of a plan for extensive works combining fiction and history while imitating the air of history; "an Utopian system of manners and government was to complete the whole".[106] The record of Brown's utopian thought, however, is not sufficiently definite to give him any real significance in a study of economic criticism in American fiction.

From the standpoint of this study the same regrettable weakness is to be found in James Kirke Paulding's "The Man Machine, or the Pupil of 'Circumstances' " in *The Merry Tales of the Three Wise Men of Gotham* (1826). The location of the community "so trained as to live without idleness, without poverty, without crime and without punishment, by the mere application of 'circumstances',"[107] is not made clear. In its general purpose the story is a satirization of those who seek the good life for society in the Hobbesian principle that self-love uniformly practised is most conducive to the social good.

---

103. Cf. William Dunlap, *Life of Charles Brockden Brown*, v. I, pp. 77-78.
104. Cf. Lillie Deming Loshe, *Early American Novel*, p. 38.
105. *Ibid.*, p. 39.
106. William Dunlap, *Life of Charles Brockden Brown*, v. I, p. 258.
107. *Merry Tales*, p. 29.

The work, however, is most significant for its protest against "little children, of six or seven years old", laboring a dozen or fourteen hours a day in the mills until their souls have "transmigrated into a spinning jenny" and "actually become a piece of machinery".[108]   Paulding has nothing but reproach for the theory of his utopian "master" that "the Man Machine may, by proper regulation, be so arranged that one man may be able to do the work of twenty".[109]

J. A. Etzler's, *The Paradise* (1833) is an expository setting forth of the Utopia into which this country allegedly could be made. It is contended that virtually all human labor may be done away if we but bethink ourselves and make the possible and proper use of the forces of nature: "1) from wind, 2) from the tide, or the rise and fall of the ocean caused by the gravity between the moon and the ocean, and 3) from the sunshine, or the heat of the sun, by which water may be transformed into steam. . . ." The powers are "sufficient to do in one year more than hitherto all men on earth could do in many thousands of years. . . ." It is further declared that "the most profitable, shortest and easiest way to put them (these forces) into operation for such great purposes is to form associations . . . so as to enable the rich and the poor to participate fully in all the possible greatest benefits of these discoveries. . . ." The way to carry out this idea of associations is to form communities to house the population in great communal dwellings "contrived for lodging thousands of families together".[110]   Each adult is to have an apartment for his exclusive use. Children may be with their parents or live in special quarters. The work of the community not requiring all, since natural forces are so well harnessed, should be "done by turns", and is indeed "an amusement and no tedious occupation or labor'. ". . . The dealings between man and man within the community consist no more in selling as dear as possible and buying as cheap as possible— there is no traffic—because everything is as cheap as water and

---

108. *Ibid.*, pp. 21-24.
109. *Ibid.*, p. 28.
110. *The Paradise,* pp. iv-vi, 71.

as free as air".[111]   Man can now give himself almost wholly to
the pursuit of the beautiful and the good.

To become a member of an association one must pay the
price of at least one share into the treasury.   There is to be
a central congress from the associations which "may extend to
any part of the world".

". . . Man will no more be a slave to work and drudgery and insipid occupations; he will be no longer under the sad necessity to struggle through
life for life; his mind will no longer be absorbed by mechanical pursuits for
his livelihood, for earning money; he will no longer, like a beast of burden,
live but for to work and work but for to live.—What, is man such a poor
miserable creature by nature, that he cannot live without living like a beast
of burden, like a slave?—Is there no better destination of the human being
to be looked for?"[112]

Etzler's answer is yes.   In the Utopia he has sketched man is
liberated from the slavery of work and his mind left free for
superior culture.

Sylvester Judd's *Margaret* (1845) is a representation of economic ideality accomplished by non-economic means.   The principles of Christianity have been applied to the everyday business of life in the New England town of Livingston and the
result is the Utopia so many have been seeking.   A committee
from the State Legislature comes to view it and report for the
benefit of other towns in the state and the nation.   Margaret
Evelyn writes to her friend Anna a 'syllabus' of their report:
"They say our roads are in fine order, in fact none are better
in the state; that the whole town has an aspect of neatness and
thrift; that during all the time of their visit they saw not one
drunken man, while in most towns such characters appeared
without looking for them; . . . that the amount paid for schools
has risen from three or four hundred dollars to two thousand;
that all taxes laid by State and county have been promptly
paid; that our poor have lessened three-quarters; they say also
that the value of real estate in Livingston has advanced twenty
per cent, . . . and that the mania for removing to the West,
which prevails all over New England, has here subsided. . . .
During the last four years, since the enlargement of the jail,

111. *Ibid.,* pp. 75, 83.
112. *Ibid.,* p. 84.

the addition to the comfort of the inmates, and the practice here adopted of visiting them frequently and attending to their moral condition, the recommitments have almost entirely ceased; whereas in former times these constituted nearly one-half of the subjects of prosecution. . . . They add, pleasantly enough, that, while they have been in a hundred houses at all hours of the day, they have not heard a woman speak scandal, or scold her children. . . . Waste lands have been redeemed; sundry improvements in agricultural and mechanical arts adopted, whereby at once is a saving and a profit. Education, Literature, Religion, Recreation, Beauty, Music, Art, Morality, and General Happiness, are things the people enjoy, and for which they are able to pay".[113]

The Crater (1847) by James Fenimore Cooper is a satirization of the socialistic scheme of life and a declaration of Cooper's belief that the only sound government is that of a wise and benevolent minority. An imaginary island in the Pacific is the setting of this tale. Mark Woolston, having discovered the island through a bit of Crusoe fortune, colonizes it and has himself elected Governor. He is supported by a council, also elected for life to prevent "the corrupting influence of politics." When there is a suggestion made "for forming an association in which all property should be shared in common", Woolston refused to entertain the idea. "He was of the opinion that civilization could not exist without property, or property without a direct personal interest in both its accumulation and its preservation".[114] He did not propose to be the "dupe of any of these visionary theories" but to govern "the Crater by precisely the same laws that he would govern Pennsylvania".[115]

"Protect all their rights equally, but that done, let every man pursue his road to happiness in his own way; conceding no more of his natural rights than were necessary to the great ends of peace, security, and law. Such was Mark's theory."[116]

For a considerable time there were in the country no newspapers—"a species of luxury which like the gallows, comes in

113. *Margaret*, pp. 22-273, 286.
114. *The Crater*, p. 324.
115. *Ibid.*, p. 325.
116. *Ibid.*, p. 351.

only as society advances to the corrupt condition. . . ." However, one finally established itself and worked up the resentment of the Craterinos against Governor Mark Woolston. A supposedly representative government by the incapable masses resulted;[117] and life in the Crater became as petty, as mercenary, as unidealistic as life in Jacksonian America.

The Blithedale Romance (1852) is only with qualifications classifiable as a utopian novel. It pictures Brook Farm; and Brook Farm intended to teach the utopian way of life. It is in this sense utopian, for despite Hawthorne's satirization of phases of this actual experiment he believed in the fundamental idea behind the project; he felt "more and more . . . that we had struck upon what ought to be a truth".[118]   The principle of communal labor and communal reward was the basis of the Blithedale project.

"We had left the rusty, iron framework of society behind us; we had broken through many hindrances that are powerful enough to keep most people on the weary treadmill of the established system, even while they feel its irksomeness almost as intolerable as we did. . . . It was our purpose—a generous one, certainly, and absurd, no doubt, in full proportion with its generosity—to give up whatever we had heretofore attained, for the sake of showing mankind the example of a life governed by other than the false and cruel principles on which human society has all along been based. . . . We meant to lessen the laboring man's great burden of toil, by performing our due share of it at the cost of our own thews and sinews. We sought our profit by mutual aid, instead of wresting it by the strong hand from an enemy, or filching it craftily from those less shrewd than ourselves, or winning it by selfish competition with a neighbor. . . ."[119]

But the true idealism of the new order is open to serious question in the mind of the experienced Hawthorne: "The peril of our new way of life was not lest we should fail in becoming practical agriculturalists, but that we should probably cease to be anything else. . . . The clods of earth, which we so constantly belabored and turned over and over, were never etherealized into thought.   Our thoughts, on the contrary, were fast becoming cloddish".[120]

---

117. *Ibid.*, p. 477.
118. *The Blithedale Romance*, p. 351.
119. *Ibid.*, pp. 22-23.
120. *Ibid.*, pp. 90-91.

The Philosopher of Foufouville (1868) by 'Radical Freelance, Esq.' is essentially like *The Blithedale Romance* in its utopian technique. It pictures the "Harmonian colony at Foufouville, New Jersey," with palpable satirization. "Perfect equality shall exist between us", declared the colonists. "All property shall be in common; and we shall depend for our subsistence on the labor of our hands".[121]   But the book devotes more space to the merely amusing than to any effort at serious satire. The disintegration of the Harmonian colony compares to the passing of Blithedale.

Edward Everett Hale's *Ten Times One is Ten* (1871) depicts a possible reformation of the world through the influence of the memory of one man. Clubs are organized to put into effect the life creed of Henry Wadsworth:

> To look forward and not back
> To look up and not down
> To look out and not in,—
> and
> To lend a hand.

In twenty-seven years this doctrine of brotherhood has spread throughout the world, has reached a thousand millions of people. The old economic problems of the earth have disappeared, without the customary economic solutions, in the vast ideality which prevails.

Utopia; or the History of an Extinct Planet (1884) by Alfred Denton Cridge is the story of an imagined civilization "from infancy to dissolution." Its constitution under the stage of life corresponding to modern industrialism was not unlike that of the United States—with fact being as ideal as theory. The spiritual and the material became fused in some pleasant but not very explicitly explained way. All but the faintest trace of private enterprise disappeared. The worker was no longer a subordinate but a part-owner in everything his 'community'— of three hundred families—controlled. Equal wealth was accepted as the proof of strength and prosperity. Money was still in use but the degree of its fluctuation in value rigidly governed by law; and into the constitution it was written that

---

121. *The Philosopher of Foufouville*, p. 9.

"no private debt shall ever be considered binding or just, and no public debt shall ever be incurred for any object or under any circumstances".[122] Much of the story is given to explaining the lighter, non-economic phenomena of the planet Utopia. Science, art, and literature flourished. Inhabitants of the Great countries of Liberia and Sunland acknowledged themselves possessors of the perfect society.

The purpose of Henry F. Allen's *The Key of Industrial Cooperative Government* (1886) is "to show advantages of the Industrial cooperative over the Competitive form of government".[123] This is done by picturing universal cooperation on the planet Venus—"a collective system: there was no individual exchange of production".[124] The products of compulsory labor went into a common fund from which each was supplied according to his wants. Thus was it possible to completely do away with money, and the enslavement of the many to the few which money has always caused. Surprisingly enough these drastic changes were accomplished by peaceful legislation.

Allen occasionally drops his utopian perspective and attacks the problems of the United States directly. The land and tax problems particularly interest him. "We must stop the sale of any more public lands" except to individuals intending to personally use them. Land should be taxed on the "accumulative plan of doubling itself for every additional quarter section of acres added to the specified first legal holding. This would stop the stealings of corporations through legislative corruption and keep the lands available to the masses, for the excessive taxes would make them unprofitable to hold for speculative or other purpose than working a limited number of acres. . . ."[125] There should be, contends Allen, a graduated capital tax after the first ten thousand dollars of property, doubling with each additional five thousand. More strenuous punishment for malfeasance in office is also advocated. Economic planning on Venus is inferred and urged for the United States: "The legisla-

---

122. *Utopia; or the History of an Extinct Planet,* p. 19.
123. *The Key to Industrial Cooperative Government,* p. 9.
124. *Ibid.,* p. 34.
125. *Ibid.,* p. 44.

tion of the future must harmonize production with distribution and prevent any interference with the natural rights of others, and thus prove the way for cooperative equity".[126]

Anna Bowman Dodd's *The Republic of the Future, or Socialism a Reality* (1887) takes a negative view of the socialist program of life. It is the year 2050, and America has been socialistic since 1900. The nationalistic plan has been tried and found wanting: everything is "run by the government on government capital", and it "has resulted in the most deadening uniformity".[127] Each house is furnished by state law exactly alike, "hideous, bare, and plain".[128] An effort is made to refute the single-tax gospel: "Machinery was the true cause of the conflict between capital and labor, and not the unequal distribution of land, as the great founder of this communal society, Henry George, asserted in this book (*Progress and Poverty*), the bible of this people. . . . Machinery needed capital to run it and was more or less indifferent to labor."[129] The mechanical wonders here are quite like those in the positive Utopias. Labor was limited to two hours a day to prevent over-production. Out of this leisure grew marked intellectual classes. Many were "mind sluggards", a minority were intellectually enterprising. And out of this grew an aristocracy of intellect "as dangerous to the state as an aristocracy founded on pride of descent or on the possession of ancestral acres. It became necessary therefore to make a law against learning and the sciences" . . . that they should "not be carried beyond a certain fixed standard attainable by all".[130] This novel is a full-fledged defense of individualism; it pictures the socialized Utopia only to satirize it.

In 1888 came the most important and best remembered of all these utopian novels—Edward Bellamy's *Looking Backward*. It was read by hundreds of thousands of people; influenced the thought of many subsequent utopian novelists — including Howells—and wrought great effect upon the social mindedness of the people as a whole. Since socialistic clubs, like the National-

---

126. *Ibid.*, p. 54.
127. *The Republic of the Future*, p. 21.
128. *Ibid.*, p. 32.
129. *Ibid.*, pp. 46-47.
130. *Ibid.*, p. 66.

ist, were in so large number born from its ideas it is interesting that the book was not intended as serious propaganda at all. Writing in the *Nationalist* for May, 1889, Bellamy stated:

In undertaking to write *Looking Backward* I had, at the outset, no idea of attempting a serious contribution to the movement of social reform. The idea was a mere literary fantasy, a fairy tale of social felicity. There was no thought of contriving a house which practical men might live in, but merely of building in mid-air, far out of reach of the sordid and material world, of the present, a cloud-palace for an ideal humanity".[131]

From an economic and social outlook the plan of reform in *Looking Backward* is all inclusive. We may say, however, that the social order of the imagined America of the year 2000 revolved around one central fact:

"The nation was organized as the one great business corporation in which all other corporations were absorbed; it became the one capitalist in the place of all other capitalists, the sole employer, the final monopoly in which all previous and lesser monopolies were swallowed up, a monopoly in the profits and economies of which all citizens shared. The Epoch of Trusts had ended in the Great Trust."[132]

All between the ages of twenty-one and forty-five, women as well as men, were required to become members of the Industrial Army. As a mmber of the Army "a man's natural endowment, mental and physical", determined what he could work at most profitably to the nation and most satisfactorily to himself. The wage system was abolished, and in place of the familiar forms of currency there were introduced "credit cards", issued annually and representing an equal share in the national wealth. (About $6,000 per citizen measured by the standard of 1887.) "The nation guarantees the nurture, education and comfortable maintenance of every citizen from the cradle to the grave."[133]

Such were the outstanding features in Bellamy's so-called Nationalism. He could not, however, resist sniping away directly at individual institutions of his own day. "Interest on Investments", he defines as "a species of tax in perpetuity upon the product of those engaged in industry, which a person possessing

---

131. "How I Came to Write Looking Backward", *Nationalist*, I:1, May, 1889.
132. Bellamy, Edward, *Looking Backward*, p. 56.
133. *Ibid.*, p. 90.

or inheriting was able to levy."[134]   Or again: "securities may
be described as so many kinds of harness, by which the masses,
broken and tamed by the pressure of want, were yoked and
strapped to the chariots of capitalists".[135]

The utopian situation of *Looking Backward* is continued in
Equality, which Bellamy published nine years later, in 1897.
In this sequel Bellamy essayed a critical examination of economic
history with a view of creating an adequate social economics.
The earlier work had drawn the outlines of the democratic
society of the future, the later supplied a .justification and a
commentary.   The theme involved a two-fold problem: an
analysis of the failure of social justice under private capitalism,
and a defense of the working of social capitalism in the new order.

Bellamy is undoubtedly much more serious in his second
treatment of the Utopian theme than in his first.   There is less
story, less art; he is preaching with his fist.

"Undoubtedly the confusion of terms in our political systems is rather cal-
culated to puzzle one at first, but if you only grasp firmly the vital point
that the rule of the rich, the supremacy of copital and its interests, as against
those of the people at large, was the central principle of our system, to which
every other interest was made subservient, you will have the key that clears
up the mystery".[136]

"The foundation principle of the whole property system was not ability,
effort, or desert of any kind whatever, but merely the accident of birth, than
which no claim could more completely mock at ethics".[137]

If competition entails irretrievable waste, Bellamy insists,
the system of competitive profit leads to economic suicide.[138]
The increased concentration of wealth through the accumulation
of profits can only result eventually in the complete destruction
of the market.[139]   The problem of achieving economic equality
is the fundamental concern of democracy; without this, liberty
and fraternity, and equality before the law are a delusion and
a snare.

Walter Besant's *The Inner House* (1888) is another protest

134. *Ibid.*, p. 10.
135. Bellamy, Edward, *Equality*, p. 96.
136. *Ibid.*, p. 13.
137. *Ibid.*, p. 109.
138. Cf. *Ibid.*, Chapter XXII.
139. Bellamy illustrates this effectively with the water-tank parable,
Equality, p. 195.

against the dead level which socialism would allegedly bring. Mechanical proficiency makes it necessary that men should work only five hours at day, but even so there is a decided "lack of zeal" in their labor.[140]   Faces are becoming ever more similar. Perhaps, Besant suggests, some day all will be alike, even sex making no difference: "Then there will be, from first to last, among the whole multitude neither distinction nor difference".[141] The significant economic thesis of this book and other satirizations of the utopian dream, is that a sound, progressive society depends upon a policy of economic individualism.

The Twentieth Century (1889) by D. Herbert Heywood has no significance as an economic treatise. Heywood is interested only in inventive, industrial accomplishment; not in the class conflict. He believes with another gullible idealist, Ulysses S. Grant, that "God is preparing the world to become one nation, to speak one language, and to attain to a state of perfection in which armies, fleets, and commerce will be no longer needed."[142]

Arthur Dudley Minton's *Looking Further Backward* (1890) is an obvious attempt to capitalize upon the popularity of the Bellamy book. Vinton believes that our present government can be legally modified to correct all evils, and has in this story endeavored "to point out wherein the Bellamy nationalism would prove disastrously weak". Bellamy's utopian "remedies for the evils which exist today are fraught with danger". But of course much of his thought has obvious merit: "the comparison of our social system to a coach whereon a few persons sit in indolence, while the vast majority, driven by hunger, toil at the ropes and drag the coach along, has appealed to every honest mind by its truthfulness".[143] Vinton like Bellamy sees a serious cancer in the social body in class inequality and injustice based on superior economic power. "Corrupt judges on the bench", he complains, "and partisan grand juries in the precincts of the courts have made one law for the rich and another for the poor".[144] The Vinton criticisms of Bellamy are these: inade-

---

140. *The Inner House*, p. 30.
141. *Ibid.*, p. 35.
142. *The Twentieth Century*, p. 47.
143. *Looking Further Backward*, p. 5.
144. *Ibid.*, p. 5.

quate national defense; individualism reduced to a minimum; woman competes with man—she should be the "handmaiden of male humanity". Although Vinton proposes to fear the ultimate lengths of Bellamy's socialism his withholding of approval impresses one as being only tentative. However, his book is of no large consequence among these utopian novels.

Of particular interest in our utopian fiction is *Caesar's Column* (1890) by Ignatius Donnelly. Probably no other writer of this group "played an important part for so long a time in the reform agitations of the nineteenth century. For several years he was president of the State Farmer's Alliance of Minnesota. In 1876 he was presiding officer of the National Anti-Monopoly Convention that nominated Peter Cooper for President. For five years he published at Minneapolis a reform journal known as *The Representative*. In 1900 he was nominated by the People's Party for the Vice-Presidency".[145]

The greater part of *Caesar's Column* is devoted to a description of the downfall of civilization in the closing years of the twentieth century. The proletariat rises and by force of arms overthrows the plutocratic bourgeoise in a great revolution beginning in 1988. World-wide anarchism ensues.

Arguing from the basis that "civilization is a gross and dreadful failure for seven-tenths of the human family",[146] and that our government, "courts, judges, and juries are the merest tools of the rich",[147] Donnelly advocates a number of remedies for the evils which exist in our society.

"I should do away with all interest on money. Interest on money is the root and ground of the world's troubles. It puts one man in a position of safety, while another is in a condition of insecurity, and thereby it at once creates a radical distinction in society. . . . If money could not be loaned, it would have to be put out by the owner of it in business enterprises which would employ labor."[148]

Donnelly would change all laws, customs or conditions which "gave any man an advantage over any other man",[149] or which

---

145. Allyn B. Forbes, "Literary Quest for Utopia" in *Social Forces*, VI:184, December, 1927.
146. *Caesar's Column*, p. 40.
147. *Ibid.*, p. 32.
148. *Ibid.*, pp. 116-117.
149. *Ibid.*, p. 119.

tended to concentrate wealth in the hands of the few. He would establish a maximum wealth limit. "It is right and wise and proper for men to accumulate sufficient wealth to maintain their age in peace, dignity, and plenty, and to be able to start their children into the arena of life sufficiently equipped".[150] But when a man makes over the prescribed limit, his surplus should be taken for the building of hospitals, colleges, galleries, and "national railroads that would bring the productions of the farmers to the workmen at the least cost of transportation, and free from the exactions of speculators and middlemen".[151] Donnelly would also limit the amount of land that one individual may hold, to from one hundred to five hundred acres; he would abolish all corporations and substitute for them partnerships; he would withdraw political patronage from the control of the Executive; he would deny office-holders the right to vote while holding office and make corruption of the voter or the office-holder an act of highest treason; he would have state ownership of all roads, streets, telephone and telegraph lines, railroads and mines; he would have Congress fix the rate of compensation for all labor; he would have a paper currency of international circulation based on "all the property of the civilized world," and "deny gold and silver any function as money except for small amounts"; he would have state medicine.[152] Donnelly's summary of the situation is this: "Government—national, state, and municipal—is the key to the future of the human race. . . . We have but to expand the powers of government to solve the enigma of the world".[153]

F. U. Worley's *Three Thousand Dollars a Year* (1890) sees Utopia attained through a gradual extension of the cooperative principle of social organization. Starting with a few stores— the successful Rochdale system in England is the model utopian fictionists have in mind when they argue in this manner—giving customers a percentage dividend on the amount of their purchases the principle gradually spread to all distributive and

---

150. *Ibid*, p. 119.
151. *Ibid.*, p. 120.
152. Cf. *Ibid.*, pp. 354-361.
153. *Ibid.*, p. 129.

productive industries. Beginning with municipalities government, too, took up the cooperative principle—assuming ownership and operation of all communication and transportation agencies: "the owners were fully indemnified for the cost of construction and equipment; all new works were afterwards built and operated by the city authorities."[154] The Federal government followed the municipal example by purchasing all railroads, mines, and finally all industries of every kind, printing a huge issue of greenbacks to finance the transactions.[155] A National Postal Savings Bank was established, paying 2% interest on all money. The population was divided into three classes; adolescent, 0-25 years; active, 25 to 50; honorary 50—. Free general education to the age of twenty-one was the order of life; this was followed by the selection of a vocation and four years of special training. Each "active" citizen received $250 a month; each family head $600 a year additional for every adolescent. Between the ages of twenty-one and twenty-five each individual received $1500 yearly.[156] All the American people were housed in a manner befitting sovereigns".[157] The new constitution adopted in 2001 abolished entirely the old governmental organization and placed the management of national affairs in the hands of a Congress of counsellors elected from the different industries. Looking at the beautiful picture he has drawn Worley concludes:

> "As Christ once drove the money-changers from the Temple, so have the Christ spirit and the Christ principle driven the money grabbers, with all their pernicious influences and false valuations of human worth from the hallowed precincts of a purified government".[158]

John Bachelder, author of *A. D. 2050* (1890) has studied Bellamy's *Looking Backward* and thinks its "scientific and material development" inadequate and unworthy of the passage of time;[159] and from the utopian perspective of the mid-twenty-first century sees the fading and supplanting of communism all

154. *Three Thousand Dollars a Year*, p. 20.
155. *Ibid.*, pp. 30-43, 72.
156. *Ibid.*, p. 50.
157. *Ibid.*, p. 54.
158. *Ibid.*, p. 98.
159. *A. D. 2050*, p. 3.

over the world in the preceding twenty-five years because of the "gaseous volcanic elements" which had arisen to prove its unsoundness. With these Bellamy weaknesses in his mind Bachelder has his Captain Jones discover the island of Atlantis and establish there the real Utopia. Among the reform measures which he advocates under this guise are: individual wealth to be limited to $100,000; rate of interest limited; amendment to the Constitution by a two-thirds vote of all the people; national hospitals and national nurseries—with parents expected to visit their children once a day; no marginal sales of stock; the right of operatives to buy shares in the companies in which they are employed.[160] The government of Atlantis makes no foolish attempt to mold all men into the same likeness; it recognizes "a wide difference in the physical as well as mental and moral conditions in the human family" and proposes to "provide for the protection of all".[161]

The Utopia which William Simpson offers in *The Man from Mars* (1891) is primarily a Henry George, single-tax accomplishment. There is no condemnation of the division of society into two classes; indeed the people of Mars believe it is "a natural and a just one"; and that "there is nothing whatever in it to prevent the largest possible amount of happiness to all. . . . "We acknowledge as the foundation of all material progress that the honest accumulation of wealth should be the privilege of all; and that the rights of property should be protected, and the enjoyment of it secured to everyone. Yet with these principles firmly and successfully carried out in our government, we have for many centuries, considered it necessary to support and sustain the interests of the labor class by special legislative attention. You have pursued a directly opposite course".[162] The great evil of American society lies in our land policy which "enables the few to dominate the many".[163] Simpson proposes to remedy this condition by dividing the land "into small farms" with rent according to the richness of the soil; there should be

---

160. *Ibid.*, pp. 9, 16, 33, 60.
161. *Ibid.*, p. 16.
162. *The Man from Mars*, p. 67.
163. *Ibid.*, p. 71.

no sub-letting. Rent graded according to the profits of the land
is the only equitable basis of taxation, declares the Man from
Mars: "Our government derives its sole support from rent, and
no other tax or exaction is known".[164]   A national economic
planning board is urged through the example of Mars which
has a bureau of statistics that has enabled it to save its population "from the distress of over-production, and the chance
occurrences of uneven labor demand".[165]   "All public necessities
(*i. e.* utilities) of general demand . . . should be provided by
the government".[166]   It should be noted that in the literary
skill of its plot structure *The Man from Mars* is, among these
utopian novels, a very able book.[167]

Walter H. McDougal's *The Hidden City* (1891), is the picturization of a lost town of twenty-five hundred people somewhere in the canyons of the Rockies, people who have never
known anything but the ancient Aztec civilization.   The lost
canyon is transformed into Utopia by organizing the 'Hidden
City' into a great stock company—its earnings to be "divided
among the people; its government is by a board of directors.[168]

Francis Howard William's *Atman* is a utopian story which is
economic only in its remotest implications.[169]   It offers no program of social reform.

Chauncey Thomas apparently felt some confusion as to how
the ideality pictured in *The Crystal Button* (1891) could be
attained.   He attempted to guard himself against the semblance
of being revolutionary by placing all of his emphasis upon
higher ethical standards and an informed public opinion. "Truth!
Truth!" is the text here, and both author and editor feel that
"whatever Socialism and Nationalism may or may not accomplish, this lesson of truth-loving and truth-observing is certainly
a kind of seed that can hardly fail to produce good fruit. . . ."
Life in Thomas' Utopia, however, has many things in common
with Bellamy's ideal Boston.   "Government and people drew

---

164.   *Ibid.,* p. 75.
165.   *Ibid.,* p. 96.
166.   *Ibid.,* p. 119.
167.   Cf. Chapter III, p. 233 of this study.
168.   *The Hidden City,* p. 309.
169.   Cf. Chapter III, p. 234 of this study.

closer in their mutual relations. . . . Even in your day", says Professor Prosper to Paul Prognosis, "it was one of the signs of the times that small interests were beginning to be absorbed by corporations, and those by giant monopolies.   By slow and peaceful steps the same movement progressed, until the Government itself came into possession of such industries as were of peculiarly public interest, including all means of communication and transportation, and life and fire insurance; and the land question was settled in the same manner".[170]   This nationalized land was then leased to individual occupants.   In taking over industries the Government simply guaranteed a "certain rate of interest to the former proprietors for a certain period".[171] Government annuities for rich and poor were the chief form of investment.   Money still existed and was used for things not free.[172]   A heavy income tax was levied for the avowed purpose of leveling the inequalities of wealth.   Doubtless suggested by Bellamy but worked out in considerably less detail is the idea of an Industrial Army.   The keystone of Thomas' program is the substitution for a gold currency of one based on the world's surplus of food products, distributed each decade in proportion to the world's population.   The old enemy of society, speculation, was thus substantially destroyed.

Amos K. Fiske, author of *Beyond the Bourn* (1891) is like Thomas in being in perfect sympathy with Bellamy's ultimate ideal, and in fearing some of Bellamy's basic propositions.   He felt, for example that the equal distribution of wealth would dull individual initiative and produce a dead level of uniformity. Fiske's ideal government is based on the principle "that the results of the united labors of the community belonged of right to that community for the satisfaction of the rational wants of every member.   No man was regarded as having any right to a superfluity while another was in need".[173]   The achievement of this state of brotherly solicitation was "attained by the growth and development of individual character. . . .   Those of

---

170. *The Crystal Button*, p. 244.
171. *Ibid.*, p. 245.
172. *Ibid.*, p. 271.
173. *Beyond the Bourn*, p. 98.

superior capacity learned that they exercised a stewardship for the benefit of others. . . . The difference between public and private interests is well nigh obliterated by the constant and universal application of the principles of unselfishness. . . ."[174] In another place, however, Fiske definitely embraces the nationalistic program with the provision for public control of "all appliances of common use", and the abolition of all private property in land. Whatever the confusion in his mind regarding the method of attainment, Fiske was in other respects thoroughly convinced that his ideal would be realized as soon as society discovered that each one's happiness depended upon his assuring every other one an opportunity equal to his own.

Published in New York in 1891 were also two utopian novels translated from the German—*Freeland* by Dr. Theodor Hertzka, a Viennese economist, and *Mr. East's Experiences in Mr. Bellamy's World*, a German's denial of the ideality of Nationalism. Both merit mention in this study: the former because it is the acknowledged source of the ideas of several of our native utopian fictionists, and the latter because it is perhaps the most explicit fictional refutation of Bellamy's socialistic brief. Conrad Wilbrandt the author of the latter novel maintains that Dr. Leete, expositor of Bellamy's new order, looked at things through rose-colored glasses. He shows that the blighting sameness and the economic inefficiency of Bellamy's scheme more than nullify its virtues.

Hertzka's influential work is based on the thesis that Labor is the only producer of wealth and that the laborer should have the "full proceeds of his own work";[175] that "thoughtlessness and inaction are, in truth, at present the only props of the existing economic and social order".[176] "I perceived he declares that capitalism stops the growth of wealth, not—as Marx has it—by stimulating 'production for the market', but by preventing the consumption of the surplus produce; and that interest, though not unjust, will nevertheless in a condition of economic justice become superfluous and objectless. . . . If interest can

174. *Ibid.*, pp. 103, 107, 109.
175. *Freeland*, p. x.
176. *Ibid.*, p. 442.

be dispensed with without introducing communistic control in its stead, then there no longer stands any positive obstacle in the way of the establishment of the free social order".[177] The establishment of a 'Freeland Colony' is proposed; it is to be based on the following principles: (1) No exclusive right of property in the land either on part of an individual or the collective community; (2) Associations sharing profits according to the several contributions to the common labor of the association; (3) Anyone may belong and leave when he wills; (4) Capital shall be furnished to the producers out of the revenue of the community, without interest, but must be reimbursed; (5) All persons incapable of labor shall receive an allowance; (6) Public revenue for public expense provided by a tax levied upon the net income of the total production.[178]

M. Louise Moore's *Al-Modad, or Life Scenes Beyond the Polar Circumflex* (1892) is "a religio-scientific solution of the problems of the present and future life". The appeal is chiefly on a religious basis. Miss Moore's chief, if not only, economic tenet is that we can do away with speculation by abolishing artificial money, and basing the price of all goods according to the labor of production.

San Salvador (1892) by Mary Agnes Tincker is as an economic treatise exceedingly indefinite. It purports to be a picture of "San Salvador, the city of the Holy King"—somewhere along the northern coast of Africa—whose ideality has been achieved by the practical application of the teachings of Jesus. "Unless the Lord build the house they labor in vain that build it", contends Miss Tincker.[179] The brotherhood of complete communism is implied.

Samuel Crocker's *That Island* (1892) attacks public utilities interests and Congress for their mutual corruption in giving hyper-profitable franchises to private interests at the expense of the public.[180] It denounces, too, mortgage oppression, and the foreclosures whereby capitalists are gradually getting all of the

---

177. *Ibid.,* p. xxi.
178. *Ibid.,* p. xxi.
179. *San Salavdor,* p. 267.
180. *That Island,* pp. 28-29.

land: "By contraction and expansion of the currency capitalists [have] amassed princely fortunes, and finally [have] depressed industry to such a degree as to force land and labor down to a point of cheapness and dependence truly alarming".[181] The chief measures of reform advocated by Crocker are these: abolition of the protective tariff, nationalization of all means of communication, and the establishment of a "postal sub-treasury system"— taking the place of banks—which should sponsor a gigantic inflation and thereby foster prosperity.[182]

Henry L. Everett's *The People's Program* (1892) chronicles a world-wide student movement in the interests of better conditions for the laboring classes. Religion is curiously, almost sacrilegiously, mixed in with the economic matter of this book. Streeter, for example, writing to James Emmet regarding a strike at Lawrence, Massachusetts, says: "I have even begun to convey by hints to all workingmen whom I meet a desire for concerted simultaneous prayer on the part of a great multitude for some proof of the power of God to answer prayer".[183]   For, argues Everett in a footnote, "The power of prayer being once conceded, the only course for us to pursue is to lead men to accept Christianity", and then pray; thereby overcoming their enemies, the capitalists, without labor and without price. Among the more earthy and commonplace reforms suggested by Everett were: boards of arbitration for all labor disputes: variation in labor—a miner, for example, should work outside half of the time; taxation of all private inheritances in estates exceeding $50,000; pensions for all persons over seventy years of age who make application for them; government ownership and operation of all railroads and telegraphs; and "free coinage". Everett wants his originality to receive its due credit; writing from his utopian perspective, he declares: "The plans which were now attaining realization for the amelioration of mankind were not the suggestions of Edward Bellamy; they were not precisely the purpose of the socialists; they were evolved from the productive brain of George Streeter, and were enlarging the happiness

---

181. *Ibid.*, pp. 32-33.
182. *Ibid.*, p. 127.
183. *The People's Program*, p. 135.

of humanity infinitely more than all the programs of socialist reformers and labor parties. In fact they achieved for the world improvements which the socialists liked better than their own plans".[184]

A fiction that out-utopias even the most extravagant of other forecasts of the future is Will N. Harben's short story "In the Year Ten Thousand", published in the *Arena* for November, 1892. Even speech no longer exists; people merely read each other's thoughts. Everyone can disengage himself from gravitation at will. Life is so changed that every economic phase of existence has long since disappeared and been forgotten. Naturally, such a conception defies any definite description.

In *The Future Commonwealth* (1892) Albert Chavannes declares his belief that the necessary changes can be made "without resorting to such revolutionary methods as would never meet with the approval of sensible and practical men". "I claim", he says, "that our economic condition is the logical outcome of our present religious belief, and that both must change together if any progress is to be achieved. . . . Nationalism, in fact, will only prove acceptable in so far as it will know how to reconcile economic organization with personal liberty. . . . I not only believe that it can be done, but I feel confident that it will be done".[185]

Picturing a country which he calls Socioland, somewhere in Africa in the year 1950, Chavannes recommends a number of social and economic reforms. He advocates State control of wholesale trade, all facilities of communication and transportation, light and water companies, mines, banks, life and fire insurance organizations, "and a portion of the manufactures"— with local control in suitable cases.[186] The commonwealth should hold the land "in trust for the whole people", and merely "sell leases, equal for practical purposes to complete ownership". Speculation would be abolished by giving the commonwealth the right to hold or reclaim what it wants at "reasonable rates".[187]

---

184. *Ibid.*, p. 207.
185. *The Future Commonwealth*, pp. iii-vi.
186. *Ibid.*, pp. 28-29.
187. *Ibid.*, p. 29.

Chavannes published a second utopian novel, *In Brighter Climes* in 1895. It continued his picture of the ideal life of Socioland.

"Every citizen of Socioland is a member of a political organization which owns and controls the largest share of the means of production, and sees to it that what is privately owned is so distributed that no citizen can appropriate more products than he can dispose of to the advantage of the community. By so doing we insure an adequate consumption for all we can produce, and as a natural result there is no difficulty to furnish every man with work".[188]

The commonwealth furnishes free bread and laundry to all. There are no taxes. A national employment bureau puts men in touch with the kinds of positions they desire. Private property is not legally forbidden, but the vast cooperative, communistic services of the State make private enterprise negligible, and undesirable. To Chavannes' mind "the unpleasant state of things in . . . the United States is not the result of the will of the capitalists, but of inherent defects in the whole system".[189]

The key which Henry Olerich offers in *A Cityless and Country-less World* (1893) for unlocking the difficulties of society is the idea of practical cooperative individualism. In essence it amounts to a developed fusion of the principles of Fourier and Owen. In a Mars setting Olerich pictures the distribution of population between urban and rural districts as done away. The country is divided into rectangular tracts the size of four American townships; in each of these is a 'big house' serving as the home for a thousand men, women, and children. Electric car lines connect the different houses. Each 'community' has its quota of factories and warehouses—with manufactures and commerce always in accordance with the nature of the resources peculiar to each area. Distribution between the various communities was carried on without profit. Agriculture followed the same procedure as manufacturing. By the very organization of society private ownership of land was not permitted.[190] The individualistic features of the Olerich Utopia lie in the arrangements as to labor and currency. The idea of money as a single commodity was abandoned. The medium of exchange was "labor

---

188. *In Brighter Climes*, p. 40.
189. *Ibid.*, p. 40.

checks", which represented the amount of each person's work, measured in time units. There were day, hour, minute, and second notes. The average labor was two hours a day.[191] The two-fold principle underlying this was that no one should receive what he had not earned by his own productive labor, and that the medium of exchange should equal the value of the actually existing wealth. Thus was abolished that type of capitalism resulting from the ability of a few to gain a monopoly, and also all forms of credit and interest.[192]

J. W. Roberts' *Looking Within* (1893) is chiefly devoted to pointing out the misleading tendencies of *Looking Backward*. Roberts feels that Bellamy's Nationalism is but a "quack nostrum" for the thousand ills the flesh is heir to, and insists that the polemical *Looking Backward* ignores "the great middle class of the people, constituting a majority of all".[193] Roberts also bitterly assails the labor unions and their 'walking delegate' methods: "It is the right of every free man to quit working for any man, firm or corporation at pleasure, when not bound by contract. . . . If he tries to prevent another workman from taking the place he has vacated, he is a tyrant." Harsh treatment of scabs by the rough element of unions is scathingly indicated: "With such a record how can labor have the face to ask for favors".[194] In the way of constructive criticism Roberts recommends the setting up of government machinery to prevent watered stock and other dishonest capitalistic schemes, and suggests, profit-sharing, cooperative operation of individual industries, if the originators and workers involved so desire. But he has only ridicule and denouncement for paternalism and communism.

Joaquin Miller's *The Building of the City Beautiful* (1893) is a religious fantasy rather than an economic treatise, but is not without definite socialistic import. 'Competition is the life of trade', Miller quotes with scorn; he declares that "these old sayings are more than millstones about the neck of the world. . . .

190. *A Cityless and Countryless World,* pp. 50-60.
191. *Ibid.,* p. 176.
192. *Ibid.,* p. 178.
193. *Looking Within,* p. 13.
194. *Ibid.,* pp. 19, 21.

Man succeeds, with all [his] evil and ill-doing, in making unequal that which God made equal".[195]   In the City Beautiful all
is equality and brotherhood.

The Beginning (1893) is "a romance of Chicago as it might
be", by an anonymous author. The proposition it first considers
is whether "the People's party's platform if adopted by the
country and put in force and extended as it would have to be
. . . would benefit the great mass of working men, that is raise
the masses". The answer of the workingmen's debating club
from whose discussions this book allegedly arose is 'no'. Its
program offers a too strict discipline, which would interfere
with American freedom of individual enterprise. "The ideal
state will be when we have arrived at that stage of moral perfection where we can dispense with all government control".[196]
How can we arrive there? The answer: levy a tax of six per
cent of every will probated (most inheritances represent "unearned increment" at any rate) and use the money for the
establishment of free national colleges, and the promoting of
other educational and social measures. More stringent child
labor laws, and legislation to more severely penalize corrupt
election and general governmental graft practices are also advocated.

Charles Elliot Niswonger's *The Isle of Feminine* (1893) has
no economic significance. However, the air of unbroken happiness about the Isle permits the unsupported inference that here
is absolute equality not only among things useful, but those
beautiful and good as well.

Solomon Schindler's *Young West* (1894) labels itself "a sequel
to Edward Bellamy's celebrated novel, Looking Backward",
and is a palpable attempt to capitalize upon the fame of the
Bellamy book, without adding a single element to its criticism.
It is the story of Julian West, Jr., as he moves from the municipal nursery through life to a ripe old age. Here, as in a number of our other utopian novels, the author's imagination and
memory bog down, and he forgets at places the marvels his
elaborate machines can do.

---

195. *The Building of the City Beautiful*, pp. 25-26, 155.
196. *The Beginning*, pp. 3-4.

King C. Gillette's *The Human Drift* (1894) advocates "material equality", and "the foundation of a united stock company by the people, of sufficient magnitude to gradually absorb and finally control production and distribution, such company having in view the destruction of all tributary industries of the present system which do not contribute or are not necessary to the production and distribution of the necessities of life".[197] The book presents a "Prospectus of The United Company": nominal capital one thousand million dollars—actual capital unlimited. Shares one dollar each. Gillette was really trying to organize such a company through this book; a certificate of subscription is printed and the reader is asked to "sign and return . . . to the publishers, Boston".[198] The organization was to be effected and stock issued when one hundred million dollars had been subscribed; but there is no record that the enterprise reached this stage.

From Earth's Center (1894) by S. Byron Welcome is a concentric-spheres Utopia with some exceedingly romantic and ridiculous features. The elements of its reform program are, however, seriously proposed; they are similar to those of the general run of our utopian novels. The Henry George single-tax, upon land values only, is the fundamental tenet of Welcome's utopian doctrine. The tax should be "levied to within ten per cent of the annual rental value of the land".[199] Railroads should be government owned and operated; street railways should be municipally owned and furnish transportation free of charge. All inventions should be common property, with royalties paid by Congress. The amount of money should be increased proportionally to the growth of the population and the growth of the products of labor.[200]

Will N. Harben's *The Land of the Changing Sun* (1894) is an extravaganza even as Utopias go. Balloonists Thorndyke and Johnston come down on an unmarked island in an unnamed sea, and a submarine takes them to the cave Kingdom of Alpha,

---

197. *The Human Drift*, p. vi.
198. *Ibid.*, p. 30.
199. *From Earth's Center*, p. 95.
200. *Ibid.*, pp. 90, 105, 158.

where everything is electrical, even the sun. There is no developed economic criticism, save what may be inferred from the fact that at the end of the story the Alphan king divides all the property of the realm equally among his people.

From William Dean Howells' brooding upon the dark days of the panic of 1893 came the first of his two Utopian romances, *The Traveller from Altruria* (1894) subjecting our system of capitalism to minute analysis. Here is a contrast of our democratic professions without plutocratic practice set against a Marxian background. The Age of Accumulation was marked by increasingly larger monopolies. And then at precisely the right moment the Altrurians by a great popular vote achieved the nationalization of all forms of business. The entire economic structure was changed to bring everything into line with what had been accomplished. Through the scrapping of a large part of the railroad system—and here is an example of Howells' attack on some specific part of the American economic structure—which had hitherto been disastrously destructive, a blow was struck at the huge urban centers which had grown up in its wake. This in turn made possible a complete revision of the conditions of labor. Money, too, could now be abolished. Each did his share of the nation's labor, and each shared equally the nation's wealth. The results were the theoretical ones outlined in other Utopias. Nationalization and the disuse of money had removed that great source of social injustice—speculation. Crime, the inevitable consequence of the institution of private property, disappeared. One hour of toil sufficed where twelve had been needed before; labor was emancipated.

Howells completed his utopian study with *Through the Eye of the Needle* in 1907. Mr. Homos, the 'Traveller' continues as the central character. Howells in urbane satire apologizes for the misapprehensions of the Altrurian:

"He is entangled in his social sophistries regarding all the competitive civilizations; he cannot apparently do full justice to the superior heroism of charity and self-sacrifice as practiced in countries where people live upon each other as the Americans do, instead of for each other as the Altrurians do. . . ."201

---

201. *Through the Eye of the Needle,* p. v.

Transferring his scene from New York to Altruria Howells sketches in fuller detail the order of life there, depicting the kindly, rational society that emerged when men learned that cooperation is better than competition, altruism than egotism. ". . . Logically" Howells argues "the Americans should be what the Altrurians are, since their polity embodies our belief that all men are born equal, with the right to life, liberty and the pursuit of happiness; but illogically they are what the Europeans are, since they still cling to the economical ideals of Europe, and hold that men are born socially unequal, and deny them the liberty and happiness which can come from equality alone."[202] The artist type is the ideal in Altruria: the Altrurians work gladly for the joy of creating.[203]

Castello N. Holford's *Aristopia* (1895) is of singular technique among utopian novels. Instead of imagining the future it pictures the present as it would have been if certain fundamental humanitarian changes would have been wrought in the past. No private ownership of land is the central economic fact in the ideal state of Aristopia; agricultural lands may be leased for no longer than fifteen years; urban no longer than fifty. Leases are renewable. All traffic in merchandise must be by public agency, with any profits as public revenue. A deceased person's wealth is to be divided equally among his heirs, though not more than $10,000 may be inherited by any one person. Whatever is over this escheats to the commonwealth.[204] An inventor is given the exclusive patent rights to his invention, unless the state desires its use—in which case a royalty of not more than $10,000 shall be paid for each invention.[205] Schools of all rank are free and attendance compulsory.

Another earth directly opposite ours in the same orbit is the locale for the Utopia of D. L. Stump's *From World to World* (1896). As in Bellamy, Howells, and other utopians the change to the good life was here brought about quietly by a great vote of the people. The new declaration of freedom known as the Philoso-

---

202. *Ibid.,* p. 25.
203. Cf. *Ibid.,* p. 172.
204. *Aristopia,* pp. 94-98.
205. *Ibid.,* p. 155.

phy of Life had the common ownership of land and the prohibition of all forms of money as its central features. Tracts of real estate are assigned and recorded under individuals' names, and children may inherit the privilege of working the same land their father held; but failure to grow a crop for two years means forfeiture of the land. A man may choose his work but must pass an examination in it in order to follow that occupation.[206] Imprisonment is used as a cure for chronic idleness. There is state control of all food-stuffs. Everything is sent from the municipal kitchen—everybody lives in moderate-sized towns —to the homes of the people, through pneumatic tubes. Free city nurseries are provided for the care of children, but they may be kept at home.

Frank Rosewater's *Utopia* (1897) essays the Brobdingnagian task of "presenting a solution of the labor problem, a new God, and a new religion". "Labor is property" and "capital is a destroyer of property", Rosewater contends. "In its very origin wealth is a surplus product representing an excess of labor sold by the capitalist, as compared with the poverty of the working classes which represents a deficiency in the sale or preservation of their property in labor".[207]   The Utopia which Rosewater has his balloonist Ross Allison dream ,is a completely communistic state in which was evolved the "gradual collective ownership of the entire capital of the country".[208]   The utopian perspective is dropped and two important suggestions directly made with reference to the contemporary condition of the United States.   The first is a proposal for unemployment insurance benefits: "The man standing ready to work when employment is due him is on duty, and wages are morally due him just as if he were working."[209]   The second is a recommendation for "the prompt issue of a bond currency, to be distributed pro rata among the states, counties, and municipalities, according to population, this currency to take the place of future local bond issues, to bear interest at the rate of four per cent, and to be

---

206. *From World to World*, pp. 25-35.
207. *Utopia*, pp. 125-127.
208. *Ibid.*, p. 122.
209. *Ibid.*, p. 127.

legal tender, with one per cent for each expired quarter elapsed since its issue".[210]   The gradual purchase of all wealth by the government is the ultimate program of Rosewater.

In *The Legal Revolution of 1902* B. J. Wellman submits a prospectus for gradual reform leading ultimately to the complete nationalization of all economic forces.   He would first of all make the machinery for amending the Constitution less cumbersome—a majority vote in each state, or two-thirds of the total national vote—and provide for the direct election of President, Vice-President, and Senators.   Graduated income and inheritance taxes, the establishment of a postal savings bank system, and government ownership and operation of railroads are advocated.[211]   Speculation based on marginal sales should be made illegal, our money expanded to double its volume, and all personal property over one-half a million dollars should be confiscated, Wellman declares.   His ultimate ideal is the government's gradual acquiring of a majority holding in the stocks of all corporations, and the nationalization of agriculture.

J. W. Sullivan's "A Modern Cooperative Colony" (in *So the World Goes,* 1898) presents a picture of complete internal communism.   Sullivan's trend of mind argues from the services already government performed toward more extended paternalism—toward complete nationalism.[212]

Among the decidedly less significant of the utopian fictions is Warren S. Rehm's *The Practical City* (1898).   It is an unimaginative description of the physical elements which contribute to a desirable city site.   Initiative and referendum are in full political force.   All religious sects have been organized into one church but there is still need for charity work conducted by that church.   Adults are given the privilege of night-school study.   The only suggestion for economic reform is a proposal for limiting the amount of land one individual may hold.

Albert Waldo Howard's *The Milltillionaire* (1898) represents

---

210. *Ibid.,* p. 138.
211. *The Legal Revolution of 1902,* pp. 56, 82-83.
212. Cf. "The Intricacies of Laissez-Faire" in *So the World Goes,* pp. 34-36.

the ultimate in communal states; the entire earth has been fused into one great commonwealth whose welfare is unselfishly supervised by the Bard Regent and The Alphabeta, twenty-six sub-bards representing the different sections of the world. There is no vestige of private property; everything is state-owned and free. All that is required of a man or woman is a Tax on Time, between the ages of twenty-four and forty,—"a few hours per day, a few days per week, seven months per year, the rest of the time not so required being at his or her own disposal".

That "the working people have produced all the wealth" while "the possession and enjoyment of it are in other hands"[213] is the contention of Alexander Craig in *Ionia; Land of Wise Men and Fair Women* (1898). And to reprove us by an example of the ideal Craig pictures an imaginary country far up in the Himalaya mountains. The excellence of the state rests on the four basic laws: Land, Inheritance, General Criminal, and Marriage. The land belongs to the whole people; inheritance is limited in amount, the surplus escheating to the state; the criminal law "exterminated the whole brood of evil doers; marriage is based on physical, moral, and mental selection looking toward the betterment of the race.[214]

The central feature of Albert A. Merrill's *The Great Awakening* (1889) is the change from the nineteenth century monetary system. "This question of money", Merrill states, "is of vast importance and is deeper than either free trade or single tax. To treat land as private property is morally wrong, but it is not such an evil as to limit the increase of money, for if it were not for the latter, land market values would not exist".[215] In the nineteenth century the issue of money was "dependent upon the amount of gold in existence" rather than on the "amount of wealth."[216] This enabled those who controlled the gold to manipulate that commodity to their advantage and to the disadvantage of the debtor class. Since effective demand "is wholly dependent on the amount of money in circulation", hard times

---

213. *Ionia, Land of Wise Men and Fair Women*, p. 43.
214. *Ibid.*, pp. 200-201.
215. *The Great Awakening*, p. 88.
216. *Ibid.*, p. 24.

cannot be due to overproduction when at the same time people are starving. "It is only explained when you understand that it was the effective demand that was stopped by the capitalists for their own benefit".[217]   Under Merrill's utopian state the old monetary system was replaced by a currency based on the total amount of wealth in existence,[218] and the circulating medium, therefore ceased to have any value of itself.   Each month on the basis of production during that period the issue of money was increased, and divided among the people in proportion to their productive labor.   Consequent to this change came the decentralizing of population and the evolving of a superior type of citizen.   In equal division of wealth and a stationary population, Merrill contends, is "the secret of all happiness".[219]

Caroline A. Mason's *A Woman of Yesterday* (1900) is the story of a Robert Owen colony in northern Vermont, an example of cooperative economic life.   Miss Mason feels with Hawthorne that "we had struck upon what ought to be a truth".   Fraternia, however, disintegrates and disbands, as did the real Owen colonies.[220]

Solaris Farm (1900) by Milan C. Edson is a study of the farmer's future in the light of increasing capitalistic oppression. "Agriculture is the true basis of industrial and commercial success, Edson maintains, but the "alarming encroachments of land monopoly . . . threaten the total extinction of all land owning farmers", and their reduction to the caste of farm laborers.   He feels that the problem of keeping farm lands in the hands of the people working them "lies at the very foundation of the permanency of this republic".[221]   Cooperative working of the farms "supplemented and reinforced by cooperative thinking" is the solution suggested.   Solaris Farm, a vast stock company embracing six hundred fifty members, is a developed example of the idea advocated.   Within the colony various businesses are conducted with Solaris scrip used as the medium of exchange.   The com-

217. *Ibid.*, p. 25.
218. *Ibid.*, p. 35.
219. *Ibid.*, p. 334.
220. Cf. Samuel P. Orth, "Utopias in America", *Our Foreigners*, p. 96.
221. *Solaris Farm*, p. 6.

munity supports a comprehensive program of insurance against accident, poverty, sickness, and old age.

Alcanoan O. Grigsby's *Nequa, or the Problem of the Ages* (1900) is another concentric spheres story. The ideal inside country is called Altruria. It is essentially communal. Governmental authorities issue "evidences of useful service rendered to society" and these are honored in exchange for anything desired.[222] Private ownership of property is permitted but since everything is obtainable free at any time there is no accumulation.[223]

Edward A. Caswell in *Toil and Self* (1900) looks back from the perspective of the year of our Lord 2400 and sees a whole series of Utopias or semi-Utopias lying in his wake. He sees the rise and fall of the 'contract system' of labor—under which the employer pledged certain wages and conditions for the life of the contract—and the successive growth and decay of the profit-sharing and cooperative schemes of industry. Complete state socialism had its day and likewise lost favor and proved unsatisfactory. Caswell concludes that it is "impossible for the great law of life to be any other than that of selfishness. . . . We decry it denounce it, and deplore it, but we must never ignore it, for looking forward or backward we see SELF as the pillar of flame which will always guide man through the wilderness of life until there is no man left to live".[224] Apparently Caswell's most serious and significant suggestion is the creation of a system of labor arbitration courts, composed of three judges, elected by popular vote for ten-year terms, supported by a jury of men "not directly connected with the business in dispute".[225]

Bradford Peck believes that "the simple religion of Christ was socialistic and cooperative", and that all of civilization ought so to be. In *The World a Department Store* (1900) he represents the pure gold idea of Associationism dropped into the sea of American life at Lewiston, Maine, spreading its influence

---

222. *Nequa*, p. 152.
223. *Ibid.*, p. 221.
224. *Toil and Self*, pp. 147, 154.
225. *Ibid.*, p. 73.

from a tiny local circle to vast rings that reach the farthest part of the nation. Cities, towns, villages are re-created by the cooperative principle of life. The more equal distribution of wealth under the great company in which all are stock-holders is the central feature of the new order. Each man is valued by the Association at — say $300 a month. This is deposited for him in the Treasury and he draws his coupon-checks against it. Each child is credited with $120 a year. General ideality prevails.

What conclusions may be drawn regarding American utopian fiction? It has been shown by the analyses of these books individually that our utopian novelists conceive of the problems of society as economic ones, and that most of them have proposed economic solutions. Some would depend for improvement of conditions upon an appeal based on the ideal of Christian brotherhood. A brief chronological summary of the salient features of the thought of each author will serve best as the basis of an analysis of the reforms suggested in this fiction.

Mercier: an attempt at equalizing the distribution of wealth; modification of tax system to favor the poor; public officials prohibited the use of money while in office; state medicine; cultivation of agriculture and interior commerce only.

Brown: general ideality; a large degree of equal work and equal wealth implied.

Paulding: (N)[226] child labor protest; appeal for more humanitarian factory legislation for all workers.

Etzler: associations, cooperative and communal (to include the world).

Cooper: (N) benevolent minority; social inequalities and property protected.

Hawthorne: (N?) communal labor and reward within an association.

'Freelance': (N) common property and labor; "perfect equality".

Hale: general ideality, through brotherhood and unselfishness.

Judd: general ideality through principles of Christianity.

---

226. "N" indicates a negative view of the socialistic schemes for Utopia.

Cridge: communal communities; equalizing of wealth; fluctuation of money fixed by law; private and public debts illegal.

Allen: collectivist society and government; no money; change accomplished by legislation; sale of land only to those who use it; accumulative land tax, doubling for each additional quarter-section; graduated capital tax after $10,000, doubling for each additional $5000; more strenuous laws for malfeasance in office; economic planning.

Dodd: (N) complete socialism and sameness—"deadening uniformity"; intellectual classes as bad as economic classes, grew out of leisure—law against learning beyond the standard attainable by all.

Bellamy: complete communism; equal work, equal pay (credit cards, $6000 a year); Industrial Army.

Besant: (N) socialism; sameness; no zeal in labor even at five hours a day; progressive society depends on economic individualism.

Heywood: general ideality.

Vinton: more severe penalties for official corruption; general approval of the Bellamy program; would like something done for individual initiative—what?

Donnelly: no interest on money; change all laws, customs, and conditions giving one man advantage over another; maximum wealth limit; limit on amount of land; partnerships substituted for corporations; withdraw political patronage from the Executive; allow no office-holder to vote; more severe penalties for malfeasance in office; government ownership and operation of public utilities; wage rate of labor to be fixed by Congress; base money on total wealth, not gold or silver; state medicine.

Worley: cooperative organization of productive and distributive agencies, progressing gradually toward government assumption of all economic activities, beginning with the railroads and mines; national postal savings bank; in the final cooperative organization equal pay from the government for all members.

Bachelder: (N?) socialism inefficient, deadening; limit maximum individual wealth to $100,000; limit rate of interest; no marginal sales; permit amending Constitution by two-thirds vote; national nurseries; profit-sharing in industry through operatives' right to buy stock.

Simpson: "special legislation" for laboring class; limit holding of land; single-tax; economic planning; government ownership and operation of public utilities.

McDougall: stock company cooperative government of communities.

Thomas: higher ethical standards; government ownership and operation of public utilities; heavy income tax to level inequalities; currency based on surplus of food products and distributed each ten years according to population — speculation thereby eliminated.

Fiske: growth of character and brotherhood; government control of public utilities; nationalization.

Wilbrandt: (N) socialism's blighting sameness and inefficiency.

Hertzka: no private property in land; associations sharing according to individual contributions; no interest on money; support for the physically incapable; income tax.

Moore: base money on all goods according to labor of production, thereby abolishing speculation.

Tincker: general Christian ideality; communism through brotherhood is implied.

Crocker: abolition of tariff; nationalization of public utilities; postal sub-treasury system sponsoring a gigantic inflation.

Everett: power of prayer; boards of labor dispute arbitration; variations in the kind of labor (mines); inheritance tax over $50,000; pensions for all over the age of seventy; government ownership and operation of public utilities; "free coinage."

Chavannes: nationalism with modification for individual initiative; state control of wholesale trade, public utilities, banks, insurance, and "a portion of the manufactures"; nationalization of land; speculation abolished by right of the state to hold or reclaim anything; national employment bureau.

Olerich: cooperative community organization for all work—distribution among them without profit; no private ownership of land; "labor checks"—money based on the time worked, equal for all labor; no credit or interest allowed.

Roberts: (N) Bellamy and the socialist program ignore the

great middle class; walking-delegate methods of labor unions assailed; legislation to prevent watered stock; profit-sharing where individually desired.

Miller: religious fantasy; communal equality and brotherhood.

The Beginning: (N) freedom of individual enterprise upheld; moral perfection the goal to strive for; heavy inheritance tax; child labor laws; more severe penalties for malfeasance in office.

Niswonger: general ideality.

Schindler: repeats Bellamy program verbatim.

Gillette: country to be made into a great stock company— equal distribution, no profits.

Welcome: single-tax; government ownership and operation of public utilities; money based on products of labor and size of population.

Harben: general ideality; equalizing of wealth may be in- ferred—not specific.

Howells: complete communism—no money, equal work and wealth.

Holford: no private ownership of land; government owner- ship and operation of public utilities; government operation of all traffic in merchandise; $10,000 limit on inheritance.

Stump: change to communism by a great vote of the people; all forms of money prohibited; no ownership of land; state con- trol of all food-stuffs; municipal nurseries.

Rosewater: completely communistic—evolved by gradual col- lective ownership of the entire capital of the country; unem- ployment insurance; issue of a bond currency for inflation.

Wellman: amend Constitution by a two-thirds vote or a ma- jority vote in each state; graduated income and inheritance taxes; postal savings bank system; government ownership and operation of public utilities; expand money to double its present volume; no marginal sales; confiscate all personal property over $500,000; nationalization of agriculture; government to gradual- ly acquire a majority holding in the stock of all companies.

Sullivan: communism within cooperative colonies.

Rehm: limit the amount of land a single individual may hold.

Howard: completely communal world; men and women work

for the government a few hours a day between the ages of twenty-four and forty.

Craig: no private property in land; inheritance limited.

Merrill: currency based on total wealth, not gold; divided each month according to productive labor; no private ownership of land.

Mason: cooperative communities.

Edson: cooperative stock company communities; social insurance.

Grigsby: socialistic state with a few vestiges of private enterprise; credit vouchers as in Bellamy.

Caswell: (N?) labor arbitration courts.

Peck: Christian spirit, plus a cooperative nation-wide stock company.

It is seen, therefore, that our utopian novelists who have criticized the present social order and pictured the good life at some future time or unfamiliar place fall roughly into three groups. First, those who depict a general ideality based for the most part upon some unexplained but very appreciable modification of the possessive impulse of human nature. They have imaginatively substituted unselfishness for selfishness. In this group are Brown, Hale, Judd, Heywood, Tincker, Miller, Niswonger, and Harben. They would improve society economically by religious and ethical methods. Christian idealism as an important background to economic devices for social betterment is also represented by Mercier, Thomas, Fiske, Everett, and Peck. The ultimate ideal of many of the writers of this group is apparently communism, but it is not so economically stated. The second group definitely espouses complete national communism, explains its economic operation, and defends its merits against individualism. They provide either for the equal distribution of the common wealth through credit cards, as in Bellamy, or for the abolition of all forms of money, as in Howells. In this group are Allen, Bellamy, Worley, Schindler, Howells, Stump, Rosewater, Howard, and Merrill. None of these writers, however, advocated the Marxian program of class war. They hoped the new social order could be accomplished in America by a great peaceful vote of the people, for in observing the unrest of their times[227] they could see in the strike and other acts of violence nothing but ultimate disaster for all concerned. Political rather than direct action was the method they espoused. Their Utopia was to be found in the all embracing strength of government rather than in the destruction of government. The third group proposes to modify our present government toward a socialistic system, although there is great variation in the degree to which these writers would carry out the socialist program. Classed here are those who advocate organizing communities into cooperative units practically communal within themselves, those who would organize society in stock companies protecting all, but definitely recognizing variations in individual value, and those who would retain the unorganized individualism of the present social order, but turn over to government the operation of those lines of business which most directly effect the public at large. In this group are Etzler, Cridge, Vinton, Donnelly, Bachelder, Simpson, McDougall, Thomas, Fiske, Hertzka, Moore, Crocker, Everett, Chavannes, Olerich, Gillette, Welcome, Holford, Wellman, Sullivan, Craig, Edson, Grigsby, and Peck.

The existence of a fourth group, among these utopians, who definitely deny the merit of the socialist program and who defend individualism, has already been indicated. Of these Paulding, Cooper, Hawthorne, 'Freelance', Dodd, Besant, Wilbrandt, and Roberts are most conspicuous. These in general hold that we had better bear those ills we have than fly to others that we know not of. Caswell, also, represents the failure of socialism in his Utopia. But it is not that he disapproves of the idea; it is that he believes the inherent selfishness of man can never be overcome.

Since even those novelists who fully espouse communism would bring it about by legislative action, and since there is such great variation in the socialist program which these different fictions advocate, the satirical extravaganza of our utopian novelists can probably be best discounted and their true thought most accurately arrived at by an analysis of their specific sup-

---

227. Cf. Chapter I and Chapter II of this study.

port of more detailed issues. Uniformity, of course, is far from absolute even in these details.

Revision of our monetary system is specifically urged by a number of novelists: notably, Donnelly, Worley, Moore, Crocker, Everett, Olerich, Wellman, Merrill, and Rosewater. In general they believe in discarding gold as the basis of currency, and basing it instead on the total value of the products of labor. This, they allege, would make it impossible for the country to have a so-called over-production while thousands lack the necessities of life. It would also have the effect of abolishing speculation.

Other specific legislative remedies for the evil of speculation —such as prohibiting marginal buying—are recommended by Bachelder, Chavannes, Roberts, and Wellman. Cridge would fix by law the permissible fluctuation of the national currency. Donnelly, Hertzka, and Olerich would abolish the system of interest. Nine writers, in addition to those who advocate the complete communistic system, would definitely limit or abolish entirely the individual holding of land: Allen, Simpson, Fiske, Hertzka, Chavannes, Olerich, Holford, Rehm, and Craig. Those who definitely advocate government ownership and operation of public utilities—and some additional enterprises—are: Donnelly, Worley, Simpson, Thomas, Fiske, Crocker, Chavannes, Welcome, Holford, Wellman, and Peck. Worley, Crocker, and Wellman would also establish a national postal savings bank system, paying two per cent interest on all deposits, controlling the country's financial policy, and gradually replacing all other banks.

Leveling economic inequalities through tax reform is an idea that receives treatment by a number of novelists. Thomas, Hertzka, Everett, Wellman, and the anonymous author of *The Beginning* advocate graduated income and inheritance taxes. Simpson and Wellman argue for the Henry George single-tax plan. Mercier wanted to shift the tax burden by exempting the poorer people entirely and having the deficiency made up by free gifts from the rich. Fixing a definite limit to the amount of wealth an individual may accumulate is urged by Allen, Donnelly, Bachelder, and Wellman. The maximum suggested varies from one hundred thousand to half a million dollars.

Holford and Craig would place a limit on the amount of wealth one may inherit.

Corruption at the polls and in legislative halls, think Allen, Vinton, Donnelly, and the author of *The Beginning,* should be combatted with legislation providing much more severe penalties for malfeasance in office. Donnelly would deny the power of political patronage to the Executive. Mercier would prohibit the use of money to all holders of office, the expenses of their livelihood to be paid by the state. Some form of social insurance, unemployment or old age, is advocated by Hertzka, Everett, Rosewater, and Edson. Rigid child labor statutes are sponsored by Paulding and the author of *The Beginning.* Courts for the arbitration of labor disputes are emphatically suggested by Everett and Caswell. Allen and Simpson plead for a program of national economic planning; Chavannes would establish a national employment bureau, designed to put laborers in touch with work. Donnelly advocates the fixing of minimum wage rates by Congress.

These, think the novelists represented here, are some of the tributary paths the American people may take in reaching the broad highway of increasing social justice that leads to Utopia, where

> Henceforth, whatever is wanting to yourselves
> In others ye shall promptly find—and all
> Enriched by mutual and reflected wealth,
> Shall with one heart honour their common kind.

CHAPTER THREE

LITERARY CHARACTERISTICS: THE EXPRESSION OF THE PROBLEM AND THE ANSWER

I

SEEDS OF REALISM IN THE ELEMENTS OF ECONOMIC CRITICISM IN FICTION, 1792 TO 1860

To him who thinks historically it is clear that the early years of fiction writing in America offered no challenging opportunity or necessity for novels of economic protest. It was not that the possible versatility of the novel as a literary form had not been increasingly demonstrated in the years since 1740. The social criticism in the work of Fielding back at the very beginning of the novel's history was a suggestion of what later developments should be. Henry MacKenzie in *The Man of Feeling* (1771) and *The Man of the World* (1773), and Thomas Day with the *History of Sanford and Merton* (1783-89) were feeling their way toward adapting the novel to the espousal of human brotherhood. This tendency in the novel is further developed in Godwin's *Caleb Williams* (1794) where aggressive benevolence wages definite war on class privilege and an iniquitous penal code. The novel was clearly capable of polemic employment. That we had at that time in America no novel which devoted as much effort to serious social criticism as did *Caleb Williams* may, I think, be at least partly explained by the fact that our social body was in better health than the English. At the end of the eighteenth century the questions agitating the American mind were essentially political rather than economic. Not even the fathers of the Constitution themselves sufficiently comprehended how much harder was the industrial than the military problem, nor how greatly its difficulties were to increase in the years that should succeed 1789. But the complex ills of urbanization and the impersonal power of big business were not yet, and consequently it is only natural that we find economic criticism but intermittently in our early fiction.

Restricting one's thought to the theme of this study it becomes apparent that the most significant fact relating to the

literary technique of the novels of our first half-century is that
in their elements of social criticism we find the most identifiable
roots of later realism—faint and fibrous though they generally
are. In my analyses of the individual novels in which I have
found economic themes, I shall follow a largely chronological
order. The significant reason for this—already given expression
in the organization of my economic content analysis—lies in the
fact that the novel treating economic themes must have close reference to the time contemporary with its writing if it is to be
considered serious economic criticism. It must definitely indict
the conditions of its own day. Such a story as Mary Johnston's
Prisoners of Hope (1898) although it treats a phase of life definitely economic in its problems—Negro and indentured slavery
in Virginia, following 1663—is historical rather than critical,
for its problems had ceased to exist long before the novel was
written. It therefore merits only passing mention in this study.
However, a satire as broad in its implications as Mark Twain's
A Connecticut Yankee in King Arthur's Court (1889) must receive consideration because its accusations ostensibly directed at
the society of legendary Britain have unmistakable application
to our own time.

After having traced the roots of realism in the expressions of
social criticism in our fiction before 1860—the literature dealing
with the Negro race excepted—I shall show that the general
novel of economic criticism was a definite phase of the more
completely developed realism of the last forty years of the century, and finally that the utopian novel was technically a continuation of romance in the midst of realism.

Modern Chivalry (1792-1805) I have already pointed out was
the first American novel in which significant economic criticism
appeared. That it was also our first fiction of genuine literary
power is generally conceded. Following the picaresque pattern
of Don Quixote it achieves a remarkable realism for its time.
Whether the picture is of the unpolished life of the sparsely
settled frontier communities—as most of it is—or of the manners of Philadelphia and the more populous East there is always the conviction of reality. The method is satire, but it is
satire that does not disturb the general illusion of life. There

is a classic restraint in the satirical style of Brackenridge that is to be definitely distinguished from the romantic satire of most of the utopian novelists treated later in this chapter; these latter too often out-Herod Herod in piling up supposed real data and pass over into the romantic and lose the appearance of truth.

The characters, whose adventures are the string of narrative between the interspersed knots of discussion in *Modern Chivalry* are Captain John Farrago and his bog-trotting servant Teague O'Regan. The Captain is apparently Brackenbridge's portrait of himself, a man well-read in the literature and life of the times. He analyzes both with intelligent non-partisan acumen; democratic he is in sympathy but unsparing in his exposure of all absurdities. Teague O'Regan is a caricature of the old-world peasant who would grasp the opportunity of American political equality to push himself into positions for which he is not fitted. The story is episodic but has much dramatic power within its several units.

Here was an excellent beginning for the novel of social criticism in America. That its progress was not always worthy of the beginning will be evident.

Charles Brockden Brown, first American professional novelist, is represented in social criticism fiction principally by *Alcuin* (1798), *Arthur Mervyn* (1798) and the unfinished *Memoirs of Carwin, the Biloquist.*[1] Brown was a political and literary romanticist of first rate power. His general method bears a relationship to the Gothic school—which had been producing novels of varying quality since 1764—although his heroes customarily fight with brain rather than brawn, as in the Gothic. William Godwin who was the author of *St. Leon* as well *Caleb Williams* was his admitted master. *Alcuin* was written in dialogue form, but the speeches are of such length as to little interfere with the effect of regular fiction. Here, as elsewhere in Brown's writing, what purports to be conversation does not always overcome a tendency toward stiltedness of style. As a character we conceive of Alcuin as a rather priggish schoolmaster; his ideas have

---

1. Cf. Loshe, *Early American Novel*, p. 38.

an importance, an emphasis, that does not arise from the character. Mrs. Carter who shares the dialogue is a convincing personality—judged by the standards of her day strikingly intelligent and independent, but in ours a quite normal and real woman. Brown is represented most typically, however, by such Gothic figures as Ormond, Walbeck, Ludloe and Carwin. But in his adequate inventive power, his sympathy with his characters under emotion—arising from crime particularly—Brown gives the unreal a dignity and a probability that mark high literary art.

Brockden Brown's social criticism is conveyed largely by the representation of alluring ideality—the intimations of Utopia in *Alcuin,* and the Carwin fragment, and in the Godwinian figure of Arthur Mervyn, one of nature's noblemen, "generous in instincts, impulsive in sociability, responsive to suffering, hating injustice, loving the pure and disinterested"![2]   It is obvious that this as economic criticism is an expression of the French romantic theory. The generality of its appeal stands in sharp contrast to the direct attack of Brackenridge. It is the Brackenridge type of criticism, I have already pointed out, that grows to the greatest significance in the realistic fiction following 1860; but the Brown method also has its echoes in our later social-purpose literature. Indeed if one does not balk on a theistic-deistic quibble all later appeals for reform on the basis of the principles of ideal Christianity may be thought of as related to Brown's economic romanticism. But it must be noted that however uniformly romantic is his material, Brown occasionally—as in his yellow fever description—becomes grippingly realistic in method. His relation to later realism in these instances must, therefore, not be entirely overlooked.

Royall Tyler's *The Algerine Captive* (1797) is frankly a romance. Its reproving glance at land speculation—a remarkable attitude for the time—and its vivid picture of the slave trade explain its inclusion in this study. As a story it reads easily, the adventure motif being well sustained. Dr. Updike Underhill is the captive and predominantly major character; he

---

2. Parrington, *Main Currents,* II:190.

fails, however, to leave the impression of a person. Emphasis is placed upon the action.

Almost nothing can or need be said of Samuel B. H. Judah's *The Buccaneers* except that it was a romance written in 1827. For an adventure story the style is extremely tedious. Despite the fact that it is concerned with describing the eagerness for prosperity in contemporary New York it contributes nothing significant to the development of realism in our early fiction. It is the kind of book a man who would adopt the pseudonym Terentius Phlogobombos would write.

The fascinating style of the *Knickerbocker History* (1809) is well known. It is the only volume of Irving's fiction that contains much economic criticism, and this largely by inference since the time of the history is the early seventeenth century. The geniality and vitality of the work are its chief literary characteristics. Irving's ability to create character was always a significant factor in raising his work to the level of art; William the Testy, Peter the Head-strong and many other valiant Dutchmen are memorable figures. However romantic was his material, Irving was frequently a realist in method—a significant fact in tracing the early roots of realism as found in social criticism.

The fiction of James K. Paulding, from the standpoint of social criticism, continues essentially in the pattern of Brackenridge and Irving. His material is romantic; his treatment realistic. The effect of the whole is that of pleasant but unmistakable satire, and it is in the elements of his criticism that his realism may be most plainly seen. *Konigsmarke* (1823) is perhaps the most representative embodiment of Paulding's social theories and literary aversions.

Westward Ho! (1832) is similar in method to the earlier novel. Paulding's best characters are generally a skillful blend of the life portrait and analytic caricature, as in Wolfgang Langfanger or Mrs. Judith Paddock. Observe in relation to the latter how Paulding's drawing of the character is made to contribute to the reality of the environment as well.

"She would go cackling about the village like unto a venerable old hen which had lost its last chicken, uttering mysterious innuendoes, and throw-

.ing out random hints which set the ears of her sister spirits buzzing almost equal to her own. The spinning wheels stood stock-still; the pots and kettles boiled over; the panting labourer, when he came home to dinner found it overdone, or not done at all; and the pussy-cats skimmed the cream of the milk-pans with perfect impunity. Such are the dire consequences of a secret in a country village!"[3]

That Paulding's work toward realistic method was not incidental is shown by the fact that in *Konigsmarke* he specifically defended the realism of setting and characters in Cooper's *Pioneers* (1823) against the charge of vulgarity and commonplaceness. It may be further inferred from his comments on the prevailing literary tastes in the dedication to *The Puritan and His Daughter* (1849):

"I am not ignorant of your preference for high-seasoned dishes of foreign cookery, most especially blood-puddings, plentifully spiced and sauced with adultery, seduction, poisoning, stabbing, suicide, and all other sublime excesses of genius. I am aware also that Your Majesty, being yourself able to perform impossibilities, believed nothing impossible. Possessing this clew to Your Majesty's royal approbation, I solemnly assure you I have gone as far as I could to secure it, with a safe conscience. I have laid about me pretty handsomely, and sprinkled a good number of pages with blood enough, I hope, to make a pudding. If I have any apology to make to Your Majesty, it is for permitting some of my people to die a natural death, a thing so unnatural that it has been banished from all works of fiction aiming at the least semblance to truth."[4]

Of course Paulding could not wholly escape the romance that was all about him; his style, too, is often discursive. He is, however, a significant figure in American fiction. His social criticism, as I pointed out in my economic analysis, was more direct in his essays than in his novels.

James Fenimore Cooper has been so thoroughly studied and interpreted in recent years that it is almost impossible in a thesis of general scope to add anything to the analyses of Parrington (*Main Currents,* 1927), Spiller (*Fenimore Cooper, Critic of His Times,* 1931), and Ross (*Social Criticism of Fenimore Cooper,* 1933). Obviously I am in this study interested only in Cooper's novels that deal primarily with social criticism—ten of them, written between 1831 and 1847: *The*

---

3. *Westward Ho!* II, p. 52.
4. *The Puritan and His Daughter,* p. 5.

Bravo, The Hiedenmauer, The Headsman, The Monikins, Home-ward Bound, Home as Found, Satanstoe, The Chainbearer, The Redskins, and *The Crater*—and not with his purely adventure stories. The most significant literary fact that can be pointed out in this connection is that the critical novels are inferior from an art standpoint as compared with the pure romances. The Cooper story formula assumes two simple opposing forces; these are precipitated into a course of flight, pursuit, capture, escape, re-pursuit, and final success of the favored force. Action pre-dominates greatly over character. The appropriateness of this formula for romance is admitted; Cooper's greatest artistic weak-ness lies in the fact he used much the same formula, very inap-propriately, for criticism as well. His lack of craftsmanship and artistic resource are manifest in his failure to integrate plot structure with the conflict of ideas. Whereas the artistic novel of criticism must have such integration in a large degree and must present well-developed characters whose philosophy of life is dramatically justified, Cooper, unable to comprehend the realistic method in its completeness, in general simply grafted explicit criticism upon the homely and unversatile framework of his adventure-story formula. The result is frequent intrusion of direct comment by the author, while characters and plot are temporarily forgotten. In the earnestness of his criticism Cooper frequently deserts the narrative abruptly in the midst of a paragraph, and only returns to it after several sentences, or sev-eral pages, of direct personal preaching with such non-illusory transitions as "but to return to the narrative" or "to return from this touch of philosophy to our ships". He was disposed to value social criticism above literary art. Writing in the person of the author he said in *The Redskins* (1846): "I write warmly, I know, but I feel warmly; and I write like a man who sees . . . a most flagitious attempt to rob him. . . . Curses—deep, deep curses—ere long will fall on all who shrink from their duty in such a crisis".[5] Cooper often ignored the qualities of tact and persuasiveness that would have made his works not only more effective as criticism but better literary art as well.

---

5. p. 227.

Despite the emphasis on social theory in the recent biographies of Cooper he is still largely remembered in our literature as a romancer—because he was a pre-eminent story-teller and because of the artistic weaknesses just cited in his critical fiction. His literary importance in this study, however, lies in the fact that in his later work there was a growing tendency toward realism, an increasingly conscious effort to substitute a critical for a romantic treatment of materials.

Catherine Maria Sedgwick had only a "modest career as a 'lady novelist'."[6] She is, however, on the whole a good story-teller. Her economic criticism as I have found it is restricted to a few very incidental comments located chiefly in *Clarence* (1830) and in *Married or Single?* (1857), as recorded earlier in this study. The character of Grace Herbert in the latter book is perhaps its chief merit. Indeed it is in general for her women and children that Miss Sedgwick deserves greatest commendation. *Clarence* is a geographical romance that succeeds in having some very extravagant moments.

Richard Edney and the Governor's Family written by Sylvester Judd in 1850 is a significant book in our tracing of the development of realism in social protest fiction. The setting is Woodylin, as industrial as New England towns could be at that period. Here then is opportunity for contrast with the later pictures of Elizabeth Phelps and Rebecca Harding. The employee-employer relationship is placed before us at the out-set in the homely figure of Labor scratching Capital "like a fowl on a dunghill". Violet, never strong, falls a prey to tuberculosis through her work in the factory. But these suggestions of potential realism are completely nullified by Judd's unsuppressible romance. The second half of the title of this novel indicates the romantic character of its method, which stands in such sharp contrast to the later picturing of the same scene by Miss Phelps. The conclusion is that though Judd had his eye on life he did not have the literary power to reproduce it in fiction.

Alice B. Haven's *Loss and Gain* (1860) is another illustration of the inadequacy of an author to make art out of materials

---

6. Parrington, V. L. *Main Currents*, II, p. 241.

which later writers used effectively. The story deals with the struggle of Margaret Grant against oppressive home conditions and the vicissitudes of department store employment. Its elements of protest contain some slight suggestions of realism. But the novel becomes utterly impossible when heroine Margaret is falsely accused of stealing a dress, and has to prove her innocence before marrying her employer's son. What might have been done with the department store situation is shown in Margaret Sherwood's *Henry Worthington* (1899). *Loss and Gain* is a decidedly sub-literary antecedent of this later novel.

The *Wide, Wide World* (1850) by Susan Warner and *The Lamplighter* (1854) by Maria Cummins have no greater significance in our day as literary accomplishments than they have as economic criticism, and have only been included here because their Christian preaching with its limitless inferences aids in the interpretation of the moralistic elements in such a really significant later critic as Elizabeth Stuart Phelps. The picturesque is coupled with the commonplace in these novels and the whole steeped in infinite moralizings. The authors' idea of reform seems to be to wash the world clean with tears.

Fiction Treating the Problem of the Negro Race Predominantly Romantic

But before the trend of social criticism turned from the insipid domestic romances just cited to the well-developed realism of Rebecca Harding in the early 60's, there was a great outburst of fiction dealing with the problems—economic and otherwise—attendant upon the presence of the Negro race in America. In this study of the relationship between social protest literature and the development of realism the significant fact about slavery fiction, anti and pro, is that it is distinctly romantic. This despite the serious treatment on both sides. The explanation lies in the organization of the life which was pictured. The slave society was a feudal society; and this by contrast with the growing industrialization of the North, if indeed not of itself, was definitely romantic. The purpose of this literature was frankly propagandistic. Its method was extravagant contrast and exaggeration. There is therefore little reality of character or situation to be found in it, despite the fact that the writers on both sides seriously thought they were telling the real and whole truth.

To this generalization there are, of course, exceptions. And one of these is *Swallow Barn* (1832) the most fully developed treatment of the slavery problem in fiction up to that time. There is much of the de Coverley method about this novel, as its infinite leisure of method reflects with considerable realism Virginia plantation life. No unqualified solution for the problem is offered; an effort is made at objectivity, and the merits and demerits of both sides of the issue analyzed. And whatever realism we find in later slavery novels is found in those which, like *Swallow Barn,* succeed in maintaining a largely unbiased outlook on the problem. Where the attitude is militant in either direction there is no consistent reality achieved.

The Partisan Leader of Nathaniel Beverley Tucker, published anonymously in 1836, is a conspicuous example of the militant Southern position. Filled with economic and political romanticisms the emphatic enlargement of which often distort the plot, the novel fails further as art through its almost wooden characters. Its attack is with the broadsword of direct preaching rather than the rapier of well-gauged satire. The extravagance in placing the time of the story toward the end of a supposed third term of Van Buren as President is palpable.

The uncompromising anti-slavery view begins to be importantly represented in the fiction of Lydia Maria Child. *Philothea* (1839)—Greek in setting but with unmistakable reference to the American slave situation, as I have already shown—is perhaps representative of Mrs. Child's literary merit, in being still a very readable book. "The Quadroons" and "The Black Saxons" in *Fact and Fiction* (1846) are further fictional treatments of the slavery question by this militant abolitionist. Emphasis upon the moral rather than the economic implications of slavery is a considerable factor in Mrs. Child's romanticism.

In Kennedy, Tucker, and Child we have represented the three possible positions on the slavery issue during the first half of the nineteenth century—the rational, the militant defense, and

the uncompromising abolitionist. As a literary artist Kennedy
was the best of these.

But the real slavery fiction pro and con stems from Harriet
Beecher Stowe's *Uncle Tom's Cabin* (1852). Greatly superior
both to the stories that echoed it and those that refuted it,
Uncle Tom's Cabin is still seriously short of being a great
novel. Its importance as a human and historical document considerably surpasses its significance as literary art. The characters are essentially types rather than individuals. The author
—as in most of the other slavery novels—frequently steps into
the midst of her narrative to deliver a personal sermon on some
phase of the problem. The book, however, makes skillful use
of emphatic contrasts, and the inherent dramatic power of its
situation cannot be overlooked. "The Two Altars" (1852)—a
short story contrasting the professions of 1776 with the actuali-
ties of 1850 as Mrs. Stowe's abolitionist eyes saw them—and
Dred (1856) do not vary greatly from the author's usual style.
The failure of the latter to match the success of *Uncle Tom's
Cabin* seems accounted for by less drama and more economics
and sociology, and by the lack of a central character of Uncle
Tom's appeal. Looked at from the perspective of our time,
however, *Dred* impresses one as being in many respects a better
written book than its more famous predecessor.

Among the crusaders who followed Mrs. Stowe, in bending
fiction to the purposes of abolition, between 1853 and 1864 were:
F. C. Adams (*Manuel Pereira,* 1853); Walter Sketch (*The Down-
Trodden,* 1853); Mary Langdon (*Ida May,* 1854); James T.
Trowbridge (*Neighbor Jackwood,* 1857, and *Cudjo's Cave,*
1863); M. R. Delany ("Blake: or, the Huts of America" in
The Anglo-African Magazine, Feb. to July, 1859); Mrs. M. V.
Victor (*Maum Guinea's Children,* 1861); James R. Gilmore
(*Among the Pines,* 1862, and *My Southern Friends,* 1863); and
Epes Sargent (*Peculiar,* 1864). Of these Trowbridge and
Gilmore came closest to the accomplishment of realism:
Trowbridge in character creation, Gilmore in setting.

I have already noted that the appeal of these novels for
emancipation was chiefly on moral rather than economic
grounds. The many real or supposititious slave biographies or

autobiographies also written during this period were exclusively moral in their argument and consequently have no place in this study.[7]

But fiction was as well the means of defense as the means of attack in the fight to abolish slavery. Fully aroused by *Uncle Tom's Cabin* to the need of counter propaganda southern apologists quickly put into the fiction lists some twenty to twenty-five refutations of Mrs. Stowe's charges.[8] Among the more important of these were: Caroline E. Rush, *The North and the South, or Slavery and Its Contrasts* (1852), J. Thornton Randolph, *Cabin and Parlor* (1852), Mrs. M. H. Eastsman, *Aunt Phillis' Cabin* (1852), Sarah Josepha Hale, *Liberia* (1853), Martha Hines Butt, *Antifanaticism* (1853), John W. Page, *Uncle Robin in His Cabin in Virginia and Tom Without One in Boston* (1853), J. H. Ingraham, *The Sunny South* (1853-4), Lucien B. Chase, *English Serfdom and American Slavery* (1854), Thomas Bangs Thorpe, *The Master's House* (1854), M. Southwood, *Tit for Tat, a Reply to Dred* (1856), (anonymous) *The Olive Branch or White Oak Farm* (1857), S. H. Elliot, *New England Chattels* (1858) W. T. Thompson, *The Slaveholder Abroad* (1860), and Mrs. G. M. Flanders, *The Ebony Idol* (1860). *Aunt Phillis' Cabin, Liberia* and *The Master's House* were probably the best of these novels from the points of view of character creation, sound reasoning, and realistic portrayal of scene. On the whole the titles themselves make evident the contrasts which are basic in these books. They pretend to picture southern life "as it is", but the pictures are almost uniformly roseate and romantic; the argument required it. Each novel brings some contention to bear upon the main proposition, mixes a few solid chunks of debate into the mush of romance, introduces a few incidents to prove minor points and ends with a wedding under the apple blossoms or the cut-glass chandelier. It is significant to remember that to the average southerner of the pre-war period the Negro was not an independently minded individual; there are, therefore, but few attempts to picture him

---

7. A representative list of such biographical writings contained in the University of Pennsylvania Library is given in my Bibliography.
8. Their argument content has already been cited p. 8, this study.

as a character with psychological reactions to the situations in which he is placed. The notable Negro character creations of Joel Chandler Harris, George W. Cable, and Thomas Nelson Page, had few antecedents in this pro-slavery fiction. These novels are on the whole sub-literary; but within that classification they show some dexterity in their use of the material treated. The earnestness of their pages contributes more to their interest as social documents than to their literary merit.[9]

I have in this study taken particular note of six writers who have treated the problem of the negro in southern society during and after the War. The literary standard of their work is on the whole much higher than the partisan propaganda which came so heatedly from both sides just prior to the civil conflict. John W. De Forest was the first of these writers. *Miss Ravenel's Conversion from Secession to Loyalty* (1867) was a realistic, non-heroic picture of the war and the days immediately after its close. The characters are convincing, the thought rational. In his picture of Charleston at the close of the War De Forest in *The Bloody Chasm* (1881) depicted the same scene that was a few years later to find more adequate treatment by the pens of Cable and Page.

The most militant espouser in post war fiction of the Negro's rights to complete equality, and the methods of obtaining them, was Albion W. Tourgée. A northern officer during the conflict, Tourgée established a residence in Charleston immediately after the surrender at Appomattox, and became identified with the Reconstruction government. In spite of an apparent effort to comprehend the race problem fairly, Tourgée never got far from his essentially carpet-bagger philosophy. He knew his idealization of the Negro, rather than the real Negro. He was by irrepressible impulse a propagandist, and could not refrain from interrupting his narrative with disquisitions on history, occasional curses loud but never deep against the northern Reconstruction policy, attacks on the South, and exuberant praise of

9. See Francis Pendleton Gaines, *The Southern Plantation,* Chapter III, and Jeanette Reid Tandy, "Pro-Slavery Propaganda in American Fiction in the Fifties", *South Atlantic Quarterly,* January-March, 1922, for a more detailed discussion of most of the anti- and pro-slavery novels here mentioned, than the scope of this study permits. Also for some not mentioned here.

the Negro. Whatever chance his characters had for reality was likely to be compromised by such ridiculous names as 'Pactolus Prime' and 'Protestatem Dedimus Smith'. *A Fool's Errand* (1879), *Bricks Without Straw* (1880), and *Pactolus Prime* (1890) are Tourgée's most important treatments of the Negro problem. In *Murvale Eastman* (1890) he advocated the Christian socialist program for the reform of northern industry. Tourgée thought of himself as a realist,[10] but he was inaccurate in that self-classification; he thought of himself as a great novelist,[11] but his works apparently do not justify that judgment.

In Mrs. J. H. Walworth's *Without Blemish* (1886) we have a less detailed development of Tourgée's program of education for the colored race. The book is the most readable after-the-war treatment of the Negro problem. Essentially romance it still makes powerful use of race contrasts and exhibits a fine psychological insight into fundamental human motives. The coincidences upon which its plot depends argue that we should scorn it as melodrama, but the fact is that we don't. In its total effect it is rational.

The Refugees, (1892) "a sequel to Uncle Tom's Cabin from a southern standpoint", by Annie Jefferson Holland is the most outstanding example of the preservation in late post-war fiction of the antagonism of the fifties. It is militant in its disapproval of the North's emancipation of the slaves and the consequent decay of the Greek civilization of the Old South to make way for an "Anglo-African race". It sees in the typical decay of the Carrington family "a foundation of Parian marble for the erection of a mud hut".[12] The novelist, however, did not have sufficient artistic restraint to mold her strong feeling into good literature.

Thomas Nelson Page in *Red Rock* (1898) and *In Ole Virginia* (short stories, 1887-96), and George W. Cable *John March, Southerner* (1894) are strictly speaking treating historical rather than contemporary material. The continuation of Reconstruc-

---

10. Cf. Preface to *A Fool's Errand*, p. 6, and Ray F. Dibble, *Albion W. Tourgée*, p. 63.
11. Cf. Ray F. Dibble, *Albion W. Tourgée*, p. 61.
12. p. 179.

tion problems into the later decades of the century gives them however, by inference a considerable place as social critics. That the southern scene received its most skillful literary treatment at their hands is generally conceded. Page is on the whole more idyllic, less realistic, than Cable. Both are able writers.

Such is the literature dealing with the economic and social problems of the Negro race from 1832 to the end of the century. From the standpoint of this study the most significant conclusion regarding it is that it contributed a great deal less to the development of realism than did our other fiction dealing with economic and social criticism.

II

The Developed Realism in the Economic Novel, 1860 to 1900

It was Rebecca Harding Davis who in American fiction first coupled unqualifiedly realistic material with unqualifiedly realistic treatment. The Pennsylvania iron district where the exploitation was harsher, more brutal, than in the textile mills was the scene of her realistic stories. In 1861 *The Atlantic* published her "Life in the Iron Mills". Mrs. Davis' appeal was candid, direct: "I want you to hide your disgust, take no heed of your clean clothes, and come right down with me—here, into the thickest of the fog and mud and foul effluvia". The Wolfes, father, Hugh and Deborah, central characters in the story, live in a damp, dark cellar. Other workers "red-faced and pale — whiskey-bloated, and heavy-brained, Irish, Dutch, black" are no whit better off; some even live on the warm ash in the mills. The neurotic temperaments of Hugh and Deborah, at the mercy of moods, driven by forces they do not understand, aggravated by physical defects—Deborah's deformed back, Hugh's tubercular lungs—these give Mrs. Davis' story a naturalism not again equalled until the end of the century. There is art in "Life in the Iron Mills": its protest lies not in carefully builded argument, but in spontaneous truth. Here was fidelity to a creed that was not put into words until the appearance of Howells' *Criticism and Fiction* thirty-three years later.

"Let fiction cease to lie about life; let it portray men and women as they are, actuated by the motives and the passions we all know. Let it leave off painting dolls and working them by springs and wires; let it show the different interests in their true proportions; let it forbear to preach pride and revenge, folly and insanity, egotism and prejudice, but frankly own these for what they are, in whatever occasions they appear; let it not put on fine literary airs; let it speak the dialect, the language most Americans know."[13]

Rebecca Harding continued her effective presentation of sordid industrialism in "A Story of Today", which ran in the *Atlantic* from October 1861 to March 1862. An Indiana woolen mill furnishes the setting of the story. The operatives are mostly women. There is still realism, genuine, unstudied: wool dust and the smell of copperas are on the pages. But quotable passages begin to appear in a not too natural manner. *Margaret Houth*, which was the book-form title of the story is, however, almost a great novel in the skill with which it digs into the vulgar and commonplace of American life and succeeds in molding those elements into art. Mrs. Davis maintained the general excellence of her writing and her distinctive character drawing in *Waiting for the Verdict* (1868), a telling protest against race injustice, and in *John Andross*, 1874, a picture of the corruption of government by big business, powerful in its non-romantic portrayal. Not to be overlooked in this study are two short stories of Mrs. Davis, "The Harmonists" (1866) and "Quella" (1875) treating respectively the communistic colony as a means to the utopian order of life, and the problem of economic and social injustices practiced toward the Cherokee Indians in North Carolina. The former of these is particularly notable for its convincingly realistic picture of the Rapp community at Economy, Pennsylvania.

Although she declined in realistic power in her later writing Mrs. Davis is an extremely important figure in the development of realism in American fiction. It was toward her work that many of the realistic elements I have cited in the efforts of our earlier novelists at economic criticism were pointing, and from her has stemmed much that is significant in the realism of our later fiction.

---

13. Howells, William D., *Chriticism and Fiction*, p. 104.

In Elizabeth Stuart Phelps' novels we find the most realistic portrayal of New England Mill conditions up to that time, and indeed a picture that is still memorable and significant in its protest. The first of her stories to attract attention was "The Tenth of January", published in *The Atlantic* for March, 1868. The central character, Arsenath Martyn, a mill girl with crippled back and large scar across her mouth, reminds us, in fundamental conception, of Mrs. Davis' Deborah Wolf. The atmosphere in this first story is not so sordid as in the later *Hedged In* (1870) and *The Silent Partner* (1871), nor is the story nearly so defensible as literary art, since its outcome depends on the collapse of the mill building—a pure accident not growing out of character, or earlier elements of the story. Miss Phelps' later novels are subject to the charge of sentimentalism and too much appeal through the principles of ideal Christianity; but even so they leave the effect of literary merit through their well-managed narratives and their vital pictures of exploited labor.

Another phase of the newly developed realism in American fiction is to be seen in the slackness and drab poverty of farm life reflected in Edward Eggleston's *The Hoosier Schoolmaster* (1871). Eggleston's later novels, *The Mystery of Metropolisville* (1873) and *Roxy* (1878) contain, as I have indicated in an earlier section of this study, more definite economic criticism; they improve, too, in literary power. In *The Faith Doctor* (1891) Eggleston essayed social satire in a New York City setting, and a picture of tenement-house conditions; but the novel is decidedly unsuccessful from the standpoint of realistic art. However for his pictures of the farm and village life of the Middle Border he is genuinely significant. These have the feeling of life about them. Note how in his description of a wake, Eggleston approaches something approximating the stream of consciousness technique of later novelists:

"So now every symptom of Mrs. Bonany's disease was gone over, and what Mrs. So-and-so said about it three days ago, and what the doctor thought, and when "the change" took place, and who were "sitting up the night she died", and whether she "died happy or not, and what she said, and whether the corpse looked "natural", and how he "took it", and whether he would stay infidel or not, and how Amanda "took it", and whether the girl had much heart or not, and whether the old man would marry again, and what he would do about his family. . . ."[14]

The Gilded Age (1873) by Mark Twain and Charles Dudly Warner is the first novel of economic criticism important for its picture of political corruption. It is specifically a satire of General Grant's administration and many of the figures which move through its pages are but slightly disguised. It definitely shows the application of a full-blown realistic method to the treatment of another phase of American life. A vivid picture it is of governmental Washington corrupted by self-seeking lobbyists. Colonel Sellers and Laura Hawkins are memorable characters despite the fact that logic says they have too much of romance about them. *The Gilded Age,* however, does not offer an exhaustive analysis of the situation it treats. The rapacious railroad robbers, than which there were none greater, are largely ignored while the satire is directed against smaller steals. The economic sources of political corruption are largely overlooked, too, and the evils simply laid to the principle of democracy. These failures of the criticism to penetrate to the heart of its problem detract somewhat, one observes, from the realism of the story. Twain is also represented in this study by *The American Claimant* (1892)— another largely political satire—*A Connecticut Yankee in King Arthur's Court* (1889) and *The Prince and the Pauper* (1881). The criticism in the last two is largely by inference. It is, however, for the realistic political satire of *The Gilded Age* that Mark Twain is significant in this study.

It will be observed from the analyses just given of Davis, Phelps, Eggleston, and Twain, that we have in their writings three different phases of the newly developed realism, as seen in the novel of economic criticism. The first two represent the exploitation of industrial labor; Eggleston reveals the beginnings of what becomes the subjection of agriculture to capitalistic oppression; Twain was the first of six standard novelists who drew realistic pictures of our national government from the viewpoint of economic criticism.

To treat the remaining regular novelists (as distinguished from

---

14. *Roxy*, p. 77.

the utopians) included in this study from the standpoint of these topical distinctions will probably foster the clearest comparison of literary merits.

Among the writers who followed in the path of Davis and Phelps as serious and comprehensive critics of the exploitation of industrial labor and who at the same time achieved more or less distinction as literary artists J. G. Holland, Amanda M. Douglass, Henry Francis Keenan, Edward Everett Hale, William Dean Howells, Henry B. Fuller, Margaret Deland, Robert Herrick, Caroline C. Walch, Margaret Sherwood, David Lubin, Florence Converse, and Mary E. Wilkins Freeman are the most important. Naturally the literary ability even within this restricted group varied considerably.

Holland's novels, *Sevenoaks* (1875) and *Nicholas Minturn* (1877) are very able examples of realistic fiction. Sustained by good narrative they are also marked by much apt phrasing. *Nicholas Minturn* has less literary power than its predecessor through its dealing more with theory than with fact. On the whole, however, there is in Holland a homeliness of realism that Davis and Phelps did not have, and that finds its most forceful use in Edward Everett Hale.

Amanda M. Douglass' *Hope Mills* (1880), as definite and serious in its criticism as the industrial novels which preceded it, is of decidedly less literary merit. Miss Douglass' weakness is that found in a large number of the lesser writers of economic fiction—particularly the utopians; it is an inability to get across her message through a general impression of truth, by the interaction of a number of characters—as for example in Howells. When in the novel of economic protest the author is not able to dramatically manage the characters to the end of getting the criticism across, the burden invariably falls upon one character who becomes idealized out of reality in order to make the message clear. That is the weakness of *Hope Mills* and the character of Jack Darcy. Romanticism of method embracing the most sentimental treatment of Victorian love-making intrudes upon what at the outset had the possibilities of being an excellent realistic novel.

Henry Francis Keenan sub-titled his novel *The Money-*

Makers (1884) "a social parable" It pictures Aaron Grimestone's--he was a "type of that consummate product of the survival of the social fittest"—strangle-hold on the town of Valedo. The book has some literary merit in its phrasing and its delineation of character but it was far below the standard Howells was soon to set for the economic novel.

I have already pointed out that Edward Everett Hale's little known novel *How They Lived at Hampton* (1888) is his most important contribution to economic criticism in fiction. It only remains to say here that it and Hale's other stories are significant from a literary point of view for the utter plainness of their realism. There is nothing of industrial sordidness here, as in Davis and Phelps, but a simplicity, a homeliness, that makes you forget that you are reading a fiction. Professor Pattee has called this the realism of "realistic extravagance",[15] making its effect through a very multitude of matter-of-fact touches. It is this that is noteworthy in Hale; his not infrequent lapses into moral and religious sentiment — as in "Ten Times One Is Ten", which I have classified as utopian—detract greatly from his art.

William Dean Howells is represented in this study by seven novels: *Annie Kilburn* (1888), *A Hazard of New Fortunes* (1889), *The Quality of Mercy* (1892), *The World of Chance* 1893), *The Traveler from Altruria* (1894), *Through the Eye of the Needle* (1907), and *New Leaf Mills* (1913). The doctrines of Howells as a social critic and his preeminent literary excellence among social critics have been admirably treated by Vernon Louis Parrington[16] and Walter Fuller Taylor.[17] In a comprehensive survey such as this, which attempts to trace the theme of economic criticism through a hundred years of our fiction and find in that theme the growing importance of realism, the perspective in which Parrington sees Howells' use of common-place material is very enlightening:

"The current school of realism is inclined to deal harshly with Howells. His

---

15. *Development of the American Short Story,* p. 185.
16. *Main Currents,* III:241 ff.
17. "William Dean Howells and the Economic Novel", in *American Literature,* March, 1932, IV:103 ff.

quiet reticences, his obtrusive morality, his genial optimism, his dislike of looking ugly facts in the face, are too old-fashioned today to please the professional purveyors of our current disgusts. They find his writings as tedious as the gossip of old ladies. To their coarser palates his respectable commonplace is as flavorless as biscuit and tea. Yet it must not be forgotten that for years he was reckoned new-fashioned. Whatever may be one's final judgment on his work it is certain that for twenty years he was a prophet of realism to his generation, the leader of a movement to turn American Literature from the path of romanticism and bring it face to face with the real and actual. It was not his fault that the ways of one generation are not those of another, and it is well to remember that if his realism seems wanting to a generation bred up on Theodore Dreiser, it seemed a debasement of the fine art of literature to a generation bred up on Thomas Baily Aldrich. Realism like dress changes its modes."[18]

With Davis and Phelps realism had been largely a sensitive reaction to the sordidness and injustice and inhumanity of industrial exploitation. With Howells it was decidedly more of a doctrine. In *Criticism and Fiction* (1894) he ascribes its rise to science and democracy, and contends that in its truthful delineation of the prosaic lives of common people realism as a literary method reveals the essential dignity and worth of all life. I would not disparage Howells' earnestness and importance as a social critic but it is occasionally difficult to reconcile his theories in their ultimate ramifications with the urbanity of his literary manner and the disciplined discretions of his artistic temperament. One cannot help noting that Howells' characters are uniformly taken from the middle and upper classes—whereas the problem chiefly concerns the blacklisted miner, the tubercular mill girl, the immigrant sweater. It is to be regretted from both the critical and literary points of view that Howells made no effort to draw characters from the lower classes.

But turning more specifically to the details of Howells' technique in the economic novel, we find an emphasis upon character and situation rather than upon narrative and plot. "The novelist's main business", Howells contended, "is to possess his reader with a due conception of his characters and the situations in which they find themselves. If he does more or less than

18. *Main Currents*, III: 241-242.

this he equally fails";[19] and Howells carried out in practice what he advocated in theory—the complete espousal of his thesis through the inter-action of character. Himself maintaining an objectivity that rarely interrupts the narrative Howells created a series of "chorus characters" whose speeches and philosophy of life express his own views. And so skillfully has this been done that a comparison of the novels with Howells' letters and utopian romances is necessary to determine just which those characters are. Peck in *Annie Kilburn,* March in *A Hazard of New Fortunes,* and Hughes in *A World of Chance* are perhaps the most identifiable.[20]

Here then is a novelist whose art has overcome most of the faults to which earlier social critics in fiction fell victim. I have already pointed out in this chapter how Cooper's obtruding of his own personality into his novels detracts from their artistic merit,[21] and how lesser writers, like Amanda Douglass,[22] failing to manage the inter-action of character had fallen into incongruous romanticism. Even so excellent a realist as Rebecca Harding Davis had spoken some of her strongest messages in the person of the author. But Howells' fine mastery of the novel form enabled him to surmount the technical difficulties that had baffled others. He must therefore rank as the American novelist up to his time who most adequately combined economic criticism and high artistic excellence.

We find much of the Howells' method and much of the Howells' excellence in the social protest fiction of Henry B. Fuller. *The Cliff-Dwellers* (1893) and *With the Procession* (1894) contribute a distinctly artistic element to the realism of American literature. Their author is a distinguished phrase-maker. Fuller's thesis in its several phases is adequately conveyed through a life-like interplay of personality and incident. There is little doubt that Fuller writes better about Chicago's civilization because he also knows other civilizations well.

19. "Henry James, Jr.," in *The Century Illustrated Magazine,* November, 1882 **XXV**: 25 ff.
20. Cf. Taylor, W. F., "William Dean Howells and the Economic Novel" in *American Literature,* March, 1932, 4:103 ff.
21. pp. 202-204.
22. pp. 135-136.

Very comparable to Fuller in material and somewhat superior to him in style is Robert Herrick, author of *The Gospel of Freedom* (1898) and *The Web of Life* (1900). The scene Chicago; the characters taken from the same social range as in Fuller. Herrick maintains an objectivity equal to Fuller's technically, but in the spirit of him there is more of the militant reformer.

The Wisdom of Fools (1897) by Margaret Deland is a series of four short stories connected rather definitely by a continuation of some of the characters. With a northwestern Pennsylvania setting Mrs. Deland's particular literary merit in these stories, as elsewhere, arises largely from well-measured moral contrast. She paints a life in which there is little glory and of which the only reward is self-respect. There is no propaganda.

Caroline Walch (*Doctor Sphinx*, 1898), Margaret Sherwood (*Henry Worthington, Idealist*, 1899), and Florence Converse (*The Burden of Christopher*, 1900) have written with about equal ability. They have not the literary strength of Howells or Fuller, nor have they delved into the sordid as did Davis and Phelps; but they do have an adequate objectivity of method based on a good sense of character conception.

David Lubin's *Let There Be Light* (1900) despite the earnestness of its examination of the causes of poverty and social inequality, has no merit at all as a novel. The narrative is broken into by stenographic reports of the meetings of a workingman's club, and the characters lack differentiation—all apparently being merely Lubin in his different phases.

The last of the novelists who have seemed to me serious critics of the exploitation of industrial labor and at the same time writers of some literary merit is Mary E. Wilkins Freeman. It is for *The Portion of Labor* (1901), that she is to be chiefly remembered in the history of the economic novel. Parrington's synopsis of the book is pithy: "It is the Cinderella story of a village girl who, refusing a chance to be sent to Vassar, enters a shoe factory, becomes a proletarian leader, engineers a strike, gains a wider vision of the function of labor, accepts the principle of exploitation, and is rewarded by marriage into the ex-

ploiting class."[23] Parrington condemns the novel by comparing it to the works of Elizabeth Stuart Phelps, and scores its
unreality. However, a review of labor union history will show
that there have been a number of local girl leaders very like
Ellen Brewster.[24] She has weaknesses to be sure, but these are
made up for by several well-drawn minor characters — Abby
Atkins, for example. The book certainly has reality in its
recognition that inequality is as old as the world, and likely
to continue as long. What invalidity then is there in Andrew
Brewster's musing conclusion that

"labor is not alone for itself, not for what it accomplishes of the tasks of
the world, not for its equivalent in silver and gold, not even for the end
of human happiness and love, but for the growth in character of the laborer."

"That is the portion of labor," he said.[25]

This study purporting as it does to summarize the doctrines
of economic criticism in our fiction is interested in its literary
evaluation primarily in ascertaining how skillfully those doctrines have been worked into the novel as a literary art form.
The excellence of a writer as a literary artist does not merit
analysis here if he has been only incidentally and generally a
social critic, for if his criticism is inconsequential in amount the
problem of how he worked it into the novel form virtually
vanishes. I have therefore grouped here several novelists of
recognized merit, whose economic criticism has been either very
general, or merely incidental, and shall treat them briefly. These
are' H. H. Boyesen, Charles Dudley Warner, Ellen Glasgow,
Harold Frederic and Theodore Dreiser—considered here only
for *Sister Carrie* (1900). Edward Bellamy's *The Duke of
Stockbridge* (1879) and Mary Johnston's *Prisoners of Hope*
(1899) while they deal with economic themes are essentially
historical. In general these novelists indict America on the

---

23. Parrington, *Main Currents*, III:67.
24. Cf. Samuel P. Orth, *The Armies of Labor*, pp. 55, 208, 225. Fanny
Wright and Elizabeth Flynn, for example. The latter, an appealing and
charming girl, was a local leader at sixteen, and was getting national pub-
licity as a labor agitator at twenty-one. p. 208.
25. *The Portion of Labor*, p. 563.

charge of philistinism without being specific on any of the large issues involved.

There is a further group of novelists whose criticism is likewise not very important, and whose literary significance is of even less moment. These are C. M. Cornwall, Clinton Ross, George Thomas Dowling, Helen Alice Nitsch, Agnes Maule Machar, Dan Beard, Randal Irving Tyler, and Finley Peter Dunne.[26]

I have reserved for mention together the names of several writers who dealt primarily with tenement-house life but whose stories deserve little recognition as literature. No one knew his material more thoroughly than they, but their stories are tracts rather than art. Helen Campbell and Jacob Riis are chief among the writers of this group. *Miss Melinda's Opportunity* (1886) and *Mrs. Herndon's Income* (1886), full length novels by Mrs. Campbell; *Nibsy's Christmas* (1893) and *Out of Mulberry Street* (1898), short story volumes, by Riis are the works primarily concerned. The lack of literary power in these writers is best seen when the incongruously romantic tendencies of their fiction are compared with the realistic moods of most of their essay and reportorial writing. There is too a picture of New York tenement conditions—drawn from considerably less adequate personal knowledge—in Joaquin Miller's *Destruction of Gotham* (1886). The novel is essentially a fantasy; its contrast between tenement sordidness and the glittering life of Fifth avenue with a dinner that cost $125,000 is not sufficiently personal to have real literary power. Others who have drawn the conventional tenement life picture with only the conventional skill are: Kate Douglass Wiggin, *Timothy's Quest* (1890) and *The Story of Patsy* (1889); Margaret Sherwood, *An Experiment in Altruism* (1885); J. W. Sullivan, *Tenement Tales of New York* (1895); Alan F. Sanborn, *Meg McIntyre's Raffle* (1896); and Hervey White, *Differences* (1889).

But the name most to be conjured with in the picturization of slum life in fiction is that of Stephen Crane. It must be em-

---

26. The novels referred to are, of course, listed in my Bibliography and citations of their content are to be found in the several sections of my economic analysis.

phatically remembered, however, that he was a naturalist in mood and had no program of reform to urge, as did the other writers in this group. Crane supplies the reader only with the raw materials for social criticism; he is himself amoral, detached, objective. His stories reproduce convincingly the language of the life they depict. *Maggie: A Girl of the Streets* (1893) has been accurately described as "an attack on everything that was respectable in American literature—a notable achievement in a world of shoddy romanticism".[27]

The beginning of a marked realism in the treatment of farm life has already been noted in *The Hoosier Schoolmaster, The Mystery of Metropolisville* and *Roxy* of Edward Eggleston. Other writers along the Middle Border were soon to take up the defense of the farmer against capitalistic exploitation. Passing mention must be made of H. H. Boyesen (for *Falconberg,* 1879, and "Liberty's Victim" in *Vagabond Tales,* 1889), although his early works contain perhaps a bit more disposition toward romance than does Eggleston's writing. His style is facile.

E. W. Howe's *The Story of a Country Town* (1882) is a significant work in the de-idyllizing of farm fiction. It is a drab, grim picturization of a small Kansas town and its rural surroundings, unrelieved by light or humor. There are no heroics in the style, as there are none in the story. Material and method combine to leave the effect of depressing drabness. Some dozen characters are sketched with convincing reality.

Joseph Kirkland's *Zury: The Meanest Man in Spring County* came in 1887 to add to the growing Middle Border literature. It is a full-length portrait of an Illinois farm boy who struggles up from poverty to prosperity. The drudgery of frontier farming reacting to produce a crabbed meanness in the man is convincingly done. Romance, however, creeps in at the end as Zury is reclaimed to human feeling by his school-teacher wife. From the standpoint of literary style the book is unevenly written.

The life of the Middle Border found its most significant expression in the work of Hamlin Garland. His creed held that the novel is the completest expression of civilization, and that

---

27. Parrington, V. L., *Main Currents,* III:328.

its method must be fidelity to fact stripped of all prudishness and convention. His pen was not without knowledge of romance but when he wrote from the soul he was a consummate realist, a reformer whose argument was truth. *Main-Travelled Roads,* which appeared in 1891, is the protest of one oppressed with the meanness of a world that takes such heavy toll of human happiness. Garland is a prophet saddened by the plight of his people:

"The main-travelled road in the West (as everywhere) is hot and dusty in summer, and desolate and drear with mud in fall and spring, and in winter the winds sweep snow across it; but it does sometimes cross a rich meadow where the songs of larks and bobolinks and blackbirds are tangled. Follow it far enough it may lead past a bend in the river where the water laughs eternally over its shallows.

"Mainly it is long and wearyful and has a dull little town at one end, and a home of toil at the other. Like the main-travelled road of life it is traversed by many classes of people, but the poor and the weary predominate."[28]

Jason Edwards was also published in 1891, *Prairie Folks* (*Other Main Travelled Roads*) in 1892, *Rose of Dutcher's Coolly,* 1895, *A Spoil of Office* in 1897. The sincerity of Garland forbids us to overlook the importance of any of these, but artistically the first two volumes were the best. *Rose of Dutcher's Coolly,* the longest of Garland's stories here cited, lacks the atmosphere of inevitability that contributes greatly to the strength of his earlier fiction of western farm life.

The plight of the western farmer is pictured with some power in two other novels of critical import. The contrast between John Thurston, equalitarian theorist farmer, and Stephen Ward, capitalist mortgage-holder, is well drawn in Mary H. Ford's *Which Wins?* (1891). Harold Frederic's *The Copperhead* (1893) has a more facile style than much of the author's later writing.

But it is not alone among the farms and villages of the Middle Border that rural life is barren and petty. In 1887 Harold Frederic in *Seth's Brother's Wife* had told the same tale of drabness about the farm life of upper New York State. It is, however, Mary E. Wilkins Freeman, writing of the New

---

28. Garland, Hamlin, Dedication to *Main-Travelled Roads.*

England scene, who most lucidly analyzes the psychology behind this life:

> "There is often to a mind from the outside world an almost repulsive nar-
> rowness and a pitiful sordidness which amounts to tragedy in the lives of
> such people as those portrayed in *Pembroke,* but quite generally the tragedy
> exists only in the comprehension of the observer and not at all in that of
> the observed. . . . Though the standard of taste of the simple villagers, and
> their complete satisfaction therewith, may reasonably be lamented, as also
> their restricted view of life, they are not to be pitied, generally speaking, for
> their unhappiness in consequence. It may be that the lack of unhappiness
> constitutes the real tragedy."[29]

The way in which the barrenness of this life has reacted to
embrittle human emotions is well portrayed in the characters
of Deborah and Barnabas Thayer. Here is a well rendered
reality only appreciably surpassed by Hamlin Garland in his
most emphatic mood.

Sarah Orne Jewett, characteristically idyllic in her outlook
upon New England life, occasionally produced a story—like
"The Town Poor"—which embodied a real complaint against
the narrowness of that life.

Kate Sanborn does not have or merit the literary reputation
of Mrs. Freeman or Miss Jewett but in several chapters of
Adopting an Abandoned Farm (1892) she tells the tale of hardships in rural New England with considerable effectiveness.

The Gilded Age (1873) by Mark Twain and Charles Dudley
Warner has been cited as the first significant political novel,
and the weakness of its lack of penetration excused by the real-
ness of its purpose. The names of other novelists who pointed
the accusing finger at governmental corruption during the last
quarter of the nineteenth century—excluding the utopians—are
pretty well known. John W. DeForest (*Honest John Vane,*
1875, and *An Inspired Lobbyist,* 1898), Henry Adams, (*Democracy,* 1880), Thomas Stewart Dennison (*An Iron Crown,* 1885)
George Cary Eggleston and Dolores Marbourg (*Juggernaut: A
Veiled Record,* 1891) and Hamlin Garland (*A Member of the
Third House,* 1897) attacked the Invisible Empire along a national front. Rebecca Harding Davis (*John Andross,* 1874)

---

29. *Pembroke,* pp. vi-vii.

H. H. Boyesen (*The Mammon of Unrighteousness* 1891) Robert Herrick (*The Gospel of Freedom* 1898), Ellen Glasgow (*The Voice of the People* 1900), and Frank Norris (*The Octopus* 1901) aimed their criticism at various state governments. Brief literary appraisal has already been made elsewhere of all the authors listed here save Adams, Dennison, Eggleston and Marbourg, and Norris. It should suffice therefore to observe that the literary merit of the politico-economic novels listed here is of about the same range as that of the other works of the several authors. It' is undeniable, I think, that there is something romantic inherent in the idea of governmental position and power; and this could not fail of reflection in fiction treating political subject matter. In general then, we find that the realism of an author when dealing with political figures seems somewhat tempered, however earnest his critical purpose may remain.

Henry Adams' *Democracy* is superior to De Forest's novels (except in criticism) though less amusing, less penetrating, less creative than *The Gilded Age*. Despite discoverable character inconsistencies the narrative is facile. *An Iron Crown* is the most comprehensive and direct denouncement among the criticisms of corrupt government. That it could also be a good novel is not to be expected. The author obtrudes upon his narrative repeatedly and occasionally attacks the robbers of the national treasury by their real names, despite the fact that he has characters in the story to represent them. *Juggernaut: A Veiled Record* is not a distinguished novel. It succumbs more and more to the unreal as it goes along; Edgar and Helen Braine are seldom convincing.

Justice, of course, cannot be done to Frank Norris by mere reference. His theory of the novel calls for a broad canvas and the tracing upon it of forces that are elemental in the life of a whole people. Within this broad outline his theory and practice are essentially like those of Howells: he feels that social doctrines must be expressed by an analysis of the characters· of the men and women composing the society depicted, and that the two must be combined and manipulated to evolve the purpose.[30]   It is sometimes difficult for Norris to maintain his objectivity; but despite the fact that he is primarily interested in man rather than men his characters are distinctly individualized. And there is poetry in the breadth of his grasp of life. *The Octopus* is decidedly his best novel.

Preserving still the idea of economic classification I have chosen to group separately even for literary analysis the three outstanding fictional defenses of the capitalistic order: *The Stillwater Tragedy* (1880) by Thomas Bailey Aldrich, *The Breadwinners·* (1884) by John Hay, and *Tom Grogan* (1896) by F. Hopkinson Smith.[31]   In tracing the relation of realism to the economic novel it is interesting that all of these stories impress us as being essentially romantic. Richard Shackford, Arthur Farnham, and Tom Grogan (Mrs.) alike fail to convince us of having any counter-parts in life. Technically Aldrich maintains an objective position with regard to his work, but his views are so unmistakably expressed by Richard Shackford and Mr. Slocum that this is largely nullified. The Aldrich attack on labor unions through these two characters is direct rather than satirical. Not so with *The Breadwinners,* the best of these novels and one which achieved a notable success. Satire is the method here—satire whose ultimate grotesqueness comes to light when the strike is broken by the women's boxing their husband's ears and chasing them back to work. Smith's satire, too, in *Tom Grogan* is excellently amusing and not without its sting. We are, for example, given this inside view of the walking delegate's philosophy of labor: "It was plainly the driver's duty, Quigg (the walking delegate, who "having been out of work himself for months at a time was admirably qualified to speak of the advantages of idleness to any other candidate for like honors") urged, to give up his job until Tom Grogan could be compelled to hire him back at advanced wages (He was getting board, room and $30 a month) . . . for there were a number of his brethren out of work and starving who would not work for less than two dollars a day if it were offered them".[32]   Nor

---

30. Cf. Parrington, V. L., *Main Currents,* III:330.
31. Cf. also various counter-Utopias, pp. 189-192, this study.
32. *Tom Grogan,* p. 63, 69.

do these novels overlook the condemning power of such epithets as 'socialism' and 'anarchism' when applied to the labor unions. Such are the literary characteristics of these rather able defenses of economic individualism.

III

The Utopian Novel a Peculiar Continuation of Romanticism

When the elements of social criticism in fiction have so clearly contributed to the development of realism from the very beginning of the novel in America, it seems paradoxial that social criticism carried to its ultimate degree in fiction should become romantic, from the standpoint of literary classification. Yet such is the case. It is impossible to classify the sixty odd utopian fictions in American literature up to 1900 as anything but romantic; their imaginings take us into the unfamiliar, of time or place; or both. Nor do they contain any characters who convince us of having counter-parts in the life we know. Indeed it may be set down as a definite inference of a lack of literary skill that these novelists seldom give us a representation of the inter-action of a number of equally important characters. The figures here are intellectual and moral super-men, and surprisingly beautiful sexless women. We are told, to be sure, that everyone else in the imagined country is for all moral, social, political, and economic purposes the equal of these heroes and heroines; but it is never demonstrated. But even the chief characters are at the best only names rather than persons. The utopian novel emphasizes action and picture, rather than character. Indeed the individual ought to become merged in the state—through principle. And those utopians who condemn the abolishing of individualism picture for us a country of the 'new' order—in which all the men and women have been "molded into the same soulless likeness". But whatever character there is in these political and economic romances is essentially Victorian and therefore strikingly incongruous amidst the imagined mechanical achievements of the twenty-first century.

The lack of literary merit of most of these novels therefore justifies their neglect by historians of our fiction, but the mere number of them is a testimony of their significance in the social and intellectual life of the last quarter of the nineteenth century. It is impossible to trace any development in the technique of utopian writing. Variations in literary skill are large and many, strictly individual, and bear no relation to chronology.

Apparently the first utopian novel published in America was *Memoirs of the Year Two Thousand Five Hundred*. It was printed by Thomas Dobson at Philadelphia in 1795. It is only incidentally interesting, however, because it was in reality the work of a Frenchman, Louis Sebastian Mercier, and further because the translation was by an Englishman, William Hooper, M. D.[33] There is some interest, however, in the fact that although the work was published in Philadelphia in 1795 the apparently first English edition did not come from a Liverpool press until 1802.[34]

"When I had closed my eye-lids", the narrator records, "I dreamed that ages had passed since I laid down to rest, and that I was awake."[35] Feeling the impulse to arise and go about the strange Paris into which he had been projected, he was fortunate in immediately meeting and receiving the personal guidance of a "man of learning". Here then we have the essential framework of many of the later Utopias: a sleep is employed for the transference of the narrator to some future time or strange place; he meets a particularly philosophic and well informed guide who is enthusiastic about the new order, and whose disquisitions upon it fill considerably more space than the actual narrative.

Our first native utopian was Charles Brockden Brown, and the work *Alcuin* (1798). The utopian machinery, however, is very inadequately described. All we know of it indeed is what we gather from Alcuin's references to it in his dialogue with Mrs. Carter: "I visited since I saw you the paradise of women". . . . "The region indeed is not far distant" . . . but he had only "various conjectures as to the position of the Isle". The journey was accomplished by "my good genius". The people seemed

---

33. Cf. *British Museum Catalogue*.
34. Cf. Mumford, Lewis, *The Story of Utopias*, p. 313.
35. *Memoirs of the Year 2500*, p. 11.

like persons of another planet but were really on our own. The language was English. A brief analysis of the literary style of *Alcuin* has already been given in my general treatment of Brown.[36]

Our second fiction of a distinguishably utopian character is "The Man Machine, or the Pupil of 'Circumstances'" in *The Merry Tales of the Three Wise Men of Gotham* (1826) by James Kirke Paulding. The location of Paulding's little Utopia is not made very clear, but its life is based on the "sublime maxim that self-love properly understood and uniformly practised is the basis of all virtue, as well as happiness in the social state".[37] That the story is intended to satirize this old Hobbesian philosophy is made clear by the fact that the treasurer is allowed to abscond with the public money and thereby wreck the struggling utopian state. Whereupon Mr. Harmony, the narrator, inheriting a distant estate from a near relative determines to apply this principle of complete equality through self-love on a smaller scale. His inculcation of the guiding maxims into the minds of the servants results in his incarceration successively in jail and insane asylum and the disintegration of his estate. This satire lacks Paulding's usual definiteness and clarity of purpose. The narrative is intangible.

J. A. Etzler's *Paradise* (1833) is not a novel, and is only fiction in the sense of being an imagined picture of a perfect nowhere. It is wholly without characters, and has no appreciable narrative movement. In general effect, however, it is not unlike a number of the later utopian novels, and it is sufficiently distinguishable from such a work as Albert Brisbane's *The Social Destiny of Man* (1840) whose Fourieristic ideas it shares, to be considered in a study of utopian fiction. Verbosity and repetition are the chief demerits of Etzler's style, but his book contains remarkable stuff for the time. An examination of later utopian literature in America cannot well be made without reference to it.

James Fenimore Cooper's *The Crater* appeared in 1847. Its situation was an imaginary island in the Pacific. Mark Woolston,

---

36. Cf. pp. 199-200.
37. *Merry Tales*, p. 34.

the main character — who seems to have much of Cooper's own personality about him—is supported by a number of fairly well individualized lesser persons. Although this is decidedly among Cooper's poorer novels, and has the faults of the author's intrusion upon his story—already pointed out in my general analysis of Cooper's critical fiction—it is, by comparison with most of the later utopian novels, of very acceptable literary quality.

It is questionable if *The Blithedale Romance* (1852) should be classified as utopian. Hawthorne was essentially describing what had been rather than what should be. It is included, however, because while he admits having Brook Farm "in his mind", he insists that his "present concern with the socialistic community is merely to establish a theatre a little removed from the highway of ordinary travel, where the creatures of his brain may play their plantasmagorical antics".[38] That is the introduction. And this is the conclusion: "More and more I feel that we had struck upon what ought to be a truth".[39] This despite Hawthorne's natural skepticism and the ac:ual failure of Brook Farm and other Fourier phalanxes. *The Blithedale Romance* is a very able novel, despite the fact that Hawthorne seems somewhat below his best in being tied to the actual scenes and some of the real characters of Brook Farm.

The Philosopher of Foufouville (1868) by 'Radical Freelance, Esq.' is the story of the Harmonian (or New Utopian) colony at Foufouville, New Jersey, allegedly established "in the spring of the year 185-". In utopian technique it may therefore be compared with *The Blithedale Romance*. Its author has perhaps even less confidence than Hawthorne in the Fourieristic (The North American phalanx at Red Bank, New Jersey, was probably the background of this novel) scheme of life; for the satire is palpable. Indeed it amounts to very enticing humor at moments. The characters are given such interpretive names as Dr. Goodenough, Charity Goodenough, Professor Malpest. A love story that is frankly burlesque carries through the novel.

Edward Everett Hale's *Ten Times One is Ten* (1871) is the

---

38. *Blithedale Romance*, Works, v. 8, p. xxix.
39. *Ibid.*, p. 351.

story of a "possible reformation". Starting with its own time it traces the geometrically increasing influence of the Henry Wadsworth Club twenty-seven years into the future. The chief literary feature of the story is the homely, matter-of-factness of its realism, already cited in connection with Hale's other economic criticism.

In *Margaret* (1882) "a tale of the real and ideal" Sylvester Judd pictured a New England town as he thought it would be if the principles of Christianity were practically applied. The novel is a series of letters in heavy semi-expository style; a sentimental, moralistic whine, with little reality in its conclusions.

Alfred Denton Cridge in *Utopia; or the History of an Extinct Planet* (1884) produced, apparently, the first utopian novel in American fiction to transfer its scene to some adequately described supposititious region arrived at through a definitely described mechanism. The narrator holds an orange-sized meteorite with Aladdin lamp properties in his hand. Rubbing it he brings to his side a venerable man, Genius Psycho, who directing him how to handle the meteorite takes him off to the planet Utopia and shows him its life "from infancy to dissolution".[40] Most of the book is given to explaining the lighter non-economic phenomena of the planet. The book is largely devoid of literary merit. No effort is made at the creation of realistic human character. The style reveals a limited imagination.

The same may be said of Henry Francis Allen's *The Key to Industrial Cooperative Government* (1886). The author lies under a locust tree and dreams himself led off over an "aerial sea" by a maid whom he names the "Queen of Grace". They eventually arrive at the planet Venus, and it is the virtues of life there that the people of earth should accept as a rebuke and an example. The Christian doctrine is emphasized.

Anna Bowman Dodd's *The Republic of the Future, or Socialism a Reality* (1887) is a denial of the advantages of a socialistic over an individualistic order. The book is a series of letters from a Swedish nobleman visiting 'New York Socialistic City' to a friend in Christiania in the twenty-first century. The same-

---

40. *Utopia*, p. 30.

ness of life under the socialistic order is revealed as "hideous, bare and plain".[41] As literary art it is as difficult to say anything for this novel as for its utopian companions. One can note nothing save a certain aptness of phrase. For example: "A man cannot have his dream and dream it too. Realization has been found before now to be exceedingly dull play".[42]

The Library of Congress "list of references on Utopias" contains Elizabeth Stuart Phelps' *The Gates Between* (1887) as well as the same author's *Beyond the Gates* (1883). These however touch not at all on economic themes and are utopian only in a spiritual sense. They are an attempt to portray the soul's experiences in the life beyond—specifically called Heaven.

Edward Bellamy's *Looking Backward* came, was seen, and conquered, in 1888. Not since *Uncle Tom's Cabin* had an American novel been so widely read.

The chief fact in the structure of the story is the mesmeric sleep in whch Julian West, hero, remained from 1887 to the year 2000; he was restored to consciousness by Dr. Leete, a retired physician of the new age, and of course fell in love with the doctor's daughter, Edith, great-granddaughter of the woman West had loved in 1887. This situation is continued in *Equality*, which Bellamy published nine years later, in 1897. In the sequel Bellamy essayed a critical examination of economic history with a view of creating an adequate social economics. The earlier work had drawn the outlines of the democratic society of the future, the later supplied a justification and a commentary. These books in their combination of the didactic and the absurdly romantic are far from having any merit as literary art. Bellamy was under no illusion regarding their quality as novels.[43] They were, however, social documents of wide popular appeal.

Walter Besant's *The Inner House* (1888) is another utopian denial of the socialistic dream. The tiresomeness of the time-less Present where all is equal finally leads to revolt against the new order. Jack Carera and Christine are pictures from a nine-

41. *Republic of the Future*, p. 36.
42. *Ibid.*, pp. 22-23.
43. Cf. Bellamy, Edward, "How I Came to Write Looking Backward", in *The Nationalist*, May, 1889, I:1-4.

teenth century album rather than real characters. But perhaps the author should receive commendation for making an attempt at character, for most of the utopian expositors fail to go even that far.

The Twentieth Century (1889), by D. Herbert Heywood is wholly without distinction. Devoid of character the narrative concerns itself largely with a rapid trip around the world by dirigible.

An indebtedness to Bellamy—such acknowledgments are numerous in the utopian novels following 1888—is implied in the title of Arthur Dudley Vinton's *Looking Further Backward* (1890). The book purports on its title page to be a "series of lectures delivered to the freshman class at Shawnut College, by Professor Won Lung Li (successor to Professor Julian West)." The purpose is to modify and strengthen Bellamy's program of nationalism. There are long quotations from Bellamy's books, which are spoken of as 'Julian West's diary'. Failing even to make the effort to change Bellamy's language it would be difficult to ascribe much merit to this book.

Ignatius Donnelly's *Caesar's Column* (1890) is at once one of the more notable and more militant of these utopias. A great anarchistic revolution is frankly predicted. And after this revolution in 1988 the scene shifts to Africa. The framework of Donnelly's romance is ridiculous in its extravagance but within it he writes better than the majority of his fellow utopians.

Three Thousand Dollars a Year (1890) by F. U. Worley is not fiction in the story sense, but pretended history. Its composition is without distinguishable merit.

John Bachelder imagined an island in the mid-Atlantic to which certain refugees from Bellamy's nationalism might escape to organize for themselves a government which fair to all would still recognize individual differences in the human family. He called the picture *A. D. 2050* (1890). It follows the almost uniformly unliterary level of its predecessors.

In *The Man From Mars* (1891) William Simpson exhibited more than the customary skill of the American utopian novelist. The Marsian visitor tells his host, the narrator, that he is "here by reflection".[44] The narrator's study of social problems and astronomy in his secluded mountain home has skillfully prepared us to accept such a spiritualistic concept. The visitor talks all night on the social contrasts of Earth and Mars, and when morning comes the narrator is not sure whether the 'Man from Mars' has really been sitting there in his easy chair or whether he has dreamed the utopian vision of Mars. The literary skill in this plot with an explanation either natural or supernatural is great in comparison with the obviousness and absurdness of the motivation of most of these novels. The style, too, is facile. The book has merit, as utopian novels go.

Walter H. McDougall placed his Utopia in a lost canyon of the Sierras; he called it *The Hidden City* (1891). A wrecked balloonist turns the primitive community into a great stock company. Ridiculous in its romantic framework, the story fails of any redeeming quality elsewhere.

Atman (1891) by Francis Howard Williams is not an economic treatise. 'Atman' is the soul, the ultimate self. Dr. Perdicaris attempts to gain control of this force through the study of eastern religions and medical theory. The accomplishment would make Utopia tangible. The author's talent was unequal to this abstruse theme.

Chauncey Thomas' *The Crystal Button* (1891) is subtitled "the adventures of Paul Prognosis in the forty-ninth century". Prognosis' unnatural dream is caused by a bump on the head, and the general literary quality of the work is in keeping with so excellent a motif.

Amos K. Fiske's *Beyond the Bourn* (1891) declares itself to be reports of a traveller returned from 'the undiscovered country'. Fiske assumes only an editor's role. If the story have merit it is probably in the utter prodigiousness of its conception of the universe: we look in upon "worlds and systems of worlds".[45]

There were published also in 1891 two translations from the German which should perhaps be noted: Conrad Wilbrandt's *Mr. East's Experiences in Mr. Bellamy's World*—a reply to the

---

44. *The Man from Mars*, p. 22.
45. *Beyond the Bourn*, p. 69.

author of *Looking Backward*—and *Freeland* by Dr. Theodor Hertzka, a Viennese economist. The first is just an ordinary utopian fiction; the second a studied economic treatise carried on the narrative framework of a projected cooperative colony.

In M. Louise Moore's *Al-Modad* (1892) the title character and a friend go a-shipping on the seas beyond the "polar circumflex" and find the perfect country which Miss Moore has imagined but inadequately described. The conception here, as in several other of the utopian novels, was based on the Symm's theory of concentric spheres. Miss Moore's use of the idea as a literary device shows no originality. I find no literary distinction in her pages.

San Salvador (1892) by Mary Agnes Tincker is a religious fantasy. As a composition it makes some effort to achieve the style of Biblical poetry, but succeeds only moderately well.

Samuel Crocker's *That Island* (1892) is technically one of the worst of these utopian novels. The author, constantly forgetting that he has taken us to a utopian spot in an unnamed sea, breaks in upon his story to personally condemn economic and political injustice in the United States and to make to Congress recommendations for their remedy.

The People's Program (1892) by Henry L. Everett involves no geographical extravagance. It is the story of imagined economic and social reform accomplished through organized public opinion and prayer. Its style is flat, stale, and unprofitable.

Albert Chavannes is represented among the utopians by two novels: *The Future Commonwealth* (1892) and *In Brighter Climes* (1895). The scene of these stories is 'Socioland' some indefinite section of Africa with climate and crops like our own middle Atlantic States. The books corroborate one another in using some of the same characters—as in Bellamy, and Howells. Chavannes was also the author of other social tracts, retailing at from five to twenty-five cents — perhaps some indication of their literary character.

In Henry Olerich's *A Cityless and Countryless World* (1893) we again encounter a man from Mars. He has shot himself to earth in a projectile, landed somewhere in the Pacific, swum to the California shore, and is now going about peddling the works of Herbert Spencer—because his author, Henry Olerich, is a disciple of the Spencerian philosophy. There is effort here at the characterization of a whole family—the Uwins—but the book is tiresome, lengthy, repetitive. It is emphatically essay rather than narrative.

In J. W. Roberts, *Looking Within* (1893), we find another Bellamy opponent who points out in a utopian way the "misleading tendencies of *Looking Backward*". The preface dates the scene of the book as 2027, but Roberts soon forgets his perspective in a direct attack on such agitators as Bellamy and a condemnation of labor union methods. His point of view changes, however, as he goes along, and at the end he is agreeing to a greatly modified individualism. Occasional aptness of phrase is the only merit of the composition.

The Beginning (1893) is very properly anonymous: it could not be considered a credit even to the lowliest hack-writer, for it is devoid alike of economic imagination and literary merit. It is a "dream of Chicago under the new system"[46] with the rough suggestion of an insipid romance tacked on.

Joaquin Miller's *The Building of the City Beautiful* (1893) is a religious fantasy. Its doctrine is that the blessing and teaching given to the Jews includes all men. Parts of the book effectively create a kind of spiritual twilight, in which the symbolical Miriam moves as the chief character. We remember her, however, as a spirit rather than as a person.

The Isle of Feminine (1893) by Charles Elliot Niswonger is a faint echo of Brown's *Alcuin*. The story—a shipwrecked sailor theme—has no significance.

A general analysis of the literary style and skill of William Dean Howells has already been given.[47] His two utopian novels though they are of necessity romantic in outline still have much of the feeling of reality about them. They do not vary appreciably from Howells' usual urbane manner. *The Traveller from Altruria* (1894) is a tactful study; Howells delivers no broadside attack on the capitalistic system; he only suggests its mean and selfish exploitation—and with such controlled satire

---

46. *The Beginning*, p. 87.
47. Cf. pp. 216-218.

that he "wakes no sleeping lions". The study is continued in
Through the Eye of the Needle (1907). Mr. Homos, the
traveller from Altruria remains the central character. A mild
love theme—there is never appreciable passion in Howells—is
introduced in the marriage of Homos to Mrs. Bellington Strange,
a New York society woman, who returns to Altruria with him,
and finds the reports of its social virtues in no way exaggerated.
The skillful, quiet reality with which Howells pictures
Altruria stands in broad contrast to the unliterary efforts of
most of his fellow utopians. Howells acknowledged indebtedness to *Looking Backward* for some of his utopian ideas.[48]

Another utopian story related directly to Bellamy is *Young
West* (1894) by Solomon Schindler. It purports to be an autobiography of Julian West, Jr. It is devoid utterly of imagination; it has no merit. This and not a few other utopian fictions
of the period were palpable attempts to capitalize, for the
pecuniary benefit of their authors, upon the great popular interest aroused by Bellamy's book.

King C. Gillette's *The Human Drift* (1894) is the most complete repetitive of all these utopian books. The first half is
essay explaining how to make the United States into a great
stock company. Then characters (*i. e.* names) and a thread
of narrative are introduced and the material gone over again,
idea by idea. It borders on the positively unreadable.

From Earth's Center (1894) by S. Byron Welcome is another
concentric spheres story. It is the inner country, 'Centralia', of
course, whose perfection condemns America. The story is extravagant but very readable.

Will N. Harben places his Utopia in a gigantic and marvelous
cave beneath an unnamed sea. In *The Land of the Changing,
Sun* (1894) everything is electrical, even the sun itself. The
story is frankly an extravaganza, but has some good dramatic
moments.

Castello N. Holford's *Aristopia* (1895) is "a romance-history
of the new world", a conjecture as to what the present would
have been if "a man of great wisdom, foresight, and genius, with

---

48. Cf. *The Traveller from Altruria*, pp. 212-213.

an unselfish devotion to the welfare of humanity"[49] had had the opportunity to direct the affairs of America three hundred years ago. Ralph Morton is the man imagined, and Jamestown, Virginia, in 1607 the opening scene of the story. It is obvious that this conception for a utopian novel has much originality. The book is very interestingly written.

D. L. Stump in *From World to World* (1896) expresses the belief that there is another earth directly opposite ours in the same orbit—hidden of course by the sun. To get there Christopher Asbury goes up in an airship that can neutralize gravity and waits for the other earth to come along. The reform that Stump advocates for our civilization has already been accomplished there. The book has some originality of imagination but not much distinction of phrase.

Frank Rosewater's *Utopia* (1887) looks back from the perspective of the year 2883. At the end, however, we find that Ross Allison, a balloonist, has only dreamed all night. The book is largely an exposition of the economic and social excellences of Lukka. It has no literary merit.

The Legal Revolution of 1902 (1898) by B. J. Wellman "purports to be a history of social conditions in the United States for a period of about fifteen years following the year 1897".[50] The predictions made compared with the actual history as we now look back upon it show how inadequately Wellman understood the great complex forces of civilization. The book has no distinction of style.

J. W. Sullivan's "A Modern Cooperative Colony" in *So the World Goes* (1898) is one of the shortest of these characteristically brief utopian fictions. Calling the story "a whimmsy" Sullivan defends himself from the criticism of being exceedingly indefinite. The work has no originality or other tangible merit.

The Practical City (1898) by Warren S. Rehm is another utopian plan of the Fourieristic pattern. The main street north and south is to be Greek Avenue; east and west, Puritan Avenue. There is little imagination. The writing is poor.

Albert Waldo Howard's *The Milltillionaire* (1898) is an ex-

---

49. *Aristopia*, p. 6.
50. *The Legal Revolution of 1902*, p. 3.

travagant conception of what the author calls the "age of bardization". Concentration of wealth has reached the ultimate degree: everything is held by one man. Fortunately he is a benevolent despot, a very god. Since he is the state, the state owns all. There is imagination here beyond the usual run. The thought and its expression are superior to the general run of these economic romances.

Ionia, Land of Wise Men and Fair Women (1898) by Alexander Craig pictures the perfect nowhere high in the Himalaya mountains. An extravagant, sexless—as usual—love story shares the pages with general social criticism. Very readable, it is still without tangible merit.

The transmigration of a soul whose reincarnation had been inexplicably delayed is the utopian mechanism employed in Albert Adams Merrill's *The Great Awakening* (1899). A brain operation on a certain Richard Pangloss is the background of the mysterious reincarnation of a full-blown nineteenth century soul in twenty-second century surroundings. There is some ingenuity apparent in this conception, but the book thereafter becomes quite conventional in plan and writing, with Professor Harding explaining the perfect life of the year 2199 to the renewed Pangloss.

Caroline A. Mason's *A Woman of Yesterday* (1900) is the pretended picture of a Robert Owen colony, Fraternia, in northern Vermont. As utopian fiction it should be compared with *The Blithedale Romance* and *The Philosopher of Foufouville*. It is a well-written novel with conspicuous reality of character drawing in John Gregory and Anna Burgess. Much sympathy is created for the ideal which the colony represents, but the author's sense of realism made her refuse to save Fraternia from dissolution—an end comparable to that of the dozen real Robert Owen colonies in America.[51]

Solaris Farm (1900) is an expression of Milan C. Edson's opinion that the Utopia for America lies in cooperative organization, particularly of the farmer. It is the old Fourier phalanx idea, though derived here through M. Godin who founded the

---

51. Cf. Samuel P. Orth, "Utopias in America", in *Our Foreigners*, Chronicles of America Series, v. 35, p. 96.

Familistere at Guise, France.[52]   The picture of the twentieth century colony, imagined here, is supposedly brightened by a love thread that gradually weaves the lives of Fillmore Flagg and Fern Fenwick into one cloth—making a romance so utterly, insipidly, moralistically Victorian that to read is to rave. This is representative of the worst type of utopian novel, making pretenses not only to noteworthiness as a social document but to importance as a literary creation—without knowing that it is neither.

Alcanoan O. Grigsby's *Nequa, or the Problem of the Ages* (1900) is the third American utopian romance to be based on the Symm's concentric spheres theory. The inner country is here called Altruria. The romance is based on the age-old motif of a woman disguising herself as a man in order to go with him she loves. It is extravagant, but readable.

Toil and Self (1900) by Edward A. Caswell purports to be a series of narrative lectures delivered at Yale University by 'Professor Winter' in the year 2400. Tracing the various utopian schemes in their supposed application during the intervening centuries he sees Self still the primary motivator of men's lives. The style is quiet, straight-forward, unpretending.

Bradford Peck's *The World a Department Store* (1900) looks only twenty-five years into the future and thereby—like *The Legal Revolution of 1902*—makes itself very absurd. It is utterly ridiculous that Percy Brantford, the sleeper in this case, should be the only one who could remember things as they were twenty-five years before.   Starting at Lewiston, Maine, the Cooperative Association of America gradually came to embrace the entire country. This picture of economic utopianism is shot through with a conventional, insipid love theme in three movements.   Here, as in about thirty-five per cent of the American utopian fictions preceding it, the brave new world, the truly good life, has been "founded on the principles and teachings of Jesus Christ".[53]

That which the introduction to this survey intimated has therefore been shown to be true: that American utopian fiction

---

52. *Solaris Farm*, preface.
53. *The World a Department Store*, p. 4.

is largely devoid of marked literary merit; that though it is seriously concerned with the social structure of civilization, it is in its narrative outlines extravagantly, absurdly romantic. The exceptions to this general conclusion are few. *The Blithedale Romance* and *A Woman of Yesterday* are good novels, and of similar structure, but utopian only in a limited sense. Comparatively able in style but extremely indefinite in physical description are Brown's *Alcuin* and Joaquin Miller's *Building of the City Beautiful.* The best of the unqualifiedly utopian novels are Howells' *Traveller from Altruria* and *Through the Eye of the Needle,* Simpson's *The Man From Mars,* and Bellamy's *Looking Backward.*[54]

---

54. Cf. Bibliography, pp. 257-260, for a list of 38 volumes of American utopian fiction, 1900 to 1932, from the catalogue and stacks of the Library of Congress, with brief descriptive notes.

CONCLUSION

What succinct and significant conclusions may be set down from a study of American fiction treating economic themes from 1792 to 1900? It is obvious that the amount of this writing is extensive. In many of the novels, however, which this study examines, the economic criticism is not the primary purpose of the book. This is more especially true of the novels written before 1850. In the decade immediately preceding the Civil War American economic fiction dealt almost wholly with the slavery issue, pro et con. Although the arguments were often not on an economic plane the implications of these novels were always in a broad sense economic. As the industrial and social problems of the nation became more acute in the years from the Civil War to 1900, so, too, did economic criticism find a more frequent and important place in American fiction. The large majority of the sixty odd utopian novels treated in this study were written during the last fifteen years of the century; they are, of course, almost exclusively economic in their import.

The novelists of economic criticism in America have conceived of the consciousness of class distinctions based upon gross inequalities of wealth as a fundamental problem in our democracy. The oppression of the weak by the strong is both wrong in itself and productive of wrong. Our government, so fine in theory, has in fact been basely degraded and grossly corrupted, the novelists charge. On the one hand the duties of government have too often fallen into the hands of those incapable of grasping the country's economic needs, and on the other officials of the State have accepted profitable personal considerations for granting favors to great private interests at the expense of the people.

In addition to these two broad problems, of class consciousness and industry in government, there are a number of smaller, more specific, evils which our economic critics in fiction have assailed. All of these stem from the subservient relationship of labor to capital under the industrial organization of society. The Machine requires capital; it becomes more and more indifferent to labor. In the increasing competition of life the owner of the

Machine has therefore been able to force the non-owner to labor and live under conditions unhealthful and inhuman. Out of this situation have come blighted bodies and seared souls, prostitution and crime, the thousand ills the social flesh is heir to. In contrast to this dark picture drawn by the many, there are a few critics who represent the present economic order as essentially sound and good. They recognize individual and social differences as deeply and inevitably human. They feel that labor movements and socialistic theories can produce nothing good.

But those who would alter the present order, what changes would they make? Some would merely have their fellow-men try to make a more practical application of the principles of Christianity. Some would reform our methods of taxation. Some would limit or abolish the private holding of land. Some would organize industry on a cooperative unit basis. Some would provide government ownership and operation of public utilities. Some—but not many—would bring about a completely communistic state.

The expression of these economic ideas in American fiction has varied greatly in literary quality. The variations, however, have been personal, and have borne no relation to chronology. It is an interesting and significant fact that the early seeds of realism in American fiction can be frequently discovered in the elements of economic criticism in our earlier novels. In the period from 1860 to 1900 the strongest of our economic critics in fiction are also in many cases our ablest writers of the realistic novel. The relationship obviously is that both economic criticism—in the regular novel—and realism demand truth to life. The utopian novel is a special species of fiction, a striking continuation of romanticism in an age of realism.

What are the reactions of a rational objective-minded individual to the ideas expressed in our economic fiction likely to be? First of all he will probably agree with an opinion expressed by a number of the novelists themselves—that too many solutions have been suggested for the problems under consideration "Every man is chasing a shadow, and the worst of it is that he doesn't know of what it is the shadow". He is likely to conclude—if he knows something of Micah and Jeremiah, of

Plato, of Savonarola and Campanella, of William Langland and Thomas More—that the problem and the solutions are alike old; that the world turns round, and all things with it, and that everything new is simply the revival of something forgotten; that the weaknesses in human nature are too deeply rooted to be overcome at once even by national collectivism. Has there been no progress? Can there be no progress? The answer is decidedly yes—in a local sense, with reference to the specific conditions of our particular age. Much has been accomplished in the way of more humane industrial legislation; a statute providing national social insurance is about to be enacted; education practical and social has been brought to a larger percentage of the people. The further advance of society depends upon a concerted social will. The novelists of economic criticism in American fiction have tried to foster the development of that will by their provoking pictures of the ills in the life about them. A great deal of thought is necessary to a little action. And action without thought is foolish and futile, for "it is the progress of ideas which ultimately determines the progress of the world. Unless these are changed, every other change is superficial, and every improvement precarious".

BIBLIOGRAPHY

FICTION

Adams, F. C.: *Manuel Pereira*. Washington, 1853.
Adams, Henry: *Democracy*. New York, 1908.
Adams, Nehemiah: *The Sable Cloud*. Boston, 1861.
Aldrich, Thomas Bailey: *The Stillwater Tragedy*. Boston, 1880.
Allen, Henry F.: *The Key of Industrial Cooperative Government*. St. Louis, 1886.
Bachelder, John: *A. D. 2050*. San Francisco, 1890.
Beard, Daniel Carter: *Moonblight and Six Feet of Romance*. New York, 1892.
Beginning, The. Chicago, 1893.
Bellamy, Edward: *Looking Backward*. New York, 1888.
Bellamy, Edward: *Equality*. New York, 1897.
Bellamy, Edward: *The Duke of Stockbridge*. New York, 1900.
Besant, Walter: *The Inner House*. New York, 1888.
Boyesen, H. H.: *Falconberg*. New York, 1879.
Boyesen, H. H.: *Daughter of the Philistines*. Boston, 1883.
Boyesen, H. H.: *Light of Her Countenance*. New York, 1889.
Boyesen, H. H.: *Vagabond Tales*. Boston, 1889.
Boyesen, H. H.: *The Mammon of Unrighteousness*. New York, 1891.
Boyesen, H. H.: *Social Strugglers*. New York, 1893.
Brackenridge, Hugh Henry: *Modern Chivalry*. Philadelphia, 1855.
    Part I 1792-3-7, 4 vols.
    Part II 1804-05, 2 vols.
Brown, Charles Brockden: *Alcuin, The Rights of Woman*. New York, 1798.
    (Second Dialogue in Dunlap's *Life*. Philadelphia, 1815.)
Brown, Charles Brockden: *Arthur Merwyn*. Philadelphia, 1799 (vol. 1). New York, 1800 (1799) (vol. 2).
Butt, Martha Haines: *Antifanaticism*. Philadelphia, 1853.
Cable, George W.: *John March, Southerner*. New York, 1907.
Campbell, Mrs. Helen: *Mrs. Hendon's Income*. Boston, 1886.
Campbell, Mrs. Helen: *Miss Melinda's Opportunity*. Boston, 1886.
Caswell, Edward A.: *Toil and Self*. Chicago, 1900.
Chase, Lucien M.: *English Serfdom and American Slavery*. New York, 1854.
Chavannes, Albert: *The Future Commonwealth*. New York, 1892.
Chavannes, Albert: *In Brighter Climes*. Knoxville, Tenn., 1895.
Child, Lydia Maria: *Philothea*. Boston, 1839 (1836).
Child, Lydia Maria: *Fact and Fiction*. New York, 1846.
Cooper, James Fenimore: *The Bravo*. New York, 1902 (1831).
Cooper, James Fenimore: *The Heidenmaner*. New York, 1902 (1832).
Cooper, James Fenimore: *The Headsman*. New York, 1902 (1833).
Cooper, James Fenimore: *The Monikins*. New York, 1902 (1835).

Cooper, James Fenimore: *Homeward Bound*. New York, 1902 (1838).
Cooper, James Fenimore: *Home as Found*. New York, 1902 (1838).
Cooper, James Fenimore: *Satanstoe*. New York, 1902 (1845).
Cooper, James Fenimore: *The Chainbearer*. New York, 1902 (1845).
Cooper, James Fenimore: *The Redskins*. New York, 1902 (1846).
Cooper, James Fenimore: *The Crater*. New York, 1902 (1847).
Cooper, James Fenimore: *The Oak Openings*. New York, 1902 (1848).
Cooper, James Fenimore: *The Sea Lions*. New York, 1902 (1849).
Converse, Florence: *The Burden of Christopher*. Boston and New York, 1900.
Cornwall, C. M.: *Free Yet Forging Their Own Chains*. New York, 1876.
Craig, Alexander: *Ionia; Land of Wise Men and Fair Women*. Chicago, 1898.
Crane, Stephen: *George's Mother*. New York, 1896.
Crane, Stephen: *Maggie, a Girl of the Streets*. New York, 1931 (1893).
Cridge, Alfred D.: *Utopia; the History of an Extinct Planet*. Oakland, Calif., 1884.
Criswell, Robert: *Uncle Tom's Cabin Contrasted with Buckingham Hall*. New York, 1852.
Crocker, Samuel (psd. Theodore Oceanic Islet): *That Island*. Kansas City, Mo., 1892.
Cummins, Maria: *The Lamplighter*. New York, 1854.
Davis, Rebecca Harding: "Life in the Iron Mills," *Atlantic*. Boston, 1861.
Davis, Rebecca Harding: "A Story of Today," *Atlantic*. Boston, 1861-2.
Davis, Rebecca Harding: "David Ganut," *Atlantic*. Boston, 1862.
Davis, Rebecca Harding: "The Harmonists," *Atlantic*. Boston, 1866.
Davis, Rebecca Harding: *John Andross*. New York, 1874.
Davis, Rebecca Harding: "Quella," *Lippincott's*. Philadelphia, 1875.
DeForest, John William: *Honest John Vane*. New Haven, 1875.
DeForest, John William: *Miss Ravenal's Conversion from Secession to Loyalty*. New York, 1881 (1867).
DeForest, John William: *Bloody Chasm*. New York, 1881.
DeForest, John William: "Inspired Lobbyist," in *Stories by American Authors*, New York, 1898 (1872).
Deland, Margaret: *The Wisdom of Fools*. Boston and New York, 1897.
Delaney, M. R.: "Blake; or, the Huts of America" in *Anglo-African Magazine*. New York, 1859.
Dennison, Thomas Scott: *An Iron Crown*. Chicago, 1885.
Dodd, Anna Bowman: *The Republic of the Future*. New York, 1887.
Donnelly, Ignatius: *Caesar's Column*. Chicago, 1890.
Douglas, Amanda M.: *Hope Mills*. Boston, 1880.
Dowling, George Thomas: *The Wreckers, a Social Study*. Philadelphia, 1886.
Dreiser, Theodore: *Sister Carrie*. New York, 1917 (1900).
Dunne, Finley Peter: *Mr. Dooley in Peace and War*. Boston, 1898.
Eastman, Mrs. M. H.: *Aunt Phillis' Cabin; or, Southern Life As It Is*. Philadelphia, 1852.

Edson, Milan C.: *Solaris Farm.* Washington, 1900.

Eggleston, Edward: *Mystery of Metropolisville.* New York, 1873.

Eggleston, Edward: *Roxy,* New York, 1878.

Eggleston, Edward: *The Hoosier Schoolmaster.* New York, 1883 (1871).

Eggleston, Edward: *The Faith Doctor.* New York, 1891.

Eggleston, George Cary and Dolores Marbourg: *Juggernaut, A Veiled Record.* New York, 1891.

Elliot, S. H.: *New England Chattels.* New York, 1858.

Everett, Henry Lexington: *The People's Program.* New York, 1892.

Etzler, J. A.: *The Paradise within the Reach of All Men.* Pittsburgh, 1833.

Fiske, Amos K.: *Beyond the Bourne.* New York, 1891.

Flanders, Mrs. G. M.: *The Ebony Idol.* New York, 1860.

Ford, Mary H.: *Which Wins?* Boston, 1891.

Frederic, Harold: *Seth's Brother's Wife.* New York, 1887.

Frederic, Harold: *The Copperhead.* New York, 1893.

'Freelance, Radical' (psd.): *The Philosopher of Foufouville.* New York, 1868.

Freeman, Mary E. Wilkins: *A Humble Romance and Other Stories.* New York, 1887.

Freeman, Mary E. Wilkins: *A New England Nun, and Other Stories.* New York, 1891.

Freeman, Mary E. Wilkins: *Pembroke.* New York, 1899 (1891).

Freeman, Mary E. Wilkins: *The Portion of Labor.* New York, 1901.

Fuller, Edward: *The Complaining Millions of Men.* New York, 1893.

Fuller, Henry Blake: *Cliff-Dwellers.* New York, 1893.

Fuller, Henry Blake: *With the Procession.* New York, 1895.

Garland, Hamlin: *A Little Norsk.* Chicago, 1890.

Garland, Hamlin: *Main-Travelled Roads.* Chicago, 1891.

Garland, Hamlin: *Jason Edwards.* New York, 1897 (1891).

Garland, Hamlin: *Prairie Folks.* Chicago, 1892.

Garland, Hamlin: *A Member of the Third House.* New York, 1897 (1892).

Garland, Hamlin: *A Spoil of Office.* New York, 1897 (1892).

Garland, Hamlin: *Rose of Dutcher's Coolly.* Chicago, 1895.

Gillette, King C.: *The Human Drift.* Boston, 1894.

Gilmore, James R.: *Among the Pines.* New York, 1862.

Gilmore, James R.: *My Southern Friends.* New York, 1863.

Glasgow, Ellen: *The Descendant.* New York, 1905 (1897).

Glasgow, Ellen: *Phases of an Inferior Planet.* New York, 1898.

Glasgow, Ellen: *Voice of the People.* New York, 1907 (1900).

Grigsby, Alcanoan O.: *Nequa; or the Problem of the Ages.* Topeka, Kans., 1900.

Hale, Edward Everett: *Ten Times One Is Ten.* Boston, 1871.

Hale, Edward Everett: *How They Lived in Hampton.* Boston, 1888.

Hale, Edward Everett: *Sibyl Knox, or Home Again.* New York, 1892.

Hale, Sara Josepha: *Liberia, or Mr. Peyton's Experiments.* New York, 1853.

Harben, William N.: "In the Year Ten Thousand" in *Arena,* 6:743. Boston, 1892.

Harben, William N.: *The Land of the Changing Sun.* New York, 1894.

Haven, Alice B.: *Loss and Gain; or Margaret's Home.* New York, 1860.

Hawthorne, Nathaniel: *The Blithedale Romance.* (In *Works,* v. 8.) Boston and New York, 1900 (1852).

Hay, John: *The Breadwinners.* New York, 1884.

Herrick, Robert: *The Gospel of Freedom.* New York, 1898.

Herrick, Robert: *The Web of Life.* New York, 1900.

Hertzka, Theodor: *Freeland.* (tr. by Arthur Ransom.) New York, 1891.

Heywood, D. Herbert: *Twentieth Century.* Boston, 1889.

Holford, Costello N.: *Aristopia.* Boston, 1895.

Holland, Annie Jefferson: *The Refugees.* Ausin, Texas, 1892.

Holland, J. G.: *Sevenoaks.* New York, 1875.

Holland, J. G.: *Nicholas Minturn.* New York, 1877 (1876).

Howard, Albert W. (psd. M. Auburre Hovarre): *The Milltillionaire.* Boston, 1898.

Howe, Edgar Watson: *The Story of a Country Town.* New York, 1926 (1882).

Howells, William Dean: *Annie Kilburn.* New York, 1888.

Howells, William Dean: *A Hazard of New Fortunes.* New York, 1889.

Howells, William Dean: *The Quality of Mercy.* New York, 1892.

Howells, William Dean: *The World of Chance.* New York, 1893.

Howells, William Dean: *A Traveller from Altruria.* New York, 1894.

Howells, William Dean: *Through the Eye of the Needle.* New York, 1907.

Howells, William Dean: *New Leaf Mills.* New York, 1913.

Ingraham, J. H.: *The Sunny South; or the Southerner's Home.* Philadelphia, 1860.

Irving, Washington: *Knickerbocker's History of New York.* New York, 1851. (1809).

Jackson, Helen Hunt: *Ramona.* Boston, 1923 (1884).

Jewett, Sarah Orne: *Tales of New England.* Boston, 1879, v. 4.

Johnston, Mary: *Prisoners of Hope.* Boston and New York, 1898.

Judah, Samuel B. H.: *The Buccaneers.* Boston, 1827.

Judd, Sylvester: *Margaret.* Boston, 1882 (1845).

Judd, Sylvester: *Richard Edney and the Governor's Family.* Boston, 1850.

Keenan, Henry Francis: *The Money Makers.* New York, 1885.

Kennedy, John P.: *Swallow Born.* New York, 1852 (1832).

Kennedy, John P.: *Quodilbet.* Philadelphia, 1840.

Kirkland, Joseph: *Zury.* Boston, 1887.

Kirkland, Joseph: *The McVeys.* Boston and New York, 1888.

Langdon, Mary: *Ida May.* Boston, 1858 (1854).

Lubin, David: *Let There Be Light.* New York, 1900

Machar, Agnes Maule: *Rolane Graeme: Knight.* New York, 1892.

Mason, Caroline A.: *A Woman of Yesterday.* New York, 1900.

McDougall, Walter H.: *The Hidden City.* New York, 1891.

Mercier, Louis Sebastian: *Memoirs of the Year Two Thousand Five Hundred.* (tr. by William Hooper.) Philadelphia, 1795.

Merrill, Albert Adams: *The Great Awakening.* Boston, 1899.

Miller, Joaquin: *Destruction of Gotham.* New York, 1886.

Miller, Joaquin: *The Building of the City Beautiful.* Trenton, 1905 (1893).

Moore, M. Louise: *Al-Modal* Cameron Point, La., 1892.

Neal, John: *Logan.* Philadelphia, 1822. 2 vols.

Neal, John: *Brother Jonathan.* Edinburgh, 1825. 3 vols.

Niswonger, Charles E.: *The Isle of Feminine.* Little Rock, Ark., 1893.

Nitsch, Helen Alice: *Gentle Breadwinners.* Boston, 1888.

Norris, Frank: *McTeague.* New York, 1924 (1899).

Norris, Frank: *The Octopus.* New York, 1901.

Norris, Frank: *The Pit.* New York, 1903.

Norris, Frank: *Vandover and the Brute.* New York, 1914.

Olerich, Henry: *A Cityless and Countryless World.* Holstein, Iowa, 1893.

Olive-Branch, or White Oak Farm. Philadelphia, 1857.

Page, John W.: *Uncle Robin in His Cabin in Virginia and Tom Without One in Boston.* Richmond, 1853.

Page, Thomas Nelson: *In Old Virginia.* New York, 1906 (1887, 1892, 1896).

Page, Thomas Nelson: *Red Rock.* New York, 1927 (1898).

Page, Thomas Nelson: *John Marvel, Assistant.* New York, 1909.

Paulding, James K.: *Konigsmarke.* New York, 1836. 2 vols. (1823).

Paulding, James K.: *Merry Tales.* New York, 1826.

Paulding, James K.: *Westward Ho!* New York, 1932. 2 vols.

Peck, Bradford: *The World a Department Store.* Lewiston, Maine, 1900.

Phelps, Elizabeth Stuart: "The Tenth of January", *Atlantic.* Boston, 1868.

Phelps, Elizabeth Stuart: *Hedged In.* Boston, 1870.

Phelps, Elizabeth Stuart: *The Silent Partner.* Boston, 1871.

Phelps, Elizabeth Stuart: *Beyond the Gates.* Boston and New York, 1883.

Phelps, Elizabeth Stuart: *The Gates Between.* Boston and New York, 1887.

Randolph, J. Thornton: *Cabin and Parlor, or, Slaves and Masters.* Philadelphia, 1852.

Rehm, Warren S.: *The Practical City.* Lancaster, Pa., 1898.

Reid, Mayne: *The Quadroon.* New York, 1856.

Riis, Jacob: *Nibsy's Christmas.* New York, 1893.

Riis, Jacob: *Out of Mulberry Street.* New York, 1897.

Roberts, J. W.: *Looking Within.* New York, 1893.

Rosewater, Frank: *'96, a Romance of Utopia.* New York, 1897.

Ross, Clinton Scollard: *The Silent Workman.* New York, 1886.

Ross, Clinton Scollard: *The Speculator.* New York, 1891.

Rush, Carolina E.: *The North and the South, or Slavery and Its Contrasts.* Philadelphia, 1852.

Sanborn, Alvan Francis: *Meg McIntyre's Raffle.* Boston, 1896.

Sanborn, Kate: *Adopting an Abandoned Farm.* New York, 1892.

Sanborn, Kate: *Abandoning an Adopted Farm*. New York, 1894.
Sargent, Epes: *Peculiar*. London, 1864. 3 vols.
Schindler, Solomon: *Young West*. Boston, 1894.
Sedgwick, Catherine Maria: *Clarence*. New York, 1849 (1830).
Sedgwick, Catherine Maria: *Married or Single?* New York, 1857.
Sherwood, Margaret: *An Experiment in Altruism*. New York, 1895.
Sherwood, Margaret: *Henry Worthington, Idealist*. New York, 1899.
Simpson, William: *The Man From Mars*. San Francisco, 1891.
Sketch, Walter: *The Down-Trodden*. New York, 1853.
Smith, F. Hopkinson: *Tom Grogan*. Boston and New York, 1896.
Smith, W. L. G.: *Life at the South: or, Uncle Tom's Cabin as It Is*. Buffalo, N. Y., 1852.
Southwood, M.: *Tit for Tat*. New York, 1856.
Stowe, Harriet B.: *The Two Altars*. Boston, 1852.
Stowe, Harriet B.: *Uncle Tom's Cabin*. Boston and New York, 1896 (1852). 2 vols.
Stowe, Harriet B.: *Dred*. Boston, 1856. 2 vols.
Stump, D. L.: *From World to World*. Asbury, Mo., 1896.
Sullivan, James William: *Tenement Tales of New York*. New York, 1895.
Sullivan, James William: *So the World Goes*. Chicago, 1898.
Thomas, Chauncey: *The Crystal Button*. Boston and New York, 1891.
Thompson, W. T.: *The Slaveholder Abroad*. Philadelphia, 1860.
Thorpe, Thomas Bangs: *The Master's House, a Tale of Southern Life*. New York, 1854.
Tincker, Mary A.: *San Salvador*. Boston and New York, 1892.
Tourgée, Albion Winegar: *A Fool's Errand*. New York, 1879.
Tourgée, Albion Winegar: *Bricks Without Straw*. New York, 1880.
Tourgée, Albion Winegar: *Pactolus Prime*. New York, 1889.
Tourgée, Albion Winegar: *Murvale Eastman, Christian Socialist*. New York, 1890.
Trowbridge, John T.: *Neighbor Jackwood*. Boston, 1887 (1857).
Trowbridge, John T.: *Cudjo's Cave*. Boston, 1892 (1863).
Trowbridge, John T.: *Coupon Bonds*. Boston, 1900 (1865).
Tucker, Nathaniel Beverly: *The Partisan Leader*. New York, 1861 (1836).
Twain, Mark: *The Prince and the Pauper*. New York, 1909 (1882).
Twain, Mark: *A Connecticut Yankee in King Arthur's Court*. New York, 1917 (1889).
Twain, Mark: *The American Claimant*. Hartford, 1903 (1892).
Twain, Mark, and Charles Dudley Warner: *The Gilded Age*. New York, n. d. (Author's National Edition). (1873). 2 vols.
Tyler, Randal Irving: *"Four Months After Date."* New York, 1898.
Tyler, Royal: *The Algerine Captive*. Hartford, 1816 (1797). 2 vols.
Victor, Mrs. M. V.: *Maum Guinea's Children*. New York, 1861.
Vinton, Arthur Dudley: *Looking Further Backward*. Albany, N. Y., 1890.
Walch, Caroline C.: *Doctor Sphinx*. New York, 1898.

Walworth, Mrs. J. H.: *Without Blemish.* New York, 1886.
Warner, Charles Dudley: *A Little Journey in the World.* Hartford, 1904 (1889).
Warner, Charles Dudley: *The Golden House.* Hartford, 1904 (1894).
Warner, Charles Dudley: *That Fortune.* Hartford, 1904 (1899).
Warner, Susan: *The Wide Wide World.* New York, 1850.
Welcome, S. Byron: *From Earth's Center.* Chicago, 1894.
Wellman, Bert J.: *The Legal Revolution of 1902.* Chicago, 1898.
White, Hervey: *Differences.* Boston, 1899.
Wiggin, Kate Douglass: *The Story of Patsy.* Boston and New York, 1889
Wiggin, Kate Douglass: *Timothy's Quest.* Boston and New York, 1895 (1890).
Wilbrandt, Conradt: *Mr. East's Experiences in Mr. Bellamy's World.* (tr. by Mary J. Safford). New York, 1891.
Williams, Francis Howard: *Atman.* New York, 1891.
Worley, Frederick W.: *Three Thousand Dollars a Year.* Washington, 1890.

GENERAL

Adams, F. C., *Uncle Tom at Home.* Philadelphia, 1853.
Adams, James Truslow: *Our Business Civilization.* New York, 1929.
Adams, James Truslow: *The Epic of America.* Boston, 1931.
Adams, Nehemiah: *A South-Side View of Slavery.* Boston, 1854.
Beard, Charles and Mary: *Rise of American Civilization.* New York, 1927. 2 vols.
Bellamy, Edward: "How I Came to Write Looking Backward," in *Nationalist,* 1:3. Boston, 1889.
Bogart, Ernest Ludlow: *Economic History of the United States.* New York, 1907.
Boyesen, H. H.: "Immigration," in *Problems of American Civilization.* New York, 1888.
Brisbane, Albert: *Social Destiny of Man.* Philadelphia, 1840.
Buck, Solon J.: *The Agrarian Crusade.* New Haven, 1919.
Cable, George W.: *The Negro Question.* New York, 1903 (1890).
Cambridge History of American Literature. New York, 1927.
Campbell, Helen: *Prisoners of Poverty.* Boston, 1895 (1887).
Campbell, Helen: *Darkness and Daylight.* Hartford, 1892.
Campbell, Helen: *Women Wage-Earners.* Boston, 1893.
Clark, David Lee: *Brockden Brown and the Rights of Woman.* Austin, Texas, 1922.
Clark, Harry Hayden, ed.: *Poems of Freneau.* New York, 1929.
Commons, John R.: *History of Labor in the United States.* New York, 1921.
Commons, John R.: *Industrial Government.* New York, 1921.
Cooper, James Fenimore: *Notions of the Americans.* Philadelphia, 1828. 2 vols.
Cooper, James Fenimore: *The American Democrat.* New York, 1931 (1838).

252   *Economic Criticism in American Fiction*

DeForest, J. W.: "Drawing Bureau Rations," in *Atlantic*, 37:74 ff. Boston, 1868.

DeForest, J. W.: "A Bureau Major's Business and Pleasures," in *Atlantic*, 37:766 ff. Boston, 1868.

Dew, Thomas R.: *The Pro-Slavery Argument*. Charleston, 1852.

Dibble, Roy F.: *Albion W. Tourgée*. New York, 1921.

Dodd, William E.: *The Cotton Kingdom*. New Haven, 1919.

Dunlap, William: *The Life of Charles Brockden Brown*. Philadelphia, 1815. 2 vols.

Dunning, William A.: *Reconstruction Political and Economic*. New York, 1907.

Dwight, Timothy: *Greenfield Hill*. New York, 1794.

Fitch, J. A.: *Causes of Industrial Unrest*. New York, 1924.

Fitzhugh, George: *Sociology for the South*. Richmond, 1854.

Flint, Timothy: *Recollections of the Last Ten Years*. Boston, 1826. Reprint, New York, 1932.

Flower, B. O.: *Civilization's Inferno, or, Studies in the Social Cellar*. Boston, 1893.

Flower, B. O.: *The Latest Social Vision*. Boston, 1897.

Forbes, Allyn B.: "Literary Quest for Utopia, The," *Social Forces*, v. 6, no. 2, p. 179 ff. Chapel Hill, N. C., 1927.

Gaines, Francis Pendleton: *The Southern Plantation*. New York, 1925.

Gee, Wilson: *Social Economics of Agriculture*. New York, 1932.

George, Henry: *Progress and Poverty*. New York, 1900 (1879).

George, Henry, Junior: *The Life of Henry George*. New York, 1900.

Gide, Charles: *Communist and Cooperative Colonies*. New York, 1928.

Griffin, Crawford S.: *Nationalism*. Boston, 1889.

Gronlund, Laurence: *The Cooperative Commonwealth*. Boston, 1884.

Hadley, Arthur Twining: *Economic Problems of Democracy*. New York, 1923.

Hakluyt, Richard: *Principal Navigation, Voyages and Discoveries of the English Nation*. Glasgow, 1904.

Hamilton, Walton Hale: *Current Economic Problems*. Chicago, 1914.

Hartwick, Harry: *The Foreground of American Fiction*. New York, 1934.

Helper, Hinton Rowan: *The Impending Crisis*. New York, 1857.

Hendrick, Burton J.: *The Age of Big Business*. New Haven, 1919.

Hertzler, Joyce O.: *The History of Utopian Thought*. New York, 1923.

"'Hon.' Charles Sumner and 'The Barbarism of Slavery'," in *The Plantation*, v. II, no. 2, New York, 1860.

Howells, Mildred (ed): *The Life in Letters of William Dean Howells*. New York, 1928.

Howells, William Dean: "Henry James, Jr." in *The Century Illustrated Magazine*, XXV:25 ff. New York, 1882.

Howells, William Dean: *Criticism and Fiction*. New York, 1891.

Howells, William Dean: *My Literary Passions*. New York, 1891.

Hulbert, Archer Butler: *Frontiers, the Genius of American Nationality.* Boston, 1929.

Imlay, Gilbert: *Topographical Description.* London, 1797 (3rd edition).

Jackson, Helen Hunt: *A Century of Dishonor.* Boston, 1913 (1885).

Jefferson, Thomas: *Notes on the State of Virginia.* Boston, 1801. (8th American edition)

Johnson, E. A. J.: *American Economic Thought in the Seventeenth Century.* London, 1932.

Johnson, J. G.: *Southern Fiction Prior to 1860.* Charlottesville, Va., 1909.

Kaufman, M.: *Utopias; or Schemes of Social Improvement.* London, 1879.

Kelly, Edmond: *Twentieth Century Socialism.* New York, 1913 (1910).

Laidler, Harry W.: *A History of Socialist Thought.* New York, 1927.

Liberty Bell, The, by Friends of Freedom. Boston, 1858.

Loshe, Lillie D.: *The Early American Novel.* (Col. thesis). New York, 1907.

Macy, Jesse: *The Anti-Slavery Crusade.* New Haven, 1919.

McMaster, John Bach: *History of the People of the United States.* New York, 1883.

Mill, John Stuart: *Principles of Political Economy.* London, 1911.

Mumford, Lewis: *The Story of Utopias.* New York, 1922.

Nearing, Scott: *Social Adjustment.* New York, 1911.

Noyes, John Humphrey: *History of American Socialisms.* Philadelphia, 1870.

Ogg, Frederic Austin: *The Reign of Andrew Jackson.* New Haven, 1919.

Orth, Samuel P.: *Our Foreigners.* New Haven, 1919.

Orth, Samuel P.: *The Armies of Labor.* New Haven, 1919.

Orth, Samuel P.: *The Boss and the Machine.* New Haven, 1919.

Page, Thomas Nelson: *The Negro: The Southerner's Problem.* New York 1904.

Parrington, Vernon Louis: *Main Current in American Thought.* New York, 1927-1930. 3 vols.

Pattee, Fred Lewis: *American Novel since 1870, The.* New York, 1917.

Pattee, Fred Lewis: *Development of American Short Story.* New York, 1923.

Patten, Simon N.: *The New Basis of Civilization.* New York, 1907.

Patterson, John Stahl: *Class Interests; Their Relation to Each Other and the Government.* New York, 1886.

Patterson, S. Howard and Karl W. H. Scholz: *Economic Problems of Modern Life.* New York, 1927.

Paulding, James K.: *Letters from the South.* New York, 1835.

Paxson, Frederic Logan: *History of the American Frontier.* Boston and New York, 1924.

Perry, Bliss: *The American Spirit in Literature.* New Haven, 1919.

Quinn, Arthur Hobson: *The Soul of America.* Philadelphia, 1932.

Riis, Jacob: *How the Other Half Lives.* New York, 1890.

Riis, Jacob: *The Children of the Poor.* New York, 1892.

Riis, Jacob: *A Ten Years' War.* Boston and New York, 1900.

Ross, John F.: *The Social Criticism of Fenimore Cooper.* Berkeley, Calif., 1933.

Rusk, Ralph Leslie: *Literature of the Midwestern Frontier.* New York, 1925.

Sanders, George A.: *Reality: or, Law and Order vs. Anarchy and Socialism.* Cleveland, 1898.

Schlesinger, Arthur Meyer: *New Viewpoints in American History.* New York, 1922.

Sinclair, Upton: *The Cry for Justice.* Philadelphia, 1915.

Smith, Adam: *Wealth of Nations.* London, 1892 (1775).

Spiller, Robert E.: *Fenimore Cooper, Critic of His Times.* New York, 1931.

Stearns, Harold E.: *Civilization in the United States.* New York, 1922.

Tandy, Jeanette Reid: "Pro-Slavery Propaganda in American Fiction of the Fifties," in *South Atlantic Quarterly,* v. XXI, nos. 1 and 2. Durham, 1922.

Taylor, Walter Fuller: "On the Origin of Howells' Interest in Economic Reform," in *American Literature,* v. II, no. 1. Durham, 1930.

Taylor, Walter Fuller: "William Dean Howells and the Economic Novel," in *American Literature,* v. IV, no. 2. Durham, 1932.

Thompson, Holland: *The New South.* New Haven, 1919.

Todd, Arthur James: *Theories of Social Progress.* New York, 1918.

Turner, Frederick Jackson: *The Frontier in American History.* New York, 1920.

Underwood, J. C.: "William Dean Howells and Altruria," in *Literature and Insurgency.* New York, 1914.

Van Doren, Carl: *The American Novel.* New York, 1921.

Veblen, Thorstein: *Absentee Ownership.* New York, 1923.

Vilas, Martin S.: *Charles Brockden Brown.* Burlington, Vt., 1904.

Wagner, Donald O.: *Social Reformers.* New York, 1934.

Wheeler, David Hilton: *Our Industrial Utopia and Its Unhappy Citizens.* Chicago, 1895.

Whittier, John Greenleaf: *Prose Works,* v. 7. (Riverside Edition). Boston and New York, 1889.

Wyckoff, Walter A.: *The Workers.* New York, 1899 (1897).

REPRESENTATIVE AUTOBIOGRAPHICAL AND BIOGRAPHICAL SLAVE WRITINGS

Biographical Sketches / and / Interesting Anecdotes / of / Persons of Colour / to which is added / A Selection / of / Pieces in Poetry / Compiled by A. Mott / New York / Mahlon Day / 1826.
>   (About 30 sketches.)

The / Life of Josiah Henson, / formerly a slave, / now an inhabitant of Canada / as / narrated by himself / Boston, / Arthur D. Phelps / 1849.
>   (After his telling, the story was read to him, to correct any errors of statement. "Not fiction but fact . . . it will be found fruitful in instruction by those who attentively consider its lessons." Fled to Canada October 28, 1830.)

The Life / of / Olandah Equiano, / or / Gustavus Vassa, / the African / written by himself / Boston / Isaac Knapp / 1837.
>   (Picture at front shows he thinks well of himself. Africa, Virginia, then many shipboards. 294 pages.)

Memoirs / of / Elleanor Eldridge / . Providence / B. T. Albro / 1838.
>   (For her financial benefit — "suffering and persecuted merit"; picture.)

Narrative / of the / Life of Moses Grandy / formerly a slave / in the / United States of America / sold for the benefit of his relations still in slavery / Boston / Oliver Johnson / 1844.
>   (Is the "second American from the last London edition.")

The / Narrative / of / Lunsford Lane, / formerly of / Raleigh, N. C. / Embracing an account of his early life, the redemption by purchase of himself and his family from slavery, and his banishment from the place of his birth for the crime of wearing a colored skin. / Published by Himself / 4th edition / Boston / 1848.

Narrative / of the / Life / of / Frederick Douglass / an / American Slave / written by himself / Boston / Published at the Anti-slavery Office / 1849.
>   (Preface by William Lloyd Garrison. Also prefatory letter to Douglass from Wendell Phillips. Maryland scene. 125 pages.)

Narrative of events / in the life of / William Green, / (formerly a slave) / Written by himself / Springfield / L. M. Guernsey / 1853.
>   (Master let him quit riding horses in the races after he joined church. Escapes to Philadelphia by boat; from Maryland.)

Twelve Years a Slave / Narrative / of / Solomon Northrup / A citizen of New York / Kidnapped in Washington City in 1841 / and Rescued in 1853 / From a Cotton Plantation near the Red River / in Louisiana / Auburn / Derby and Miller / 1853.
>   (Dedicated to Harriet Beecher Stowe . . . "affording another key to Uncle Tom's Cabin.")

Captain Canot; / or, / Twenty Years of An African Slaver; / being an account of / His career and adventures on the coast, / in the interior, on shipboard, and in / the West Indies / written out and edited from the / Captain's Journals, Memoranda and Conversations, / by / Branty Mayer. / New York / D. Appleton and Co. / 1854.

Memoir / of / Pierre Toussaint / born a slave / in / St. Domingo / by (Mrs. Hanna Lee) / Boston: / Crosby, Nichols, and Co. / 1854 / (picture).

My Bondage / and / My Freedom. Part I — Life as a slave. Part II — Life as a freeman / By Frederick Douglass / with / an introduction / by Dr. James M'Cune Smith / New York and Auburn / Miller, Orton & Mulligan / 1855.

> (Lectured in England and through North on slavery from 1846 on. 464 pages. Picture.)

The Kidnapped / and / The Ransomed. / Being the personal recollections of / Peter Still and His Wife "Vina", / after forty years of Slavery / by / Mrs. Kate E. R. Pickard. / Syracuse / William T. Hamilton. / 1856.

> (409 pages.)

A North-Side View of Slavery / The Refugee: / or the / Narratives of fugitive slaves in Canada. / Related by themselves / with / an account of the history and condition of the / colored population of upper Canada. / by Benjamin Drew. / Boston / John P. Jewett and Co. / 1856.

> ("Nowhere else can be found such a mass of direct and unimpeachable testimony as to the true character of the Peculiar Institution. 30,000 colored people in Upper Canada 1852, mostly slaves, says Anti-Slavery Society of Canada. These "narratives were gathered promiscuously." 116 of them.)

Autobiography / of a / Female Slave / Redfield / New York / 1857.

> (401 pages, an effort at depicting life on a rather detailed canvas —many things extraneous to a slave's life.)

Truth Stranger than Fiction / Father Henson's Story / of / His Own Life / with an introduction / by Mrs. H. B. Stowe / Boston / John P. Jewett and Company / 1858.

> (Picture.)

The Child's / Anti-Slavery Book: / Containing a / Few Words about American Slave Children / and / Stories of Slave-Life. / New York / Carlton & Porter / 1859.

> (Ten illustrations.)

A / Narrative / of / the Life / of / Rev. Noah Davis / a colored man / Written by himself, at the age of fifty-four. / Printed solely for the author's benefit. / Baltimore / John F. Werschampel, Jr. / 1859.

> (Virginia. Quotes much scripture. Picture.)

Incidents / in the / Life of a Slave Girl / written by herself / Edited by L. Maria Child / Boston / Published for the Author / 1861.

(Linda Brent — slave until 27 years old. "Some of my adventures may seem incredible; but they are, nevertheless, strictly true.")

Twenty-Two Years a Slave, / and / Forty Years a Freeman; / embracing a / correspondence of several years, while / president of Wilberforce Colony / London, Canada, West, / by / Austin Steward / Rochester, N. Y. / 1861.

(3rd edition. Picture. Virginia. Taken to 'great house' at 8, as in most of these biographies. Death, bridal scenes, slave whipping. Far South is bourne from which no negro returns.)

Black Man, / His Antecedents, His Genius / And His Achievements / by / William Wells Brown / Boston / Robert F. Wallcut / 1865.

(Fourth edition. Copyright 1863. 58 biographical sketches.)

Scenes / in the life of / Harriet Tubman / by / Sarah H. Bradford. / Auburn / W. J. Moses / 1869.

(Picture. For benefit of Harriet.)

The New Man / Twenty-nine Years a Slave / Twenty-nine Years a Free Man / Recollections of / H. C. Bruce / York, Pa. / P. Anstadt & Sons / 1895.

(". . . impartial and unprejudiced view of that system." Picture.)

REPRESENTATIVE AMERICAN UTOPIAN
FICTION SINCE 1900

Taylor, William Alexander: *Intermere*. The XX Century Pub. Co., Columbus, Ohio, 1901.

> ("The Tourist lost in mid-ocean is mysteriously introduced into Intermere, and meets the first citizen and other chief officials." Customary mechanical idealism asserted but not very scientifically explained. Social happiness.)

Frisbie, Henry S.: *Prophet of the Kingdom*. Neale Publishing Company, Washington, 1901.

> (Written as a Biblical narrative, chapter and verse divisions, with plentiful teaching between narrative verses.)

Bennet, Robert Ames: *Thyra, a Romance of the Polar Pit*. Henry Holt & Co., New York, 1901.

> (Dr. Godfrey and company lost on North Pole ice. Balloon. Discusses communistic government.)

Wooldridge, C. W.: *Perfecting the Earth,* a piece of possible history. Utopia Publishing Company, Cleveland, Ohio, 1902.

> ("Utopias from Bellamy back to Plato are in cloudland." This is an attempt to "make Utopia scientific and plant it on the rocks." Purports to be history of the United States, industrial, social, moral, from 1913 to 1947.)

Davis, Nathan (Capt.): *Beulah; or a Parable of Social Regeneration*. Hudson-Kimberly Pub. Co., Kansas City, Mo., 1904.

> (Essay and narrative, Missouri and Iowa setting, with intense religious emphasis.)

Peterson, Ephraim: *An Ideal City for an Ideal People*. By the author, Independence, Mo., 1905.

> (This is descriptive rather than narrative fiction in that it is the author's alleged plan for an ideal city—based on the Bible definitions and "common sense" — in Jackson, Missouri.)

Noto, Cosimo, M. D.: *The Ideal City*. By the author, New York, 1908.

> (The world through a physician's eyes, today and in 1953.)

Hatfield, Richard: *Geyserland*. Empiricisms in Social Reform. Published by author, Washington, D. C., 1908.

> (Geyserland land north of Canada; latitude of central Greenland. After narrative beginning, becomes essay. Communism urged.)

Teed, Cyrus R. (Lord Chester, pseud.): *The Great Red Dragon,* or the Flaming Devil of the Orient. Guiding Star Publishing House, Estero, Florida, 1909.

> (Evils of competitive system and Biblical prophecy indicate rise of Red Dragon (China) for "punishment of the Christian world for its departure from the communistic spirit in which the Lord in-

augurated the Christian dispensation.")

Phelps, George H. (P. Q. Tangent, pseud.): *The New Columbia; or, the Re-united States.* New Columbia Publishing Company, Findlay, Ohio, 1909.

(A small town lawyer's "purpose to record our prophecy as to what this people of the United States . . . are going to do in the near future . . ." Mildly given to legal language.)

Kirwan, Thomas (William Wonder, pseud.): *Reciprocity (Social and Economic) in the Thirtieth Century.* The coming co-operative age. A Forecast of the World's Future. Cochrane Publishing Company, New York, 1909.

(More story than some; claims however to be "a work of fiction, but not a novel.")

Brant, John Ira: *The New Regime. A. D. 2202.* Cochrane Publishing Co., New York, 1909.

(This has a definitely worked up narrative frame on which to present its Utopian picture.)

Schuette, H. George: *Anthonia; or, the Original Four Hundred.* The Lakeside Co., Manitowoc, Wisconsin, 1911.

Horner, Jacob W. (Dr. Walter H. Sensney, pseud.): *Military Socialism.* By the author, Indianapolis, 1911.

————?: *Our Sister Republic.* A single tax story. Cochrane Publishing Co., New York, 1911.

Swift, Morrison I.: *The Horroboos.* Liberty Press, Boston, 1911.

House, Edward Mandell: *Philip Dru: Administrator.* A story of tomorrow. 1920-1935. B. W. Huebsch, New York, 1912.

(This is decidedly more of a novel than most of these stories. Utopian in the sense of picturing the future. Not so extravagant as most.)

Olerich, Henry (Prof.): *Modern Paradise,* an Outline or Story of how some of the cultured people will probably live, work and organize in the near future. Equality Publishing Company, Omaha, 1915.

(Essay, not narrative at all.)

Henry, Walter O. (Dr.): *Equitania, or the Land of Equity.* By the author, Omaha, 1915.

(Story is told largely in dialogue—much essay interspersed. Lengthy "ideal constitution", for United States.)

Stauffer, Mack: *Humanity and the Mysterious Knight.* Roxburgh Publishing Co., Boston, 1915.

(More a romance than a solid criticism.)

Marshall, James and Margaret Scott: *1960: (A Retrospect).* J. F. Rowny Press, Los Angeles, 1919.

("Tomorrow's history told today."—Emphasis on war. Continuous narrative.)

Fairfield, Frederick Pease: *Story of the City of Works*. By the author, Boston, 1919.
> (Declares itself both anti-capitalistic and anti-socialistic. Narrative.)

Bruce, Stewart E.: *The World in 1931*. F. L. Searl & Co., New York, 1921.
> (No fancy imagining. A narrative criticism of the succeeding decade.)

Kayser, Martha: *The Aerial Flight, to the Realm of Peace*. Lincoln Press and Pub. Co., St. Louis, 1922.
> (Balloon flight to another planet.)

Clough, Fred M.: *The Golden Age, or the Depth of Time*. Roxburgh Publishing Co., Boston, 1923.

Griesser, Wilhelm: *The Welcome Island, Story and Laws*. Tucker-Kenworthy Co., Chicago, 1923.

Olerich, Henry: *The Story of the World a Thousand Years Hence*. Olerich Publishing Co., Omaha, 1923.
> (Really an essay, not a story.)

Paner, Louis: *The Day of Judgment and the Celestial Missionaries of Life*. By the author, (?), 1923.

Paner, Louis: *Eurekanian Paternalism*. By the author, Cleveland, 1923.
> (Not fiction in a story sense.)

Harvey, William H.: *Paul's School of Statesmanship*. Mundus Publishing Co., Chicago, 1924.
> (A story that names real American places.)

Willoughby, Frank: *Through the Needle's Eye*. The Palestine Press, New York, 1925.
> ("A narrative of the restoration of the Davidic Kingdom of Israel in Palestine with Jesus Christ as King." But withal definitely economic.)

Williams, Arthur: *Looking Forward*. Published by the author, Los Angeles, 1925.
> (Essay style. World in five countries. Constitutions given, 75 pages, big type, skipped space. Material appearing since at least 1885. Author sent copies around asking people to send $1.00 or return postpaid!)

Hodgson, John L.: *The Time Journey of Dr. Barton*. Egginton (?), 1929.

Baxter, Garrett: *Bamboa*. The Economic Press, Norfolk, Va., 1930.
> (Story.)

Schinagel, Geza, M. D.: *Possibilities*. Meador Publishing Co., Boston, 1930.
> (Narrative, but grave thought.)

Schuette, H. George: *The Grand Mysterious Secret Marriage Temple*. Manitowoc, Wisconsin, 1931.
> (Something of an extravaganza. Not literary.)

Wilkins, Hilliard: *Altrurian Farms*. Employment Extension Society, Washington, D. C., 1931.

(A treatment of periodical unemployment under a story form. Co-operative farms.)

Blanchard, Charles Elton, M. D.: *A New Day Dawns.* A Brief History of the Altruistic Era (1930 to 2162 A. D.) Medical Success Press, Youngstown, Ohio, 1932.

("A diagnosis and possible prognosis of the ills of our present social order." Not strictly fiction. Historical in form.)